MW00579889

The Modern C++ Challenge

Become an expert programmer by solving
real-world problems

Marius Bancila

BIRMINGHAM - MUMBAI

The Modern C++ Challenge

Copyright © 2018 Packt Publishing

All rights reserved. No part of this book may be reproduced, stored in a retrieval system, or transmitted in any form or by any means, without the prior written permission of the publisher, except in the case of brief quotations embedded in critical articles or reviews.

Every effort has been made in the preparation of this book to ensure the accuracy of the information presented. However, the information contained in this book is sold without warranty, either express or implied. Neither the author, nor Packt Publishing or its dealers and distributors, will be held liable for any damages caused or alleged to have been caused directly or indirectly by this book.

Packt Publishing has endeavored to provide trademark information about all of the companies and products mentioned in this book by the appropriate use of capitals. However, Packt Publishing cannot guarantee the accuracy of this information.

Commissioning Editor: Aaron Lazar
Acquisition Editors: Nitin Dasan, Chaitanya Nair
Content Development Editor: Nikhil Borkar
Technical Editor: Jijo Maliyekal
Copy Editor: Safis Editing
Project Coordinator: Ulhas Kambali
Proofreader: Safis Editing
Indexer: Mariammal Chettiyar
Graphics: Tania Dutta
Production Coordinator: Shantanu Zagade

First published: May 2018

Production reference: 1210518

Published by Packt Publishing Ltd.
Livery Place
35 Livery Street
Birmingham
B3 2PB, UK.

ISBN 978-1-78899-386-9

www.packtpub.com

`mapt.io`

Mapt is an online digital library that gives you full access to over 5,000 books and videos, as well as industry leading tools to help you plan your personal development and advance your career. For more information, please visit our website.

Why subscribe?

- Spend less time learning and more time coding with practical eBooks and Videos from over 4,000 industry professionals

- Improve your learning with Skill Plans built especially for you

- Get a free eBook or video every month

- Mapt is fully searchable

- Copy and paste, print, and bookmark content

PacktPub.com

Did you know that Packt offers eBook versions of every book published, with PDF and ePub files available? You can upgrade to the eBook version at `www.PacktPub.com` and as a print book customer, you are entitled to a discount on the eBook copy. Get in touch with us at `service@packtpub.com` for more details.

At `www.PacktPub.com`, you can also read a collection of free technical articles, sign up for a range of free newsletters, and receive exclusive discounts and offers on Packt books and eBooks.

Contributors

About the author

Marius Bancila is a software engineer with 15 years of experience in developing solutions for the industrial and financial sectors. He is the author of *Modern C++ Programming Cookbook*. He focuses on Microsoft technologies and mainly develops desktop applications with C++ and C#.

He is passionate about sharing his technical expertise with others, and for that reason, he was recognized as a Microsoft MVP for more than a decade. He can be contacted on Twitter at `@mariusbancila`.

I would like to thank Nikhil Borkar, Jijo Maliyekal, Chaitanya Nair, Nitin Dasan, and all the other people at Packt who contributed to this book. I would also like to thank the reviewers who provided great feedback and steered the book in a better direction. Finally, a special thanks to my wife and family, who supported me to work on this project.

About the reviewers

Aivars Kalvāns is the lead software architect at Tieto Latvia. He has been working on a Card Suite payment card system for more than 16 years and maintains many of core C++ libraries and programs. He is also responsible for C++ programming guidelines, secure coding training, and code reviews. He organizes and speaks at internal C++ developer meetups.

I would like to thank my lovely wife, Anete, and sons, Kārlis, Gustavs, and Leo, for making life much more interesting.

Arun Muralidharan is a software developer with over 8 years of experience as a systems and full-stack developer. Distributed system design, architecture, event systems, scalability, performance, and programming languages are some of the aspects of a product that interest him the most.

He is an ardent fan of C++ and its template metaprogramming; he likes how the language keeps his ego in check. So, one would find him working on C++ most of the time.

I would like to take this moment to thank the C++ community, from whom I have learned a lot over the years.

Nibedit Dey is a technopreneur with a multidisciplinary technology background. He has a bachelor's in biomedical engineering and a master's in digital design and embedded systems. Before starting his entrepreneurial journey, he worked for L&T and Tektronix for several years in different R&D roles. He has been using C++ to build complex software-based systems for the last 8 years.

Packt is searching for authors like you

If you're interested in becoming an author for Packt, please visit authors.packtpub.com and apply today. We have worked with thousands of developers and tech professionals, just like you, to help them share their insight with the global tech community. You can make a general application, apply for a specific hot topic that we are recruiting an author for, or submit your own idea.

Table of Contents

Preface

C++ is a general-purpose programming language that combines different paradigms such as object-oriented, imperative, generic, and functional programming. C++ is designed for efficiency and is the primary choice in applications where performance is key. Over the last few decades, C++ has been one of the most widely used programming languages in industry, academia, and elsewhere. The language is standardized by the International Organization for Standardization (ISO), which is currently working on the next version of the standard, called C++20, due to be completed in 2020.

With the standard covering almost 1500 pages, C++ is not the simplest language to learn and master. Skills are not acquired only by reading about them or watching others exercising them, but by practicing them again and again. Programming is no different; we developers do not learn new languages or technologies just by reading books, articles, or watching video tutorials. Instead, we need practice to sediment and develop the new things we learn so that we can eventually master them. Many a times, however, finding good exercises to put our knowledge to test is a difficult task. Although there are many websites that feature problems for different programming languages, most of these are mathematical problems, algorithms, or problems for student competitions. These kinds of problems do not help you exercise a large variety of a programming language functionalities. That is where this book steps in.

This book is a collection of 100 real-world problems designed for you to practice a large variety of the C++ language and standard library features as well as many third-party, cross-platform libraries. Yet, a few of these problems are C++ specific and, in general, can be solved in many programming languages. Of course, the intention is to help you master C++ and therefore you are expected to solve them in C++. All the solutions provided in the book are in C++. However, you can use the book as a reference for its collection of proposed problems when you learn other programming languages, although in this case, you will not benefit from the solutions.

The problems in this book are grouped into 12 chapters. Each chapter contains problems on similar or related topics. The problems have different levels of difficulty; some of them are easy, some are moderate, and some are difficult. The book has a relatively equal number of problems for each difficulty level. Each chapter starts with the description of the proposed problems. The solutions to these problems ensue with recommendations, explanations, and source code. Although you can find the solutions in the book, it is recommended that you try to implement them by yourself first, and only afterward—or if you have difficulties completing them—look at the proposed solutions. There is only one thing that is missing in the source code presented in the book—the headers you have to include. This was left out on purpose so that you figure those out by yourself. On the other hand, the source code provided with the book is complete, and you can find all the required headers there.

At the time of writing this book, the C++20 version of the standard is in progress and will continue for the next couple of years. However, some features have already been voted in, and one of these features is the extension to the `chrono` library with calendars and time zones. There are several problems in the fifth chapter on this topic, and although no compiler supports these yet, you can solve them using the `date` library, based on which the new standard additions have been designed. Many other libraries are used for solving problems in the book. The list includes Asio, Crypto++, Curl, NLohmann/json, PDF-Writer, PNGWriter, pugixml, SQLite, and ZipLib. Also, as an alternative to the `std::optional` and the `filesystem` libraries used throughout the book, you can use Boost with compilers where these are not available. All these libraries are open source and cross-platform. They were chosen for reasons that include performance, good documentation, and wide use within the community. However, you are free to use any other libraries you would like to solve the problems.

Who this book is for

Are you trying to learn C++ and are looking for challenges to practice what you're learning? If so, this book is for you. The book is intended for people learning C++, regardless of their experience with other programming languages, as a valuable resource of practical exercises and real-world problems. This book does not teach you the features of the language or the standard library. You are expected to learn that from other resources, such as books, articles, or video tutorials. This book is a learning companion and challenges you to solve tasks of various difficulties, utilizing the skills you have previously learned from other resources. Nevertheless, many of the problems proposed in this book are language agnostic, and you can use them when learning other programming languages; however, in this case, you won't be benefiting from the solutions provided here.

What this book covers

`Chapter 1`, *Math Problems*, contains a series of math exercises to warm you up for the more challenging problems in the next chapters.

`Chapter 2`, *Language Features*, proposes problems for you to practice operator overloading, move semantics, user-defined literals, and template metaprogramming aspects such as variadic functions, fold expressions, and type traits.

`Chapter 3`, *Strings and Regular Expressions*, has several problems for string manipulation, such as converting between strings and other data types, splitting and joining strings, and also for working with regular expressions.

`Chapter 4`, *Streams and Filesystems*, covers output stream manipulation and working with files and directories using the C++17 `filesystem` library.

`Chapter 5`, *Date and Time*, prepares you for the upcoming C++20 extensions to the `chrono` library, with several calendar and time zone problems that you can solve with the `date` library, on which the new standard additions are based.

`Chapter 6`, *Algorithms and Data Structures*, is one of the largest chapters and contains a variety of problems where you need to utilize the existing standard algorithms; others are where you need to implement your own general-purpose algorithms or data structures, such as circular buffer and priority queue. The chapter ends with two rather fun problems, Dawkins' Weasel program and Conway's Game of Life program, where you can learn about evolutionary algorithms and cellular automata.

`Chapter 7`, *Concurrency*, is where we use threads and asynchronous functions to implement general-purpose parallel algorithms, but also solve some real-word problems involving concurrency.

`Chapter 8`, *Design Patterns*, proposes a series of problems suited to be solved with design patterns such as decorator, composite, chain of responsibility, template method, and others.

`Chapter 9`, *Data Serialization*, covers most common formats of serialized data, JSON, and XML, with several problems; but it also challenges you to create PDF files, all with the use of third-party, open-source, and cross-platform libraries.

`Chapter 10`, *Archives, Images, and Databases*, teaches you to solve problems for working with zip archives, creating PNG files for real-world problems, such as Captcha-like systems and barcodes, and embedding and utilizing SQLite databases in your applications.

Chapter 11, *Cryptography*, mostly covers the user of the Crypto++ library for data encryption and signing. It also challenges you to implement your own Base64 encoding and decoding utilities.

Chapter 12, *Networking and Services*, is where you have to implement your own client-server application communicating on TCP/IP, and also consume various REST services such as bitcoin exchange rates or text translation APIs.

To get the most out of this book

As previously mentioned, you need a basic familiarity with the C++ language and the standard library in order to be able to utilize this book, or you can learn that along the way. In any case, this book will teach you how to solve problems, but it will not teach you about the language and features utilized in the solutions. You will need a compiler with C++17 support; a complete list of required libraries as well as possible compilers you can use can be found in the *Software Hardware List* available in the code bundle. In the following sections, you will find detailed instructions for downloading and building the code from this book.

Download the example code files

You can download the code files with the solutions to the problems in this book from your account at www.packtpub.com. If you purchased this book elsewhere, you can visit www.packtpub.com/support and register to have the files emailed directly to you.

You can download the code files by following these steps:

1. Log in or register at www.packtpub.com.
2. Select the **SUPPORT** tab.
3. Click on **Code Downloads & Errata**.
4. Enter the name of the book in the **Search** box and follow the onscreen instructions.

Once the file is downloaded, please make sure that you unzip or extract the folder using the latest version of:

- WinRAR/7-Zip for Windows
- Zipeg/iZip/UnRarX for Mac
- 7-Zip/PeaZip for Linux

The code bundle for the book is also hosted on GitHub at `https://github.com/PacktPublishing/The-Modern-Cpp-Challenge`. We also have other code bundles from our rich catalog of books and videos available at `https://github.com/PacktPublishing/`. Check them out!

Building the code

Although a large number of 3rd party libraries are used throughout the book, all these libraries, as well as all the solutions provided in the book are cross-platform and run on all platforms. However, the code has been developed and tested with Visual Studio 2017 v15.6/7 on Windows 10 and Xcode 9.3 on Mac OS 10.13.x.

If you are using Xcode on a Mac, there are two features used in the book that are not available with the LLVM toolset included in Xcode; these are the `filesystem` library and `std::optional`. However, these have been designed based on the `Boost.Filesystem` and `Boost.Optional` libraries and the use of the mentioned standard libraries in the proposed solutions is easily interchangeable with the Boost libraries. In fact, the accompanying code is written so that it works with either of the two; controlling which one to use is done with several macros. Instructions for building either with one or another are provided below, although the same information is also available in the source archive.

In order to support most of the development environments and build systems you could use on various platforms, the code is provided with CMake scripts. These are used to generate projects or build scripts for your preferred toolset. If you do not have CMake installed on your machine, you can get it from `https://cmake.org/`. Below, you can find instructions for using CMake to generate Visual Studio and Xcode scripts. For other tools, please refer to the CMake documentation, if necessary.

How to generate projects for Visual Studio 2017

Do the following in order to generate Visual Studio 2017 projects to target the x86 platform:

1. Open a command prompt and go to the `build` directory in the source code root folder.
2. Execute the following CMake command:

```
cmake -G "Visual Studio 15 2017" .. -DCMAKE_USE_WINSSL=ON -
DCURL_WINDOWS_SSPI=ON -DCURL_LIBRARY=libcurl -
DCURL_INCLUDE_DIR=..\libs\curl\include -DBUILD_TESTING=OFF -
DBUILD_CURL_EXE=OFF -DUSE_MANUAL=OFF
```

3. After completion, the Visual Studio solution can be found
   at `build/cppchallenger.sln`.

If you want to target the x64 platform instead, use the generator called `"Visual Studio 15 2017 Win64"`. Visual Studio 2017 15.4 supports both `filesystem` (as an experimental library) and `std::optional`. If you use a previous version, or just want to use the Boost libraries instead, you can generate the projects using the following command, after you properly install Boost:

```
cmake -G "Visual Studio 15 2017" .. -DCMAKE_USE_WINSSL=ON -
DCURL_WINDOWS_SSPI=ON -DCURL_LIBRARY=libcurl -
DCURL_INCLUDE_DIR=..\libs\curl\include -DBUILD_TESTING=OFF -
DBUILD_CURL_EXE=OFF -DUSE_MANUAL=OFF -DBOOST_FILESYSTEM=ON -
DBOOST_OPTIONAL=ON -DBOOST_INCLUDE_DIR=<path_to_headers> -
DBOOST_LIB_DIR=<path_to_libs>
```

Make sure that the paths to the headers and static library files do not include trailing backslashes (i.e. \).

How to generate projects for Xcode

Several solutions in the last chapter utilize the `libcurl` library. For SSL support, this library needs to be linked with the `OpenSSL` library. Do the following to install OpenSSL:

1. Download the library from `https://www.openssl.org/`.
2. Unzip the archive and, in a terminal, go to its root directory.
3. Build and install the library with the following commands (executed in this order):

```
./Configure darwin64-x86_64-cc shared enable-
ec_nistp_64_gcc_128 no-ssl2 no-ssl3 no-comp --
openssldir=/usr/local/ssl/macos-x86_64

make depend

sudo make install
```

Until `std::optional` and the `filesystem` library will be available with Xcode's Clang, you need to use Boost. Do the following to install and build the Boost libraries:

1. Install Homebrew from `https://brew.sh/`.
2. Run the following command to download and install Boost automatically.

   ```
   brew install boost
   ```
3. After installation, the Boost library will be available at `/usr/local/Cellar/boost/1.65.0`.

In order to generate projects for Xcode from the sources you have to:

1. Open a terminal and go to the `build` directory in the source code root directory.
2. Execute the following CMake command:

   ```
   cmake -G Xcode .. -DOPENSSL_ROOT_DIR=/usr/local/bin -
   DOPENSSL_INCLUDE_DIR=/usr/local/include/ -DBUILD_TESTING=OFF -
   DBUILD_CURL_EXE=OFF -DUSE_MANUAL=OFF -DBOOST_FILESYSTEM=ON -
   DBOOST_OPTIONAL=ON -
   DBOOST_INCLUDE_DIR=/usr/local/Cellar/boost/1.65.0 -
   DBOOST_LIB_DIR=/usr/local/Cellar/boost/1.65.0/lib
   ```
3. After completion, the Xcode project can be found at `build/cppchallenger.xcodeproj`.

Conventions used

There are a number of text conventions used throughout this book.

`CodeInText`: Indicates code words in the text, database table names, folder names, filenames, file extensions, pathnames, dummy URLs, user input, and Twitter handles. Here is an example: "Mount the downloaded `WebStorm-10*.dmg` disk image file as another disk in your system."

A block of code is set as follows:

```
int main()
{
    std::cout << "Hello, World!\n";
}
```

When we wish to draw your attention to a particular part of a code block, the relevant lines or items are set in bold:

```
template<typename C, typename... Args>
void push_back(C& c, Args&&... args)
{
    (c.push_back(args), ...);
}
```

Any command-line input or output is written as follows:

```
$ mkdir build
$ cd build
```

Bold: Indicates a new term, an important word, or words that you see onscreen. For example, words in menus or dialog boxes appear in the text like this. Here is an example: "Select **System info** from the **Administration** panel."

Warnings or important notes appear like this.

Tips and tricks appear like this.

Get in touch

Feedback from our readers is always welcome.

General feedback: Email feedback@packtpub.com and mention the book title in the subject of your message. If you have questions about any aspect of this book, please email us at questions@packtpub.com.

Errata: Although we have taken every care to ensure the accuracy of our content, mistakes do happen. If you have found a mistake in this book, we would be grateful if you would report this to us. Please visit www.packtpub.com/submit-errata, selecting your book, clicking on the Errata Submission Form link, and entering the details.

Piracy: If you come across any illegal copies of our works in any form on the Internet, we would be grateful if you would provide us with the location address or website name. Please contact us at copyright@packtpub.com with a link to the material.

If you are interested in becoming an author: If there is a topic that you have expertise in and you are interested in either writing or contributing to a book, please visit authors.packtpub.com.

Reviews

Please leave a review. Once you have read and used this book, why not leave a review on the site that you purchased it from? Potential readers can then see and use your unbiased opinion to make purchase decisions, we at Packt can understand what you think about our products, and our authors can see your feedback on their book. Thank you!

For more information about Packt, please visit packtpub.com.

1
Math Problems

Problems

1. Sum of naturals divisible by 3 and 5

Write a program that calculates and prints the sum of all the natural numbers divisible by either 3 or 5, up to a given limit entered by the user.

2. Greatest common divisor

Write a program that, given two positive integers, will calculate and print the greatest common divisor of the two.

3. Least common multiple

Write a program that will, given two or more positive integers, calculate and print the least common multiple of them all.

4. Largest prime smaller than given number

Write a program that computes and prints the largest prime number that is smaller than a number provided by the user, which must be a positive integer.

5. Sexy prime pairs

Write a program that prints all the sexy prime pairs up to a limit entered by the user.

6. Abundant numbers

Write a program that prints all abundant numbers and their abundance, up to a number entered by the user.

7. Amicable numbers

Write a program that prints the list of all pairs of amicable numbers smaller than 1,000,000.

8. Armstrong numbers

Write a program that prints all Armstrong numbers with three digits.

9. Prime factors of a number

Write a program that prints the prime factors of a number entered by the user.

10. Gray code

Write a program that displays the normal binary representations, Gray code representations, and decoded Gray code values for all 5-bit numbers.

11. Converting numerical values to Roman

Write a program that, given a number entered by the user, prints its Roman numeral equivalent.

12. Largest Collatz sequence

Write a program that determines and prints which number up to 1 million produces the longest Collatz sequence and what its length is.

13. Computing the value of Pi

Write a program that computes the value of Pi with a precision of two decimal digits.

14. Validating ISBNs

Write a program that validates that 10-digit values entered by the user, as a string, represent valid ISBN-10 numbers.

Solutions

1. Sum of naturals divisible by 3 and 5

The solution to this problem is to iterate through all numbers from 3 (1 and 2 are not divisible by 3 so it does not make sense to test them) up to the limit entered by the user. Use the modulo operation to check that the rest of the division of a number by 3 and 5 is 0. However, the trick to being able to sum up to a larger limit is to use `long long` and not `int` or `long` for the sum, which would result in an overflow before summing up to 100,000:

```cpp
int main()
{
    unsigned int limit = 0;
    std::cout << "Upper limit:";
    std::cin >> limit;

    unsigned long long sum = 0;
    for (unsigned int i = 3; i < limit; ++i)
    {
        if (i % 3 == 0 || i % 5 == 0)
            sum += i;
    }

    std::cout << "sum=" << sum << std::endl;
}
```

2. Greatest common divisor

The greatest common divisor (*gcd* in short) of two or more non-zero integers, also known as the greatest common factor (*gcf*), highest common factor (*hcf*), greatest common measure (*gcm*), or highest common divisor, is the greatest positive integer that divides all of them. There are several ways the gcd could be computed; an efficient method is Euclid's algorithm. For two integers, the algorithm is:

```
gcd(a,0) = a
gcd(a,b) = gcd(b, a mod b)
```

This can be very simply implemented in C++ using a recursive function:

```cpp
unsigned int gcd(unsigned int const a, unsigned int const b)
{
    return b == 0 ? a : gcd(b, a % b);
}
```

A non-recursive implementation of Euclid's algorithm should look like this:

```cpp
unsigned int gcd(unsigned int a, unsigned int b)
{
    while (b != 0) {
        unsigned int r = a % b;
        a = b;
        b = r;
    }
    return a;
}
```

In C++17 there is a `constexpr` function called `gcd()` in the header `<numeric>` that computes the greatest common divisor of two numbers.

3. Least common multiple

The **least common multiple (lcm)** of two or more non-zero integers, also known as the lowest common multiple, or smallest common multiple, is the smallest positive integer that is divisible by all of them. A possible way to compute the least common multiple is by reducing the problem to computing the greatest common divisor. The following formula is used in this case:

```cpp
lcm(a, b) = abs(a, b) / gcd(a, b)
```

A function to compute the least common multiple may look like this:

```cpp
int lcm(int const a, int const b)
{
    int h = gcd(a, b);
    return h ? (a * (b / h)) : 0;
}
```

To compute the *lcm* for more than two integers, you could use the `std::accumulate` algorithm from the header `<numeric>`:

```cpp
template<class InputIt>
int lcmr(InputIt first, InputIt last)
{
    return std::accumulate(first, last, 1, lcm);
}
```

In C++17 there is a `constexpr` function called `lcm()` in the header `<numeric>` that computes the least common multiple of two numbers.

4. Largest prime smaller than given number

A prime number is a number that has only two divisors, 1 and the number itself. To find the largest prime smaller than a given number you should first write a function that determines if a number is prime and then call this function, starting from the given number, towards 1 until the first prime is encountered. There are various algorithms for determining if a number is prime. Common implementations for determining the primality appear as follows:

```cpp
bool is_prime(int const num)
{
    if (num <= 3) { return num > 1; }
    else if (num % 2 == 0 || num % 3 == 0)
    {
        return false;
    }
    else
    {
        for (int i = 5; i * i <= num; i += 6)
        {
            if (num % i == 0 || num % (i + 2) == 0)
            {
                return false;
            }
        }
        return true;
    }
}
```

This function can be used as follows:

```
int main()
{
    int limit = 0;
    std::cout << "Upper limit:";
    std::cin >> limit;

    for (int i = limit; i > 1; i--)
    {
        if (is_prime(i))
        {
            std::cout << "Largest prime:" << i << std::endl;
            return 0;
        }
    }
}
```

5. Sexy prime pairs

Sexy prime numbers are prime numbers that differ from each other by six (for example 5 and 11, or 13 and 19). There are also *twin primes*, which differ by two, and *cousin primes*, which differ by four.

In the previous challenge, we implemented a function that determines whether an integer is a prime number. We will reuse that function for this exercise. What you have to do is check that if a number n is prime, the number n+6 is also prime, and in this case print the pair to the console:

```
int main()
{
    int limit = 0;
    std::cout << "Upper limit:";
    std::cin >> limit;

    for (int n = 2; n <= limit; n++)
    {
        if (is_prime(n) && is_prime(n+6))
        {
            std::cout << n << "," << n+6 << std::endl;
        }
    }
}
```

You could take it as a further exercise to compute and displays the sexy prime triples, quadruplets, and quintuplets.

6. Abundant numbers

An abundant number, also known as an excessive number, is a number for which the sum of its proper divisors is greater than the number itself. The proper divisors of a number are the positive prime factors of the number, other than the number itself. The amount by which the sum of proper divisors exceeds the number itself is called abundance. For instance, the number 12 has the proper divisors 1, 2, 3, 4, and 6. Their sum is 16, which makes 12 an abundant number. Its abundance is 4 (that is, 16 - 12).

To determine the sum of proper divisors, we try all numbers from 2 to the square root of the number (all prime factors are less than or equal to this value). If the current number, let's call it i, divides the number, then i and num/i are both divisors. However, if they are equal (for example, if i = 3, and n = 9, then i divides 9, but n/i = 3), we add only i because proper divisors must only be added once. Otherwise, we add both i and num/i and continue:

```cpp
int sum_proper_divisors(int const number)
{
    int result = 1;
    for (int i = 2; i <= std::sqrt(number); i++)
    {
        if (number%i == 0)
        {
            result += (i == (number / i)) ? i : (i + number / i);
        }
    }
    return result;
}
```

Printing abundant numbers is as simple as iterating up to the specified limit, computing the sum of proper divisors and comparing it to the number:

```
void print_abundant(int const limit)
{
    for (int number = 10; number <= limit; ++number)
    {
        auto sum = sum_proper_divisors(number);
        if (sum > number)
        {
            std::cout << number << ", abundance="
                      << sum - number << std::endl;
        }
    }
}

int main()
{
    int limit = 0;
    std::cout << "Upper limit:";
    std::cin >> limit;

    print_abundant(limit);
}
```

7. Amicable numbers

Two numbers are said to be amicable if the sum of the proper divisors of one number is equal to that of the other number. The proper divisors of a number are the positive prime factors of the number other than the number itself. Amicable numbers should not be confused with *friendly numbers*. For instance, the number 220 has the proper divisors 1, 2, 4, 5, 10, 11, 20, 22, 44, 55, and 110, whose sum is 284. The proper divisors of 284 are 1, 2, 4, 71, and 142; their sum is 220. Therefore, the numbers 220 and 284 are said to be amicable.

The solution to this problem is to iterate through all the numbers up to the given limit. For each number, compute the sum of its proper divisors. Let's call this `sum1`. Repeat the process and compute the sum of the proper divisors of `sum1`. If the result is equal to the original number, then the number and `sum1` are amicable numbers:

```cpp
void print_amicables(int const limit)
{
    for (int number = 4; number < limit; ++number)
    {
        auto sum1 = sum_proper_divisors(number);
        if (sum1 < limit)
        {
            auto sum2 = sum_proper_divisors(sum1);
            if (sum2 == number && number != sum1)
            {
                std::cout << number << "," << sum1 << std::endl;
            }
        }
    }
}
```

In the above sample, `sum_proper_divisors()` is the function seen in the solution to the abundant numbers problem.

The above function prints pairs of numbers twice, such as 220,284 and 284,220. Modify this implementation to only print each pair a single time.

8. Armstrong numbers

An Armstrong number (named so after Michael F. Armstrong), also called a narcissistic number, a pluperfect digital invariant, or a plus perfect number, is a number that is equal to the sum of its own digits when they are raised to the power of the number of digits. As an example, the smallest Armstrong number is 153, which is equal to $1^3 + 5^3 + 3^3$.

To determine if a number with three digits is a narcissistic number, you must first determine its digits in order to sum their powers. However, this involves division and modulo operations, which are expensive. A much faster way to compute it is to rely on the fact that a number is a sum of digits multiplied by 10 at the power of their zero-based position. In other words, for numbers up to 1,000, we have $a*10^2 + b*10^2 + c$. Since you are only supposed to determine numbers with three digits, that means a would start from 1. This would be faster than other approaches because multiplications are faster to compute than divisions and modulo operations. An implementation of such a function would look like this:

```
void print_narcissistics()
{
   for (int a = 1; a <= 9; a++)
   {
      for (int b = 0; b <= 9; b++)
      {
         for (int c = 0; c <= 9; c++)
         {
            auto abc = a * 100 + b * 10 + c;
            auto arm = a * a * a + b * b * b + c * c * c;
            if (abc == arm)
            {
               std::cout << arm << std::endl;
            }
         }
      }
   }
}
```

You could take it as a further exercise to write a function that determines the narcissistic numbers up to a limit, regardless their number of digits. Such a function would be slower because you first have to determine the sequence of digits of the number, store them in a container, and then sum together the digits raised to the appropriate power (the number of the digits).

9. Prime factors of a number

The prime factors of a positive integer are the prime numbers that divide that integer exactly. For instance, the prime factors of 8 are 2 x 2 x 2, and the prime factors of 42 are 2 x 3 x 7. To determine the prime factors you should use the following algorithm:

1. While n is divisible by 2, 2 is a prime factor and must be added to the list, while n becomes the result of n/2. After completing this step, n is an odd number.
2. Iterate from 3 to the square root of n. While the current number, let's call it i, divides n, i is a prime factor and must be added to the list, while n becomes the result of n/i. When i no longer divides n, increment i by 2 (to get the next odd number).
3. When n is a prime number greater than 2, the steps above will not result in n becoming 1. Therefore, if at the end of step 2 n is still greater than 2, then n is a prime factor.

```cpp
std::vector<unsigned long long> prime_factors(unsigned long long n)
{
    std::vector<unsigned long long> factors;
    while (n % 2 == 0) {
        factors.push_back(2);
        n = n / 2;
    }
    for (unsigned long long i = 3; i <= std::sqrt(n); i += 2)
    {
        while (n%i == 0) {
            factors.push_back(i);
            n = n / i;
        }
    }

    if (n > 2)
        factors.push_back(n);
    return factors;
}

int main()
{
    unsigned long long number = 0;
    std::cout << "number:";
    std::cin >> number;
```

```
auto factors = prime_factors(number);
std::copy(std::begin(factors), std::end(factors),
    std::ostream_iterator<unsigned long long>(std::cout, " "));
}
```

As a further exercise, determine the largest prime factor for the number 600,851,475,143.

10. Gray code

Gray code, also known as reflected binary code or simply reflected binary, is a form of binary encoding where two consecutive numbers differ by only one bit. To perform a binary reflected Gray code encoding, we need to use the following formula:

```
if b[i-1] = 1 then g[i] = not b[i]
else g[i] = b[i]
```

This is equivalent to the following:

```
g = b xor (b logically right shifted 1 time)
```

For decoding a binary reflected Gray code, the following formula should be used:

```
b[0] = g[0]
b[i] = g[i] xor b[i-1]
```

These can be written in C++ as follows, for 32-bit unsigned integers:

```
unsigned int gray_encode(unsigned int const num)
{
    return num ^ (num >> 1);
}

unsigned int gray_decode(unsigned int gray)
{
    for (unsigned int bit = 1U << 31; bit > 1; bit >>= 1)
    {
        if (gray & bit) gray ^= bit >> 1;
    }
    return gray;
}
```

To print the all 5-bit integers, their binary representation, the encoded Gray code representation, and the decoded value, we could use the following code:

```cpp
std::string to_binary(unsigned int value, int const digits)
{
    return std::bitset<32>(value).to_string().substr(32-digits, digits);
}

int main()
{
    std::cout << "Number\tBinary\tGray\tDecoded\n";
    std::cout << "------\t------\t----\t-------\n";

    for (unsigned int n = 0; n < 32; ++n)
    {
        auto encg = gray_encode(n);
        auto decg = gray_decode(encg);

        std::cout
            << n << "\t" << to_binary(n, 5) << "\t"
            << to_binary(encg, 5) << "\t" << decg << "\n";
    }
}
```

11. Converting numerical values to Roman

Roman numerals, as they are known today, use seven symbols: I = 1, V = 5, X = 10, L = 50, C = 100, D = 500, and M = 1000. The system uses additions and subtractions in composing the numerical symbols. The symbols from 1 to 10 are I, II, III, IV, V, VI, VII, VIII, IX, and X. Romans did not have a symbol for zero and used to write *nulla* to represent it. In this system, the largest symbols are on the left, and the least significant are on the right. As an example, the Roman numeral for 1994 is MCMXCIV. If you are not familiar with the rules for Roman numerals, you should read more on the web.

To determine the Roman numeral of a number, use the following algorithm:

1. Check every Roman base symbol from the highest (M) to the lowest (I)
2. If the current value is greater than the value of the symbol, then concatenate the symbol to the Roman numeral and subtract its value from the current one
3. Repeat until the current value reaches zero

For example, consider 42: the first Roman base symbol smaller than 42 is XL, which is 40. We concatenate it to the numeral, resulting in XL, and subtract from the current number, resulting in 2. The first Roman base symbol smaller than 2 is I, which is 1. We add that to the numeral, resulting in XLI, and subtract 1 from the number, resulting in 1. We add one more I to the numeral, which becomes XLII, and subtract again 1 from the number, reaching 0 and therefore stopping:

```cpp
std::string to_roman(unsigned int value)
{
    std::vector<std::pair<unsigned int, char const*>> roman {
        { 1000, "M" },{ 900, "CM" }, { 500, "D" },{ 400, "CD" },
        { 100, "C" },{ 90, "XC" }, { 50, "L" },{ 40, "XL" },
        { 10, "X" },{ 9, "IX" }, { 5, "V" },{ 4, "IV" }, { 1, "I" }};

    std::string result;
    for (auto const & kvp : roman) {
        while (value >= kvp.first) {
            result += kvp.second;
            value -= kvp.first;
        }
    }
    return result;
}
```

This function can be used as follows:

```cpp
int main()
{
    for(int i = 1; i <= 100; ++i)
    {
        std::cout << i << "\t" << to_roman(i) << std::endl;
    }

    int number = 0;
    std::cout << "number:";
    std::cin >> number;
    std::cout << to_roman(number) << std::endl;
}
```

12. Largest Collatz sequence

The Collatz conjecture, also known as the Ulam conjecture, Kakutani's problem, the Thwaites conjecture, Hasse's algorithm, or the Syracuse problem, is an unproven conjecture that states that a sequence defined as explained in the following always reaches 1. The series is defined as follows: start with any positive integer n and obtain each new term from the previous one: if the previous term is even, the next term is half the previous term, or else it is 3 times the previous term plus 1.

The problem you are to solve is to generate the Collatz sequence for all positive integers up to one million, determine which of them is the longest, and print its length and the starting number that produced it. Although we could apply brute force to generate the sequence for each number and count the number of terms until reaching 1, a faster solution would be to save the length of all the sequences that have already been generated. When the current term of a sequence that started from a value n becomes smaller than n, then it is a number whose sequence has already been determined, so we could simply fetch its cached length and add it to the current length to determine the length of the sequence started from n. This approach, however, introduces a limit to the Collatz sequences that could be computed, because at some point the cache will exceed the amount of memory the system can allocate:

```cpp
std::pair<unsigned long long, long> longest_collatz(
   unsigned long long const limit)
{
   long length = 0;
   unsigned long long number = 0;
   std::vector<int> cache(limit + 1, 0);
   for (unsigned long long i = 2; i <= limit; i++)
   {
      auto n = i;
      long steps = 0;
      while (n != 1 && n >= i)
      {
         if ((n % 2) == 0) n = n / 2;
         else n = n * 3 + 1;
         steps++;
      }
      cache[i] = steps + cache[n];

      if (cache[i] > length)
      {
         length = cache[i];
         number = i;
```

```
      }
   }

   return std::make_pair(number, length);
}
```

13. Computing the value of Pi

A suitable solution for approximately determining the value of Pi is using a Monte Carlo simulation. This is a method that uses random samples of inputs to explore the behavior of complex processes or systems. The method is used in a large variety of applications and domains, including physics, engineering, computing, finance, business, and others.

To do this we will rely on the following idea: the area of a circle with diameter d is PI * d^2 / 4. The area of a square that has the length of its sides equal to d is d^2. If we divide the two we get PI/4. If we put the circle inside the square and generate random numbers uniformly distributed within the square, then the count of numbers in the circle should be directly proportional to the circle area, and the count of numbers inside the square should be directly proportional to the square's area. That means that dividing the total number of hits in the square and circle should give PI/4. The more points generated, the more accurate the result shall be.

For generating pseudo-random numbers we will use a Mersenne twister and a uniform statistical distribution:

```
template <typename E = std::mt19937,
          typename D = std::uniform_real_distribution<>>
double compute_pi(E& engine, D& dist, int const samples = 1000000)
{
   auto hit = 0;
   for (auto i = 0; i < samples; i++)
   {
      auto x = dist(engine);
      auto y = dist(engine);
      if (y <= std::sqrt(1 - std::pow(x, 2))) hit += 1;
   }
   return 4.0 * hit / samples;
}

int main()
{
   std::random_device rd;
   auto seed_data = std::array<int, std::mt19937::state_size> {};
   std::generate(std::begin(seed_data), std::end(seed_data),
```

```
                    std::ref(rd));
std::seed_seq seq(std::begin(seed_data), std::end(seed_data));
auto eng = std::mt19937{ seq };
auto dist = std::uniform_real_distribution<>{ 0, 1 };

for (auto j = 0; j < 10; j++)
    std::cout << compute_pi(eng, dist) << std::endl;
}
```

14. Validating ISBNs

The **International Standard Book Number (ISBN)** is a unique numeric identifier for books. Currently, a 13-digit format is used. However, for this problem, you are to validate the former format that used 10 digits. The last of the 10 digits is a checksum. This digit is chosen so that the sum of all the ten digits, each multiplied by its (integer) weight, descending from 10 to 1, is a multiple of 11.

The `validate_isbn_10` function, shown as follows, takes an ISBN as a string, and returns `true` if the length of the string is 10, all ten elements are digits, and the sum of all digits multiplied by their weight (or position) is a multiple of 11:

```
bool validate_isbn_10(std::string_view isbn)
{
    auto valid = false;
    if (isbn.size() == 10 &&
        std::count_if(std::begin(isbn), std::end(isbn), isdigit) == 10)
    {
        auto w = 10;
        auto sum = std::accumulate(
            std::begin(isbn), std::end(isbn), 0,
            [&w](int const total, char const c) {
                return total + w-- * (c - '0'); });

        valid = !(sum % 11);
    }
    return valid;
}
```

You can take it as a further exercise to improve this function to also correctly validate ISBN-10 numbers that include hyphens, such as 3-16-148410-0. Also, you can write a function that validates ISBN-13 numbers.

2
Language Features

Problems

15. IPv4 data type

Write a class that represents an IPv4 address. Implement the functions required to be able to read and write such addresses from or to the console. The user should be able to input values in dotted form, such as `127.0.0.1` or `168.192.0.100`. This is also the form in which IPv4 addresses should be formatted to an output stream.

16. Enumerating IPv4 addresses in a range

Write a program that allows the user to input two IPv4 addresses representing a range and list all the addresses in that range. Extend the structure defined for the previous problem to implement the requested functionality.

17. Creating a 2D array with basic operations

Write a class template that represents a two-dimensional array container with methods for element access (`at()` and `data()`), capacity querying, iterators, filling, and swapping. It should be possible to move objects of this type.

18. Minimum function with any number of arguments

Write a function template that can take any number of arguments and returns the minimum value of them all, using `operator` < for comparison. Write a variant of this function template that can be parameterized with a binary comparison function to use instead of `operator` <.

19. Adding a range of values to a container

Write a general-purpose function that can add any number of elements to the end of a container that has a method `push_back(T&& value)`.

20. Container any, all, none

Write a set of general-purpose functions that enable checking whether any, all, or none of the specified arguments are present in a given container. These functions should make it possible to write code as follows:

```
std::vector<int> v{ 1, 2, 3, 4, 5, 6 };
assert(contains_any(v, 0, 3, 30));

std::array<int, 6> a{ { 1, 2, 3, 4, 5, 6 } };
assert(contains_all(a, 1, 3, 5, 6));

std::list<int> l{ 1, 2, 3, 4, 5, 6 };
assert(!contains_none(l, 0, 6));
```

21. System handle wrapper

Consider an operating system handle, such as a file handle. Write a wrapper that handles the acquisition and release of the handle, as well as other operations such as verifying the validity of the handle and moving handle ownership from one object to another.

22. Literals of various temperature scales

Write a small library that enables expressing temperatures in the three most used scales, Celsius, Fahrenheit, and Kelvin, and converting between them. The library must enable you to write temperature literals in all these scales, such as 36.5_deg for Celsius, 97.7_f for Fahrenheit, and 309.65_K for Kelvin; perform operations with these values; and convert between them.

Solutions

15. IPv4 data type

The problem requires writing a class to represent an IPv4 address. This is a 32-bit value, usually represented in decimal dotted format, such as 168.192.0.100; each part of it is an 8-bit value, ranging from 0 to 255. For easy representation and handling, we can use four unsigned char to store the address value. Such a value could be constructed either from four unsigned char or from an unsigned long. In order to be able to read a value directly from the console (or any other input stream) and be able to write the value to the console (or any other output stream), we have to overload operator>> and operator<<. The following listing shows a minimal implementation that can meet the requested functionality:

```cpp
class ipv4
{
   std::array<unsigned char, 4> data;
public:
   constexpr ipv4() : data{ {0} } {}
   constexpr ipv4(unsigned char const a, unsigned char const b,
                  unsigned char const c, unsigned char const d):
      data{{a,b,c,d}} {}
   explicit constexpr ipv4(unsigned long a) :
      data{ { static_cast<unsigned char>((a >> 24) & 0xFF),
              static_cast<unsigned char>((a >> 16) & 0xFF),
              static_cast<unsigned char>((a >> 8) & 0xFF),
              static_cast<unsigned char>(a & 0xFF) } } {}
   ipv4(ipv4 const & other) noexcept : data(other.data) {}
   ipv4& operator=(ipv4 const & other) noexcept
   {
      data = other.data;
      return *this;
   }

   std::string to_string() const
   {
      std::stringstream sstr;
      sstr << *this;
      return sstr.str();
   }

   constexpr unsigned long to_ulong() const noexcept
   {
      return (static_cast<unsigned long>(data[0]) << 24) |
```

```
                    (static_cast<unsigned long>(data[1]) << 16) |
                    (static_cast<unsigned long>(data[2]) << 8) |
                     static_cast<unsigned long>(data[3]);
    }

    friend std::ostream& operator<<(std::ostream& os, const ipv4& a)
    {
        os << static_cast<int>(a.data[0]) << '.'
           << static_cast<int>(a.data[1]) << '.'
           << static_cast<int>(a.data[2]) << '.'
           << static_cast<int>(a.data[3]);
        return os;
    }

    friend std::istream& operator>>(std::istream& is, ipv4& a)
    {
        char d1, d2, d3;
        int b1, b2, b3, b4;
        is >> b1 >> d1 >> b2 >> d2 >> b3 >> d3 >> b4;
        if (d1 == '.' && d2 == '.' && d3 == '.')
            a = ipv4(b1, b2, b3, b4);
        else
            is.setstate(std::ios_base::failbit);
        return is;
    }
};
```

The `ipv4` class can be used as follows:

```
int main()
{
    ipv4 address(168, 192, 0, 1);
    std::cout << address << std::endl;

    ipv4 ip;
    std::cout << ip << std::endl;
    std::cin >> ip;
    if(!std::cin.fail())
        std::cout << ip << std::endl;
}
```

16. Enumerating IPv4 addresses in a range

To be able to enumerate IPv4 addresses in a given range, it should first be possible to compare IPv4 values. Therefore, we should implement at least `operator<`, but the following listing contains implementation for all comparison operators: ==, !=, <, >, <=, and >=. Also, in order to increment an IPv4 value, implementations for both the prefix and postfix `operator++` are provided. The following code is an extension of the IPv4 class from the previous problem:

```cpp
ipv4& operator++()
{
    *this = ipv4(1 + to_ulong());
    return *this;
}

ipv4& operator++(int)
{
    ipv4 result(*this);
    ++(*this);
    return *this;
}

friend bool operator==(ipv4 const & a1, ipv4 const & a2) noexcept
{
    return a1.data == a2.data;
}

friend bool operator!=(ipv4 const & a1, ipv4 const & a2) noexcept
{
    return !(a1 == a2);
}

friend bool operator<(ipv4 const & a1, ipv4 const & a2) noexcept
{
    return a1.to_ulong() < a2.to_ulong();
}

friend bool operator>(ipv4 const & a1, ipv4 const & a2) noexcept
{
    return a2 < a1;
}

friend bool operator<=(ipv4 const & a1, ipv4 const & a2) noexcept
{
    return !(a1 > a2);
}
```

```
friend bool operator>=(ipv4 const & a1, ipv4 const & a2) noexcept
{
    return !(a1 < a2);
}
```

With these changes to the `ipv4` class from the previous problem, we can write the following program:

```
int main()
{
    std::cout << "input range: ";
    ipv4 a1, a2;
    std::cin >> a1 >> a2;
    if (a2 > a1)
    {
        for (ipv4 a = a1; a <= a2; a++)
        {
            std::cout << a << std::endl;
        }
    }
    else
    {
        std::cerr << "invalid range!" << std::endl;
    }
}
```

17. Creating a 2D array with basic operations

Before looking at how we could define such a structure, let's consider several test cases for it. The following snippet shows all the functionality that was requested:

```
int main()
{
    // element access
    array2d<int, 2, 3> a {1, 2, 3, 4, 5, 6};
    for (size_t i = 0; i < a.size(1); ++i)
        for (size_t j = 0; j < a.size(2); ++j)
        a(i, j) *= 2;

    // iterating
    std::copy(std::begin(a), std::end(a),
        std::ostream_iterator<int>(std::cout, " "));

    // filling
    array2d<int, 2, 3> b;
    b.fill(1);
```

```
    // swapping
    a.swap(b);

    // moving
    array2d<int, 2, 3> c(std::move(b));
}
```

Note that for element access, we are using `operator()`, such as in `a(i,j)`, and not `operator[]`, such as in `a[i][j]`, because only the former can take multiple arguments (one for the index on each dimension). The latter can only have a single argument, and in order to enable expressions like `a[i][j]`, it has to return an intermediate type (one that basically represents a row) that in turn overloads `operator[]` to return a single element.

There are already standard containers that store either fixed or variable-length sequences of elements. This two-dimensional array class should be just an adapter for such a container. In choosing between `std::array` and `std::vector`, we should consider two things:

- The `array2d` class should have move semantics to be able to move objects
- It should be possible to list initialize an object of this type

The `std::array` container is movable only if the elements it holds are move-constructible and move-assignable. On the other hand, it cannot be constructed from an `std::initializer_list`. Therefore, the more viable option remains an `std::vector`.

Internally, this adapter container can store its data either in a vector of vectors (each row is a `vector<T>` with `C` elements, and the 2D array has `R` such elements stored in a `vector<vector<T>>`) or single vector of $R \times C$ elements of type `T`. In the latter case, the element on row `i` and column `j` is found at index `i * C + j`. This approach has a smaller memory footprint, stores all data in a single contiguous chunk, and is also simpler to implement. For these reasons, it is the preferred solution.

A possible implementation of the two-dimensional array class with the requested functionality is shown here:

```
template <class T, size_t R, size_t C>
class array2d
{
    typedef T                  value_type;
    typedef value_type*        iterator;
    typedef value_type const*  const_iterator;
    std::vector<T>             arr;
public:
    array2d() : arr(R*C) {}
    explicit array2d(std::initializer_list<T> l):arr(l) {}
```

```cpp
constexpr T* data() noexcept { return arr.data(); }
constexpr T const * data() const noexcept { return arr.data(); }

constexpr T& at(size_t const r, size_t const c)
{
   return arr.at(r*C + c);
}

constexpr T const & at(size_t const r, size_t const c) const
{
   return arr.at(r*C + c);
}

constexpr T& operator() (size_t const r, size_t const c)
{
   return arr[r*C + c];
}

constexpr T const & operator() (size_t const r, size_t const c) const
{
   return arr[r*C + c];
}

constexpr bool empty() const noexcept { return R == 0 || C == 0; }

constexpr size_t size(int const rank) const
{
   if (rank == 1) return R;
   else if (rank == 2) return C;
   throw std::out_of_range("Rank is out of range!");
}

void fill(T const & value)
{
   std::fill(std::begin(arr), std::end(arr), value);
}

void swap(array2d & other) noexcept { arr.swap(other.arr); }

const_iterator begin() const { return arr.data(); }
const_iterator end() const   { return arr.data() + arr.size(); }
iterator       begin()       { return arr.data(); }
iterator       end()         { return arr.data() + arr.size(); }
};
```

18. Minimum function with any number of arguments

It is possible to write function templates that can take a variable number of arguments using variadic function templates. For this, we need to implement compile-time recursion (which is actually just calls through a set of overloaded functions). The following snippet shows how the requested function could be implemented:

```
template <typename T>
T minimum(T const a, T const b) { return a < b ? a : b; }

template <typename T1, typename... T>
T1 minimum(T1 a, T... args)
{
    return minimum(a, minimum(args...));
}

int main()
{
    auto x = minimum(5, 4, 2, 3);
}
```

In order to be able to use a user-provided binary comparison function, we need to write another function template. The comparison function must be the first argument because it cannot follow the function parameter pack. On the other hand, this cannot be an overload of the previous minimum function, but a function with a different name. The reason is that the compiler would not be able to differentiate between the template parameter lists `<typename T1, typename... T>` and `<class Compare, typename T1, typename... T>`. The changes are minimal and should be easy to follow in this snippet:

```
template <class Compare, typename T>
T minimumc(Compare comp, T const a, T const b)
{ return comp(a, b) ? a : b; }

template <class Compare, typename T1, typename... T>
T1 minimumc(Compare comp, T1 a, T... args)
{
    return minimumc(comp, a, minimumc(comp, args...));
}

int main()
{
    auto y = minimumc(std::less<>(), 3, 2, 1, 0);
}
```

19. Adding a range of values to a container

Writing functions with any number of arguments is possible using variadic function templates. The function should have the container as the first parameter, followed by a variable number of arguments representing the values to be added at the back of the container. However, writing such a function template can be significantly simplified using fold expressions. Such an implementation is shown here:

```
template<typename C, typename... Args>
void push_back(C& c, Args&&... args)
{
    (c.push_back(args), ...);
}
```

Examples of using this function template, with various container types, can be seen in the following listing:

```
int main()
{
    std::vector<int> v;
    push_back(v, 1, 2, 3, 4);
    std::copy(std::begin(v), std::end(v),
            std::ostream_iterator<int>(std::cout, " "));

    std::list<int> l;
    push_back(l, 1, 2, 3, 4);
    std::copy(std::begin(l), std::end(l),
            std::ostream_iterator<int>(std::cout, " "));
}
```

20. Container any, all, none

The requirement to be able to check the presence or absence of a variable number of arguments suggests that we should write variadic function templates. However, these functions require a helper function, a general-purpose one that checks whether an element is found in a container or not and returns a `bool` to indicate success or failure. Since all these functions, which we could call `contains_all`, `contains_any`, and `contains_none`, do is apply logical operators on the results returned by the helper function, we would use fold expressions to simplify the code. Short circuit evaluation is enabled after the expansion of the fold expression, which means we are evaluating only the elements that lead to a definitive result. So if we are looking for the presence of all 1, 2, and 3, and 2 is missing, the function will return after looking up value 2 in the container without checking value 3:

```
template<class C, class T>
bool contains(C const & c, T const & value)
{
    return std::end(c) != std::find(std::begin(c), std::end(c), value);
}

template<class C, class... T>
bool contains_any(C const & c, T &&... value)
{
    return (... || contains(c, value));
}

template<class C, class... T>
bool contains_all(C const & c, T &&... value)
{
    return (... && contains(c, value));
}

template<class C, class... T>
bool contains_none(C const & c, T &&... value)
{
    return !contains_any(c, std::forward<T>(value)...);
}
```

21. System handle wrapper

System handles are a form of reference to system resources. Because all operating systems were at least initially written in C, creating and releasing the handles is done through dedicated system functions. This increases the risk of leaking resources because of erroneous disposal, such as in the case of an exception. In the following snippet, specific to Windows, you can see a function where a file is opened, read from, and eventually closed. However, this has a couple of problems: in one case, the developer forgot to close the handle before leaving the function; in another case, a function that throws is called before the handle is properly closed, without the exception being caught. However, since the function throws, that cleanup code never executes:

```cpp
void bad_handle_example()
{
    bool condition1 = false;
    bool condition2 = true;
    HANDLE handle = CreateFile(L"sample.txt",
                               GENERIC_READ,
                               FILE_SHARE_READ,
                               nullptr,
                               OPEN_EXISTING,
                               FILE_ATTRIBUTE_NORMAL,
                               nullptr);

    if (handle == INVALID_HANDLE_VALUE)
        return;

    if (condition1)
    {
        CloseHandle(handle);
        return;
    }

    std::vector<char> buffer(1024);
    unsigned long bytesRead = 0;
    ReadFile(handle,
             buffer.data(),
             buffer.size(),
             &bytesRead,
             nullptr);

    if (condition2)
    {
        // oops, forgot to close handle
        return;
    }
```

```
    // throws exception; the next line will not execute
    function_that_throws();

    CloseHandle(handle);
}
```

A C++ wrapper class can ensure proper disposal of the handle when the wrapper object goes out of scope and is destroyed (whether that happens through a normal execution path or as the result of an exception). A proper implementation should account for different types of handles, with a range of values to indicate an invalid handle (such as 0/null or -1). The implementation shown next provides:

- Explicit acquisition and automatic release of the handle when the object is destroyed
- Move semantics to enable transfer of ownership of the handle
- Comparison operators to check whether two objects refer to the same handle
- Additional operations such as swapping and resetting

 The implementation shown here is a modified version of the handle class implemented by Kenny Kerr and published in the article *Windows with C++ - C++ and the Windows API*, MSDN Magazine, July 2011, `https://msdn.microsoft.com/en-us/magazine/hh288076.aspx`. Although the handle traits shown here refer to Windows handles, it should be fairly simple to write traits appropriate for other platforms.

```
template <typename Traits>
class unique_handle
{
    using pointer = typename Traits::pointer;
    pointer m_value;
public:
    unique_handle(unique_handle const &) = delete;
    unique_handle& operator=(unique_handle const &) = delete;

    explicit unique_handle(pointer value = Traits::invalid()) noexcept
        :m_value{ value }
    {}

    unique_handle(unique_handle && other) noexcept
        : m_value{ other.release() }
    {}

    unique_handle& operator=(unique_handle && other) noexcept
    {
        if (this != &other)
```

```cpp
        reset(other.release());
        return *this;
    }

    ~unique_handle() noexcept
    {
        Traits::close(m_value);
    }

    explicit operator bool() const noexcept
    {
        return m_value != Traits::invalid();
    }

    pointer get() const noexcept { return m_value; }

    pointer release() noexcept
    {
        auto value = m_value;
        m_value = Traits::invalid();
        return value;
    }

    bool reset(pointer value = Traits::invalid()) noexcept
    {
        if (m_value != value)
        {
            Traits::close(m_value);
            m_value = value;
        }
        return static_cast<bool>(*this);
    }

    void swap(unique_handle<Traits> & other) noexcept
    {
        std::swap(m_value, other.m_value);
    }
};

template <typename Traits>
void swap(unique_handle<Traits> & left, unique_handle<Traits> & right)
noexcept
{
    left.swap(right);
}

template <typename Traits>
bool operator==(unique_handle<Traits> const & left,
```

```cpp
                    unique_handle<Traits> const & right) noexcept
{
    return left.get() == right.get();
}

template <typename Traits>
bool operator!=(unique_handle<Traits> const & left,
                unique_handle<Traits> const & right) noexcept
{
    return left.get() != right.get();
}

struct null_handle_traits
{
    using pointer = HANDLE;
    static pointer invalid() noexcept { return nullptr; }
    static void close(pointer value) noexcept
    {
        CloseHandle(value);
    }
};

struct invalid_handle_traits
{
    using pointer = HANDLE;
    static pointer invalid() noexcept { return INVALID_HANDLE_VALUE; }
    static void close(pointer value) noexcept
    {
        CloseHandle(value);
    }
};

using null_handle = unique_handle<null_handle_traits>;
using invalid_handle = unique_handle<invalid_handle_traits>;
```

With this handle type defined, we can rewrite the previous example in simpler terms, avoiding all those problems with handles not properly closed because of exceptions occurring that are not properly handled, or simply because developers forget to release resources when no longer needed. This code is both simpler and more robust:

```
void good_handle_example()
{
    bool condition1 = false;
    bool condition2 = true;

    invalid_handle handle{
        CreateFile(L"sample.txt",
                    GENERIC_READ,
                    FILE_SHARE_READ,
                    nullptr,
                    OPEN_EXISTING,
                    FILE_ATTRIBUTE_NORMAL,
                    nullptr) };

    if (!handle) return;

    if (condition1) return;

    std::vector<char> buffer(1024);
    unsigned long bytesRead = 0;
    ReadFile(handle.get(),
            buffer.data(),
            buffer.size(),
            &bytesRead,
            nullptr);

    if (condition2) return;

    function_that_throws();
}
```

22. Literals of various temperature scales

To meet this requirement, we need to provide an implementation for several types, operators, and functions:

- An enumeration of supported temperature scales called `scale`.
- A class template to represent a temperature value, parameterized with the scale, called `quantity`.

- Comparison operators ==, !=, <, >, <=, and >= that compare two quantities of the same time.
- Arithmetic operators + and – that add and subtract values of the same quantity type. Additionally, we could implement member operators += and –+.
- A function template to convert temperatures from one scale to another, called `temperature_cast`. This function does not perform the conversion itself but uses type traits to do that.
- Literal operators ""_deg, ""_f, and ""_k for creating user-defined temperature literals.

For brevity, the following snippet only contains the code that handles Celsius and Fahrenheit temperatures. You should take it as a further exercise to extend the code with support for the Kelvin scale. The code accompanying the book contains the full implementation of all three required scales.

The `are_equal()` function is a utility function used to compare floating-point values:

```
bool are_equal(double const d1, double const d2,
               double const epsilon = 0.001)
{
    return std::fabs(d1 - d2) < epsilon;
}
```

The enumeration of possible temperature scales and the class that represents a temperature value are defined as follows:

```
namespace temperature
{
    enum class scale { celsius, fahrenheit, kelvin };

    template <scale S>
    class quantity
    {
        const double amount;
    public:
        constexpr explicit quantity(double const a) : amount(a) {}
        explicit operator double() const { return amount; }
    };
}
```

The comparison operators for the quantity<S> class can be seen here:

```
namespace temperature
{
   template <scale S>
   inline bool operator==(quantity<S> const & lhs, quantity<S> const & rhs)
   {
      return are_equal(static_cast<double>(lhs), static_cast<double>(rhs));
   }

   template <scale S>
   inline bool operator!=(quantity<S> const & lhs, quantity<S> const & rhs)
   {
      return !(lhs == rhs);
   }

   template <scale S>
   inline bool operator< (quantity<S> const & lhs, quantity<S> const & rhs)
   {
      return static_cast<double>(lhs) < static_cast<double>(rhs);
   }

   template <scale S>
   inline bool operator> (quantity<S> const & lhs, quantity<S> const & rhs)
   {
      return rhs < lhs;
   }

   template <scale S>
   inline bool operator<=(quantity<S> const & lhs, quantity<S> const & rhs)
   {
      return !(lhs > rhs);
   }

   template <scale S>
   inline bool operator>=(quantity<S> const & lhs, quantity<S> const & rhs)
   {
      return !(lhs < rhs);
   }

   template <scale S>
   constexpr quantity<S> operator+(quantity<S> const &q1,
                                   quantity<S> const &q2)
   {
      return quantity<S>(static_cast<double>(q1) +
                  static_cast<double>(q2));
   }
```

```
      template <scale S>
      constexpr quantity<S> operator-(quantity<S> const &q1,
                                      quantity<S> const &q2)
      {
         return quantity<S>(static_cast<double>(q1) -
                            static_cast<double>(q2));
      }
   }
```

To convert between temperature values of different scales, we will define a function template called `temperature_cast()` that utilizes several type traits to perform the actual conversion. All these are shown here, although not all type traits; the others can be found in the code accompanying the book:

```
namespace temperature
{
   template <scale S, scale R>
   struct conversion_traits
   {
      static double convert(double const value) = delete;
   };

   template <>
   struct conversion_traits<scale::celsius, scale::fahrenheit>
   {
      static double convert(double const value)
      {
         return (value * 9) / 5 + 32;
      }
   };

   template <>
   struct conversion_traits<scale::fahrenheit, scale::celsius>
   {
      static double convert(double const value)
      {
         return (value - 32) * 5 / 9;
      }
   };

   template <scale R, scale S>
   constexpr quantity<R> temperature_cast(quantity<S> const q)
   {
      return quantity<R>(conversion_traits<S, R>::convert(
         static_cast<double>(q)));
   }
}
```

The literal operators for creating temperature values are shown in the following snippet. These operators are defined in a separate namespace, called temperature_scale_literals, which is a good practice in order to minimize the risk of name collision with other literal operators:

```
namespace temperature
{
    namespace temperature_scale_literals
    {
        constexpr quantity<scale::celsius> operator "" _deg(
            long double const amount)
        {
            return quantity<scale::celsius> {static_cast<double>(amount)};
        }

        constexpr quantity<scale::fahrenheit> operator "" _f(
            long double const amount)
        {
            return quantity<scale::fahrenheit> {static_cast<double>(amount)};
        }
    }
}
```

The following example shows how to define two temperature values, one in Celsius and one in Fahrenheit, and convert between the two:

```
int main()
{
    using namespace temperature;
    using namespace temperature_scale_literals;

    auto t1{ 36.5_deg };
    auto t2{ 79.0_f };

    auto tf = temperature_cast<scale::fahrenheit>(t1);
    auto tc = temperature_cast<scale::celsius>(tf);
    assert(t1 == tc);
}
```

3
Strings and Regular Expressions

Problems

23. Binary to string conversion

Write a function that, given a range of 8-bit integers (such as an array or vector), returns a string that contains a hexadecimal representation of the input data. The function should be able to produce both uppercase and lowercase content. Here are some input and output examples:

Input: `{ 0xBA, 0xAD, 0xF0, 0x0D }`, output: `"BAADF00D"` or `baadf00d`
Input: `{ 1,2,3,4,5,6 }`, output: `"010203040506"`

24. String to binary conversion

Write a function that, given a string containing hexadecimal digits as the input argument, returns a vector of 8-bit integers that represent the numerical deserialization of the string content. The following are examples:

Input: `"BAADF00D"` or `baadF00D`, output: `{0xBA, 0xAD, 0xF0, 0x0D}`
Input `"010203040506"`, output: `{1, 2, 3, 4, 5, 6}`

25. Capitalizing an article title

Write a function that transforms an input text into a capitalized version, where every word starts with an uppercase letter and has all the other letters in lowercase. For instance, the text "`the c++ challenger`" should be transformed to "`The C++ Challenger`".

26. Joining strings together separated by a delimiter

Write a function that, given a list of strings and a delimiter, creates a new string by concatenating all the input strings separated with the specified delimiter. The delimiter must not appear after the last string, and when no input string is provided, the function must return an empty string.

Example: input { `"this"`,`"is"`,`"an"`,`"example"` } and delimiter '` `' (space), output: "`this is an example`".

27. Splitting a string into tokens with a list of possible delimiters

Write a function that, given a string and a list of possible delimiter characters, splits the string into tokens separated by any of the delimiters and returns them in an `std::vector`.

Example: input: "`this,is.a sample!!`" with delimiters "`,.! `", output: {`"this"`, `"is"`, `"a"`, `"sample"`}.

28. Longest palindromic substring

Write a function that, given an input string, locates and returns the longest sequence in the string that is a palindrome. If multiple palindromes of the same length exist, the first one should be returned.

29. License plate validation

Considering license plates with the format `LLL-LL DDD` or `LLL-LL DDDD` (where L is an uppercase letter from *A* to *Z* and D is a digit), write:

- One function that validates that a license plate number is of the correct format
- One function that, given an input text, extracts and returns all the license plate numbers found in the text

30. Extracting URL parts

Write a function that, given a string that represents a URL, parses and extracts the parts of the URL (protocol, domain, port, path, query, and fragment).

31. Transforming dates in strings

Write a function that, given a text containing dates in the format `dd.mm.yyyy` or `dd-mm-yyyy`, transforms the text so that it contains dates in the format `yyyy-mm-dd`.

Solutions

23. Binary to string conversion

In order to write a general-purpose function that can handle various sorts of ranges, such as an std::array, std::vector, a C-like array, or others, we should write a function template. In the following, there are two overloads; one that takes a container as an argument and a flag indicating the casing style, and one that takes a pair of iterators (to mark the first and then one past the end element of the range) and the flag to indicate casing. The content of the range is written to an std::ostringstream object, with the appropriate I/O manipulators, such as width, filling character, or case flag:

```cpp
template <typename Iter>
std::string bytes_to_hexstr(Iter begin, Iter end,
                            bool const uppercase = false)
{
   std::ostringstream oss;
   if(uppercase) oss.setf(std::ios_base::uppercase);
   for (; begin != end; ++begin)
     oss << std::hex << std::setw(2) << std::setfill('0')
        << static_cast<int>(*begin);
   return oss.str();
}

template <typename C>
std::string bytes_to_hexstr(C const & c, bool const uppercase = false)
{
   return bytes_to_hexstr(std::cbegin(c), std::cend(c), uppercase);
}
```

These functions can be used as follows:

```cpp
int main()
{
   std::vector<unsigned char> v{ 0xBA, 0xAD, 0xF0, 0x0D };
   std::array<unsigned char, 6> a{ {1,2,3,4,5,6} };
   unsigned char buf[5] = {0x11, 0x22, 0x33, 0x44, 0x55};

   assert(bytes_to_hexstr(v, true) == "BAADF00D");
   assert(bytes_to_hexstr(a, true) == "010203040506");
   assert(bytes_to_hexstr(buf, true) == "1122334455");

   assert(bytes_to_hexstr(v) == "baadf00d");
   assert(bytes_to_hexstr(a) == "010203040506");
```

```
    assert(bytes_to_hexstr(buf) == "1122334455");
}
```

24. String to binary conversion

The operation requested here is the opposite of the one implemented in the previous problem. This time, however, we could write a function and not a function template. The input is an `std::string_view`, which is a lightweight wrapper for a sequence of characters. The output is a vector of 8-bit unsigned integers. The following `hexstr_to_bytes` function transforms every two text characters into an `unsigned char` value ("A0" becomes `0xA0`), puts them into an `std::vector`, and returns the vector:

```cpp
unsigned char hexchar_to_int(char const ch)
{
    if (ch >= '0' && ch <= '9') return ch - '0';
    if (ch >= 'A' && ch <= 'F') return ch - 'A' + 10;
    if (ch >= 'a' && ch <= 'f') return ch - 'a' + 10;
        throw std::invalid_argument("Invalid hexadecimal character");
}

std::vector<unsigned char> hexstr_to_bytes(std::string_view str)
{
    std::vector<unsigned char> result;
    for (size_t i = 0; i < str.size(); i += 2)
    {
        result.push_back(
            (hexchar_to_int(str[i]) << 4) | hexchar_to_int(str[i+1]));
    }
    return result;
}
```

This function assumes the input string contains an even number of hexadecimal digits. In cases where the input string contains an odd number of hexadecimal digits, the last one is discarded (so that "BAD" becomes {0xBA}). As a further exercise, modify the preceding function so that, instead of discarding the last odd digit, it considers a leading zero so that "BAD" becomes {0x0B, 0xAD}. Also, as yet another exercise, you can write a version of the function that deserializes content that has the hexadecimal digits separated by a delimiter, such as space (for example "BA AD F0 0D").

The next code sample shows how this function can be used:

```
int main()
{
    std::vector<unsigned char> expected{ 0xBA, 0xAD, 0xF0, 0x0D, 0x42 };
    assert(hexstr_to_bytes("BAADF00D42") == expected);
    assert(hexstr_to_bytes("BaaDf00d42") == expected);
}
```

25. Capitalizing an article title

The function template `capitalize()`, implemented as follows, works with strings of any type of characters. It does not modify the input string but creates a new string. To do so, it uses an `std::stringstream`. It iterates through all the characters in the input string and sets a flag indicating a new word to `true` every time a space or punctuation is encountered. Input characters are transformed to uppercase when they represent the first character in a word and to lowercase otherwise:

```
template <class Elem>
using tstring = std::basic_string<Elem, std::char_traits<Elem>,
                                  std::allocator<Elem>>;
template <class Elem>
using tstringstream = std::basic_stringstream<
    Elem, std::char_traits<Elem>, std::allocator<Elem>>;

template <class Elem>
tstring<Elem> capitalize(tstring<Elem> const & text)
{
    tstringstream<Elem> result;
    bool newWord = true;
    for (auto const ch : text)
    {
        newWord = newWord || std::ispunct(ch) || std::isspace(ch);
        if (std::isalpha(ch))
        {
            if (newWord)
            {
                result << static_cast<Elem>(std::toupper(ch));
                newWord = false;
            }
            else
                result << static_cast<Elem>(std::tolower(ch));
        }
        else result << ch;
```

```
    }
    return result.str();
}
```

In the following program you can see how this function is used to capitalize texts:

```
int main()
{
    using namespace std::string_literals;
    assert("The C++ Challenger"s ==
           capitalize("the c++ challenger"s));
    assert("This Is An Example, Should Work!"s ==
           capitalize("THIS IS an ExamplE, should wORk!"s));
}
```

26. Joining strings together separated by a delimiter

Two overloads called `join_strings()` are listed in the following code. One takes a container of strings and a pointer to a sequence of characters representing a separator, while the other takes two random access iterators, representing the first and one past the last element of a range, and a separator. They both return a new string created by concatenating all the input strings, using an output string stream and the `std::copy` function. This general-purpose function copies all the elements in the specified range to an output range, represented by an output iterator. We are using here an `std::ostream_iterator` that uses `operator<<` to write the assigned value to the specified output stream each time the iterator is assigned a value:

```
template <typename Iter>
std::string join_strings(Iter begin, Iter end,
                         char const * const separator)
{
    std::ostringstream os;
    std::copy(begin, end-1,
              std::ostream_iterator<std::string>(os, separator));
    os << *(end-1);
    return os.str();
}

template <typename C>
std::string join_strings(C const & c, char const * const separator)
{
    if (c.size() == 0) return std::string{};
```

```
        return join_strings(std::begin(c), std::end(c), separator);
}

int main()
{
    using namespace std::string_literals;
    std::vector<std::string> v1{ "this","is","an","example" };
    std::vector<std::string> v2{ "example" };
    std::vector<std::string> v3{ };

    assert(join_strings(v1, " ") == "this is an example"s);
    assert(join_strings(v2, " ") == "example"s);
    assert(join_strings(v3, " ") == ""s);
}
```

 As a further exercise, you should modify the overload that takes iterators as arguments so that it works with other types of iterators, such as bidirectional iterators, thereby enabling the use of this function with lists or other containers.

27. Splitting a string into tokens with a list of possible delimiters

Two different versions of a splitting function are listed as follows:

- The first one uses a single character as the delimiter. To split the input string it uses a string stream initialized with the content of the input string, using `std::getline()` to read chunks from it until the next delimiter or an end-of-line character is encountered.
- The second one uses a list of possible character delimiters, specified in an `std::string`. It uses `std:string::find_first_of()` to locate the first position of any of the delimiter characters, starting from a given position. It does so in a loop until the entire input string is being processed. The extracted substrings are added to the result vector:

```
template <class Elem>
using tstring = std::basic_string<Elem, std::char_traits<Elem>,
                                  std::allocator<Elem>>;

template <class Elem>
using tstringstream = std::basic_stringstream<
    Elem, std::char_traits<Elem>, std::allocator<Elem>>;
```

```
template<typename Elem>
inline std::vector<tstring<Elem>> split(tstring<Elem> text,
                                        Elem const delimiter)
{
    auto sstr = tstringstream<Elem>{ text };
    auto tokens = std::vector<tstring<Elem>>{};
    auto token = tstring<Elem>{};
    while (std::getline(sstr, token, delimiter))
    {
        if (!token.empty()) tokens.push_back(token);
    }
    return tokens;
}

template<typename Elem>
inline std::vector<tstring<Elem>> split(tstring<Elem> text,
                                        tstring<Elem> const & delimiters)
{
    auto tokens = std::vector<tstring<Elem>>{};
    size_t pos, prev_pos = 0;
    while ((pos = text.find_first_of(delimiters, prev_pos)) !=
    std::string::npos)
    {
        if (pos > prev_pos)
        tokens.push_back(text.substr(prev_pos, pos - prev_pos));
        prev_pos = pos + 1;
    }
    if (prev_pos < text.length())
    tokens.push_back(text.substr(prev_pos, std::string::npos));
    return tokens;
}
```

The following sample code shows two examples of how different strings can be split using either one delimiter character or multiple delimiters:

```
int main()
{
    using namespace std::string_literals;
    std::vector<std::string> expected{"this", "is", "a", "sample"};
    assert(expected == split("this is a sample"s, ' '));
    assert(expected == split("this,is a.sample!!"s, ",.! "s));
}
```

28. Longest palindromic substring

The simplest solution to this problem is to try a brute-force approach, checking if each substring is a palindrome. However, this means we need to check *C(N, 2)* substrings (where *N* is the number of characters in the string), and the time complexity would be $O(N^3)$. The complexity could be reduced to $O(N^2)$ by storing results of sub problems. To do so we need a table of Boolean values, of size $N \times N$, where the element at [i, j] indicates whether the substring from position i to j is a palindrome. We start by initializing all elements [i, i] with true (one-character palindromes) and all the elements [i, i+i] with true for all consecutive two identical characters (for two-character palindromes). We then go on to inspect substrings greater than two characters, setting the element at [i, j] to true if the element at [i+i, j-1] is true and the characters on the positions i and j in the string are also equal. Along the way, we retain the start position and length of the longest palindromic substring in order to extract it after finishing computing the table.

In code, this solution appears as follows:

```
std::string longest_palindrome(std::string_view str)
{
    size_t const len = str.size();
    size_t longestBegin = 0;
    size_t maxLen = 1;
    std::vector<bool> table(len * len, false);
    for (size_t i = 0; i < len; i++)
        table[i*len + i] = true;

    for (size_t i = 0; i < len - 1; i++)
    {
        if (str[i] == str[i + 1])
        {
            table[i*len + i + 1] = true;
            if (maxLen < 2)
            {
                longestBegin = i;
                maxLen = 2;
            }
        }
    }

    for (size_t k = 3; k <= len; k++)
    {
        for (size_t i = 0; i < len - k + 1; i++)
        {
            size_t j = i + k - 1;
            if (str[i] == str[j] && table[(i + 1)*len + j - 1])
```

```
        {
            table[i*len +j] = true;
            if (maxLen < k)
            {
                longestBegin = i;
                maxLen = k;
            }
        }
    }
}
    return std::string(str.substr(longestBegin, maxLen));
}
```

Here are some test cases for the `longest_palindrome()` function:

```
int main()
{
    using namespace std::string_literals;
    assert(longest_palindrome("sahararahnide") == "hararah");
    assert(longest_palindrome("level") == "level");
    assert(longest_palindrome("s") == "s");
}
```

29. License plate validation

The simplest way to solve this problem is by using regular expressions. The regular expression that meets the described format is "`[A-Z]{3}-[A-Z]{2} \d{3,4}`".

The first function only has to validate that an input string contains only text that matches this regular expression. For that, we can use `std::regex_match()`, as follows:

```
bool validate_license_plate_format(std::string_view str)
{
    std::regex rx(R"([A-Z]{3}-[A-Z]{2} \d{3,4})");
    return std::regex_match(str.data(), rx);
}

int main()
{
    assert(validate_license_plate_format("ABC-DE 123"));
    assert(validate_license_plate_format("ABC-DE 1234"));
    assert(!validate_license_plate_format("ABC-DE 12345"));
    assert(!validate_license_plate_format("abc-de 1234"));
}
```

The second function is slightly different. Instead of matching the input string, it must identify all occurrences of the regular expression within the string. The regular expression would therefore change to "`([A-Z]{3}-[A-Z]{2} \d{3,4})*`". To iterate through all matches we have to use `std::sregex_iterator`, which is as follows:

```
std::vector<std::string> extract_license_plate_numbers(
                         std::string const & str)
{
   std::regex rx(R"(([A-Z]{3}-[A-Z]{2} \d{3,4})*)");
   std::smatch match;
   std::vector<std::string> results;

   for(auto i = std::sregex_iterator(std::cbegin(str), std::cend(str), rx);
       i != std::sregex_iterator(); ++i)
   {
      if((*i)[1].matched)
      results.push_back(i->str());
   }
   return results;
}

int main()
{
   std::vector<std::string> expected {
      "AAA-AA 123", "ABC-DE 1234", "XYZ-WW 0001"};
   std::string text("AAA-AA 123qwe-ty 1234 ABC-DE 123456..XYZ-WW 0001");
   assert(expected == extract_license_plate_numbers(text));
}
```

30. Extracting URL parts

This problem is also suited to being solved using regular expressions. Finding a regular expression that could match any URL is, however, a difficult task. The purpose of this exercise is to help you practice your skills with the regex library, and not to find the ultimate regular expression for this particular purpose. Therefore, the regular expression used here is provided only for didactic purposes.

 You can try regular expressions using online testers and debuggers, such as `https://regex101.com/`. This can be useful in order to work out your regular expressions and try them against various datasets.

For this task we will consider that a URL has the following parts: `protocol` and `domain` are mandatory, and `port`, `path`, `query`, and `fragment` are all optional. The following structure is used to return results from parsing an URL (alternatively, you could return a tuple and use structured binding to bind variables to the various sub parts of the tuple):

```
struct uri_parts
{
    std::string              protocol;
    std::string              domain;
    std::optional<int>       port;
    std::optional<std::string> path;
    std::optional<std::string> query;
    std::optional<std::string> fragment;
};
```

A function that can parse a URL and extract and return its parts could have the following implementation. Note that the return type is an `std::optional<uri_parts>` because the function might fail in matching the input string to the regular expression; in this case, the return value is `std::nullopt`:

```
std::optional<uri_parts> parse_uri(std::string uri)
{
    std::regex rx(R"(^(\w+):\/\/([\w.-
]+)(:(\d+))?([\w\/\.]+)?(\?([\w=&]*)(#?(\w+))?)?$)");
    auto matches = std::smatch{};
    if (std::regex_match(uri, matches, rx))
    {
        if (matches[1].matched && matches[2].matched)
        {
            uri_parts parts;
            parts.protocol = matches[1].str();
            parts.domain = matches[2].str();
            if (matches[4].matched)
                parts.port = std::stoi(matches[4]);
            if (matches[5].matched)
                parts.path = matches[5];
            if (matches[7].matched)
                parts.query = matches[7];
            if (matches[9].matched)
                parts.fragment = matches[9];
            return parts;
        }
    }
    return {};
}
```

The following program tests the `parse_uri()` function with two URLs that contain different parts:

```
int main()
{
    auto p1 = parse_uri("https://packt.com");
    assert(p1.has_value());
    assert(p1->protocol == "https");
    assert(p1->domain == "packt.com");
    assert(!p1->port.has_value());
    assert(!p1->path.has_value());
    assert(!p1->query.has_value());
    assert(!p1->fragment.has_value());

    auto p2 = parse_uri("https://bbc.com:80/en/index.html?lite=true#ui");
    assert(p2.has_value());
    assert(p2->protocol == "https");
    assert(p2->domain == "bbc.com");
    assert(p2->port == 80);
    assert(p2->path.value() == "/en/index.html");
    assert(p2->query.value() == "lite=true");
    assert(p2->fragment.value() == "ui");
}
```

31. Transforming dates in strings

Text transformation can be performed with regular expressions using `std::regex_replace()`. A regular expression that can match dates with the specified formats is `(\d{1,2})(\.|-|/)(\d{1,2})(\.|-|/)(\d{4})`. This regex defines five capture groups; the 1st is for the day, the 2nd is for the separator (. or –), the 3rd is for the month, the 4th is again for the separator (. or –), and the 5th is for the year.

Since we want to transform dates from the format dd.mm.yyyy or dd-mm-yyyy to yyyy-mm-dd, the regex replacement format string for std::regex_replace() should be "($5-$3-$1)":

```
std::string transform_date(std::string_view text)
{
    auto rx = std::regex{ R"((\d{1,2})(\.|-|/)(\d{1,2})(\.|-|/)(\d{4}))" };
    return std::regex_replace(text.data(), rx, R"($5-$3-$1)");
}

int main()
{
    using namespace std::string_literals;
    assert(transform_date("today is 01.12.2017!"s) ==
           "today is 2017-12-01!"s);
}
```

4
Streams and Filesystems

Problems

32. Pascal's triangle

Write a function that prints up to 10 rows of Pascal's triangle to the console.

33. Tabular printing of a list of processes

Suppose you have a snapshot of the list of all processes in a system. The information for each process includes name, identifier, status (which can be either *running* or *suspended*), account name (under which the process runs), memory size in bytes, and platform (which can be either 32-bit or 64-bit). Your task is to write a function that takes such a list of processes and prints them to the console alphabetically, in tabular format. All columns must be left-aligned, except for the memory column which must be right-aligned. The value of the memory size must be displayed in KB. The following is an example of the output of this function:

```
chrome.exe     1044    Running    marius.bancila    25180  32-bit
chrome.exe     10100   Running    marius.bancila   227756  32-bit
cmd.exe        512     Running    SYSTEM               48  64-bit
explorer.exe   7108    Running    marius.bancila    29529  64-bit
skype.exe      22456   Suspended  marius.bancila      656  64-bit
```

34. Removing empty lines from a text file

Write a program that, given the path to a text file, modifies the file by removing all empty lines. Lines containing only whitespaces are considered empty.

35. Computing the size of a directory

Write a function that computes the size of a directory, in bytes, recursively. It should be possible to indicate whether symbolic links should be followed or not.

36. Deleting files older than a given date

Write a function that, given the path to a directory and a duration, deletes all the entries (files or subdirectories) older than the specified duration, in a recursive manner. The duration can represent anything, such as days, hours, minutes, seconds, and so on, or a combination of that, such as one hour and twenty minutes. If the specified directory is itself older than the given duration, it should be deleted entirely.

37. Finding files in a directory that match a regular expression

Write a function that, given the path to a directory and a regular expression, returns a list of all the directory entries whose names match the regular expression.

38. Temporary log files

Create a logging class that writes text messages to a discardable text file. The text file should have a unique name and must be located in a temporary directory. Unless specified otherwise, this log file should be deleted when the instance of the class is destroyed. However, it should be possible to retain the log file by moving it to a permanent location.

Solutions

32. Pascal's triangle

Pascal's triangle is a construction representing binomial coefficients. The triangle starts with a row that has a single value of 1. Elements of each row are constructed by summing the numbers above, to the left and right, and treating blank entries as 0. Here is an example of the triangle with five rows:

```
        1
      1   1
    1   2   1
  1   3   3   1
1   4   6   4   1
```

To print the triangle, we must:

- Shift the output position to the right with an appropriate number of spaces, so that the top is projected on the middle of the triangle's base.
- Compute each value by summing the above left and right values. A simpler formula is that for a row `i` and column `j`, each new value `x` is equal to the previous value of `x` multiplied by `(i - j) / (j + 1)`, where `x` starts at 1.

The following is a possible implementation of a function that prints the triangle:

```cpp
unsigned int number_of_digits(unsigned int const i)
{
    return i > 0 ? (int)log10((double)i) + 1 : 1;
}

void print_pascal_triangle(int const n)
{
    for (int i = 0; i < n; i++)
    {
        auto x = 1;
        std::cout << std::string((n - i - 1)*(n / 2), ' ');
        for (int j = 0; j <= i; j++)
        {
            auto y = x;
            x = x * (i - j) / (j + 1);
            auto maxlen = number_of_digits(x) - 1;
            std::cout << y << std::string(n - 1 - maxlen - n%2, ' ');
        }
        std::cout << std::endl;
```

```
        }
    }
```

The following program asks the user to enter the number of levels and prints the triangle to the console:

```
int main()
{
    int n = 0;
    std::cout << "Levels (up to 10): ";
    std::cin >> n;
    if (n > 10)
        std::cout << "Value too large" << std::endl;
    else
        print_pascal_triangle(n);
}
```

33. Tabular printing of a list of processes

To solve this problem, we will consider the following class representing information about a process:

```
enum class procstatus {suspended, running};
enum class platforms {p32bit, p64bit};

struct procinfo
{
    int         id;
    std::string name;
    procstatus  status;
    std::string account;
    size_t      memory;
    platforms   platform;
};
```

In order to print the status and platform as text and not as numerical values, we need conversion functions from the enumerations to std::string:

```
std::string status_to_string(procstatus const status)
{
    if (status == procstatus::suspended) return "suspended";
    else return "running";
}

std::string platform_to_string(platforms const platform)
{
```

```
        if (platform == platforms::p32bit) return "32-bit";
        else return "64-bit";
    }
```

The processes are required to be sorted alphabetically by process name. Therefore, the first step would be to sort the input range of processes. For the printing itself, we should use the I/O manipulators:

```cpp
void print_processes(std::vector<procinfo> processes)
{
    std::sort(
        std::begin(processes), std::end(processes),
        [](procinfo const & p1, procinfo const & p2) {
            return p1.name < p2.name; });

    for (auto const & pi : processes)
    {
        std::cout << std::left << std::setw(25) << std::setfill(' ')
                  << pi.name;
        std::cout << std::left << std::setw(8) << std::setfill(' ')
                  << pi.id;
        std::cout << std::left << std::setw(12) << std::setfill(' ')
                  << status_to_string(pi.status);
        std::cout << std::left << std::setw(15) << std::setfill(' ')
                  << pi.account;
        std::cout << std::right << std::setw(10) << std::setfill(' ')
                  << (int)(pi.memory/1024);
        std::cout << std::left << ' ' << platform_to_string(pi.platform);
        std::cout << std::endl;
    }
}
```

The following program defines a list of processes (you can actually retrieve the list of running processes using operating system-specific APIs) and prints it to the console in the requested format:

```cpp
int main()
{
    using namespace std::string_literals;

    std::vector<procinfo> processes
    {
        {512, "cmd.exe"s, procstatus::running, "SYSTEM"s,
            148293, platforms::p64bit },
        {1044, "chrome.exe"s, procstatus::running, "marius.bancila"s,
            25180454, platforms::p32bit},
        {7108, "explorer.exe"s, procstatus::running, "marius.bancila"s,
```

```
                2952943, platforms::p64bit },
        {10100, "chrome.exe"s, procstatus::running, "marius.bancila"s,
                227756123, platforms::p32bit},
        {22456, "skype.exe"s, procstatus::suspended, "marius.bancila"s,
                16870123, platforms::p64bit },
    };

    print_processes(processes);
}
```

34. Removing empty lines from a text file

A possible approach to solving this task is to do the following:

1. Create a temporary file to contain only the text you want to retain from the original file
2. Read line by line from the input file and copy to the temporary file all lines that are not empty
3. Delete the original file after finishing processing it
4. Move the temporary file to the path of the original file

An alternative is to move the temporary file and overwrite the original one. The following implementation follows the steps listed. The temporary file is created in the temporary directory returned by `filesystem::temp_directory_path()`:

```
namespace fs = std::experimental::filesystem;

void remove_empty_lines(fs::path filepath)
{
    std::ifstream filein(filepath.native(), std::ios::in);
    if (!filein.is_open())
        throw std::runtime_error("cannot open input file");
    auto temppath = fs::temp_directory_path() / "temp.txt";
    std::ofstream fileout(temppath.native(),
    std::ios::out | std::ios::trunc);
    if (!fileout.is_open())
        throw std::runtime_error("cannot create temporary file");

    std::string line;
    while (std::getline(filein, line))
    {
        if (line.length() > 0 &&
        line.find_first_not_of(' ') != line.npos)
        {
```

```
            fileout << line << '\n';
         }
      }
      filein.close();
      fileout.close();

      fs::remove(filepath);
      fs::rename(temppath, filepath);
   }
```

35. Computing the size of a directory

To compute the size of a directory, we have to iterate through all the files and sum the size of individual files.

`filesystem::recursive_directory_iterator` is an iterator from the `filesystem` library that allows iterating all the entries of a directory in a recursive manner. It has various constructors, some of them taking a value of the type `filesystem::directory_options` that indicates whether symbolic links should be followed or not. The general purpose `std::accumulate()` algorithm can be used to sum together the file sizes. Since the total size of a directory could exceed 2 GB, you should not use `int` or `long`, but `unsigned long long` for the sum type. The following function shows a possible implementation for the required task:

```cpp
namespace fs = std::experimental::filesystem;

std::uintmax_t get_directory_size(fs::path const & dir,
                                  bool const follow_symlinks = false)
{
   auto iterator = fs::recursive_directory_iterator(
      dir,
      follow_symlinks ? fs::directory_options::follow_directory_symlink :
                        fs::directory_options::none);

   return std::accumulate(
      fs::begin(iterator), fs::end(iterator),
      0ull,
      [](std::uintmax_t const total,
         fs::directory_entry const & entry) {
            return total + (fs::is_regular_file(entry) ?
                     fs::file_size(entry.path()) : 0);
      });
}
```

```
int main()
{
    std::string path;
    std::cout << "Path: ";
    std::cin >> path;
    std::cout << "Size: " << get_directory_size(path) << std::endl;
}
```

36. Deleting files older than a given date

To perform filesystem operations, you should be using the `filesystem` library. For working with time and duration, you should be using the `chrono` library. A function that implements the requested functionality has to do the following:

1. Check whether the entry indicated by the target path exists and is older than the given duration, and if so, delete it
2. If it is not older and it's a directory, iterate through all its entries and call the function recursively:

```
namespace fs = std::experimental::filesystem;
namespace ch = std::chrono;

template <typename Duration>
bool is_older_than(fs::path const & path, Duration const duration)
{
    auto ftimeduration = fs::last_write_time(path).time_since_epoch();
    auto nowduration = (ch::system_clock::now() - duration)
                        .time_since_epoch();
    return ch::duration_cast<Duration>(nowduration - ftimeduration)
                        .count() > 0;
}

template <typename Duration>
void remove_files_older_than(fs::path const & path,
                             Duration const duration)
{
    try
    {
        if (fs::exists(path))
        {
            if (is_older_than(path, duration))
            {
                fs::remove(path);
            }
            else if(fs::is_directory(path))
```

```
        {
            for (auto const & entry : fs::directory_iterator(path))
            {
                remove_files_older_than(entry.path(), duration);
            }
        }
    }
    catch (std::exception const & ex)
    {
        std::cerr << ex.what() << std::endl;
    }
}
```

An alternative to using `directory_iterator` and recursively calling `remove_files_older_than()` would be to use `recursive_directory_iterator` and simply delete the entry if older than the given duration. However, this approach would employ undefined behavior, because if a file or a directory is deleted or added to the directory tree after the recursive directory iterator has been created, it is not specified whether the change would be observed through the iterator. Therefore, this method should be avoided.

The `is_older_than()` function template determines the time that has passed since the system's clock epoch for the current moment and the last file writing operation and checks whether the difference of the two is greater than the specified duration.

The `remove_files_older_than()` function can be used as follows:

```
int main()
{
    using namespace std::chrono_literals;

#ifdef _WIN32
    auto path = R"(..\Test\)";
#else
    auto path = R"(../Test/)";
#endif

    remove_files_older_than(path, 1h + 20min);
}
```

37. Finding files in a directory that match a regular expression

Implementing the specified functionality should be straightforward: iterate recursively through all the entries of the specified directory and retain all the entries that are regular files and whose name matches the regular expression. To do that, you should use the following:

- `filesystem::recursive_directory_iterator` to iterate through directory entries
- `regex` and `regex_match()` to check whether the filename matches the regular expression
- `copy_if()` and `back_inserter` to copy, at the end of a `vector`, the directory entries that match a specific criteria.

Such a function may look like this:

```
namespace fs = std::experimental::filesystem;

std::vector<fs::directory_entry> find_files(
    fs::path const & path,
    std::string_view regex)
{
    std::vector<fs::directory_entry> result;
    std::regex rx(regex.data());

    std::copy_if(
        fs::recursive_directory_iterator(path),
        fs::recursive_directory_iterator(),
        std::back_inserter(result),
        [&rx](fs::directory_entry const & entry) {
            return fs::is_regular_file(entry.path()) &&
                    std::regex_match(entry.path().filename().string(), rx);
    });

    return result;
}
```

With this available, we can write the following code:

```
int main()
{
    auto dir = fs::temp_directory_path();
    auto pattern = R"(wct[0-9a-zA-Z]{3}\.tmp)";
    auto result = find_files(dir, pattern);

    for (auto const & entry : result)
    {
        std::cout << entry.path().string() << std::endl;
    }
}
```

38. Temporary log files

The logging class that you have to implement for this task should:

- Have a constructor that creates a text file in a temporary directory and opens it for writing
- During destruction, if the file still exists, close and delete it
- Have a method that closes the file and moves it to a permanent path
- Overloads `operator<<` to write a text message to the output file

In order to create unique names for the file, you could use a UUID (also known as GUID). The C++ standard does not support any functionality related to that, but there are third-party libraries, such as `boost::uuid`, *CrossGuid*, or `stduuid`, which is actually a library that I created. For this implementation, I will use the last one. You can find it at `https://github.com/mariusbancila/stduuid`:

```
namespace fs = std::experimental::filesystem;

class logger
{
    fs::path logpath;
    std::ofstream logfile;
public:
    logger()
    {
        auto name = uuids::to_string(uuids::uuid_random_generator{}());
        logpath = fs::temp_directory_path() / (name + ".tmp");
        logfile.open(logpath.c_str(), std::ios::out|std::ios::trunc);
    }
```

```
    ~logger() noexcept
    {
       try {
          if(logfile.is_open()) logfile.close();
          if (!logpath.empty()) fs::remove(logpath);
       }
       catch (...) {}
    }

    void persist(fs::path const & path)
    {
       logfile.close();
       fs::rename(logpath, path);
       logpath.clear();
    }

    logger& operator<<(std::string_view message)
    {
       logfile << message.data() << '\n';
       return *this;
    }
};
```

An example of using this class is as follows:

```
int main()
{
    logger log;
    try
    {
        log << "this is a line" << "and this is another one";
        throw std::runtime_error("error");
    }
    catch (...)
    {
        log.persist(R"(lastlog.txt)");
    }
}
```

5
Date and Time

Problems

39. Measuring function execution time

Write a function that can measure the execution time of a function (with any number of arguments) in any required duration (such as seconds, milliseconds, microseconds, and so on).

40. Number of days between two dates

Write a function that, given two dates, returns the number of days between the two dates. The function should work regardless of the order of the input dates.

41. Day of the week

Write a function that, given a date, determines the day of the week. This function should return a value between 1 (for Monday) and 7 (for Sunday).

42. Day and week of the year

Write a function that, given a date, returns the day of the year (from 1 to 365 or 366 for leap years) and another function that, for the same input, returns the calendar week of the year.

43. Meeting time for multiple time zones

Write a function that, given a list of meeting participants and their time zones, displays the local meeting time for each participant.

44. Monthly calendar

Write a function that, given a year and month, prints to the console the month calendar. The expected output format is as follows (the example is for December 2017):

```
Mon  Tue  Wed  Thu  Fri  Sat  Sun
                         1    2    3
  4    5    6    7    8    9   10
 11   12   13   14   15   16   17
 18   19   20   21   22   23   24
 25   26   27   28   29   30   31
```

Solutions

39. Measuring function execution time

To measure the execution time of a function, you should retrieve the current time before the function execution, execute the function, then retrieve the current time again and determine how much time passed between the two time points. For convenience, this can all be put in a `variadic` function template that takes as arguments the function to execute and its arguments, and:

- Uses `std::high_resolution_clock` by default to determine the current time.
- Uses `std::invoke()` to execute the function to measure, with its specified arguments.
- Returns a duration and not a number of ticks for a particular duration. This is important so that you don't lose resolution. It enables you to add execution time duration of various resolutions, such as seconds and milliseconds, which would not be possible by returning a tick count:

```
template <typename Time = std::chrono::microseconds,
          typename Clock = std::chrono::high_resolution_clock>
struct perf_timer
{
   template <typename F, typename... Args>
   static Time duration(F&& f, Args... args)
   {
      auto start = Clock::now();
      std::invoke(std::forward<F>(f), std::forward<Args>(args)...);
      auto end = Clock::now();

      return std::chrono::duration_cast<Time>(end - start);
   }
};
```

This function template can be used as follows:

```
void f()
{
   // simulate work
   std::this_thread::sleep_for(2s);
}
```

```
void g(int const a, int const b)
{
   // simulate work
   std::this_thread::sleep_for(1s);
}

int main()
{
   auto t1 = perf_timer<std::chrono::microseconds>::duration(f);
   auto t2 = perf_timer<std::chrono::milliseconds>::duration(g, 1, 2);

   auto total = std::chrono::duration<double, std::nano>(t1 + t2).count();
}
```

40. Number of days between two dates

As of C++17, the `chrono` standard library does not have support for working with dates, weeks, calendars, time zones, and other useful related features. This will change in C++20, as time zones and calendar support have been added to the standard at the Jacksonville meeting, in March 2018. The new additions are based on an open source library called `date`, built on top of `chrono`, developed by Howard Hinnant and available on GitHub at `https://github.com/HowardHinnant/date`. We will use this library to solve several of the problems in this chapter. Although in this implementation the namespace is `date`, in C++20 it will be part of `std::chrono`. However, you should be able to simply replace the namespace without any further code changes.

To solve this task, you could use the `date::sys_days` class, available in the `date.h` header. It represents a count of days since the `std::system_clock` epoch. This is a `time_point` with a resolution of a day and is implicitly convertible to `std::system_clock::time_point`. Basically, you have to construct two objects of this type and subtract them. The result is exactly the number of days between the two dates. The following is a simple implementation of such a function:

```
inline int number_of_days(
   int const y1, unsigned int const m1, unsigned int const d1,
   int const y2, unsigned int const m2, unsigned int const d2)
{
   using namespace date;

   return (sys_days{ year{ y1 } / month{ m1 } / day{ d1 } } -
           sys_days{ year{ y2 } / month{ m2 } / day{ d2 } }).count();
}
```

```
inline int number_of_days(date::sys_days const & first,
                          date::sys_days const & last)
{
    return (last - first).count();
}
```

Here are a couple of examples of how these overloaded functions could be used:

```
int main()
{
    auto diff1 = number_of_days(2016, 9, 23, 2017, 5, 15);

    using namespace date::literals;
    auto diff2 = number_of_days(2016_y/sep/23, 15_d/may/2017);
}
```

41. Day of the week

Solving this problem is again relatively straightforward if you use the `date` library. However, this time, you have to use the following types:

- `date::year_month_day`, a structure that represents a day with fields for year, month (1 to 12), and day (1 to 31).
- `date::iso_week::year_weeknum_weekday`, from the `iso_week.h` header, is a structure that has fields for year, number of weeks in a year, and number of days in a week (1 to 7). This class is implicitly convertible to and from `date::sys_days`, which makes it explicitly convertible to any other calendar system that is implicitly convertible to and from `date::sys_days`, such as `date::year_month_day`.

With that being said, the problem resolves to creating a `year_month_day` object to represent the desired date and then a `year_weeknum_weekday` object from it, and retrieving the day of the week with `weekday()`:

```
unsigned int week_day(int const y, unsigned int const m,
                      unsigned int const d)
{
    using namespace date;

    if(m < 1 || m > 12 || d < 1 || d > 31) return 0;

    auto const dt = date::year_month_day{year{ y }, month{ m }, day{ d }};
    auto const tiso = iso_week::year_weeknum_weekday{ dt };
```

```
      return (unsigned int)tiso.weekday();
}

int main()
{
   auto wday = week_day(2018, 5, 9);
}
```

42. Day and week of the year

The solution to this two-part problem should be straightforward from the previous two:

- To compute the day of the year, you subtract two date::sys_days objects, one representing the given day and the other January 0 of the same year. Alternatively, you could start from January 1 and add 1 to the result.
- To determine the week number of the year, construct a year_weeknum_weekday object, like in the previous problem, and retrieve the weeknum() value:

```
int day_of_year(int const y, unsigned int const m,
                unsigned int const d)
{
   using namespace date;

   if(m < 1 || m > 12 || d < 1 || d > 31) return 0;

   return (sys_days{ year{ y } / month{ m } / day{ d } } -
           sys_days{ year{ y } / jan / 0 }).count();
}

unsigned int calendar_week(int const y, unsigned int const m,
                           unsigned int const d)
{
   using namespace date;

   if(m < 1 || m > 12 || d < 1 || d > 31) return 0;

   auto const dt = date::year_month_day{year{ y }, month{ m }, day{ d }};
   auto const tiso = iso_week::year_weeknum_weekday{ dt };

   return (unsigned int)tiso.weeknum();
}
```

These functions can be used as follows:

```
int main()
{
    int y = 0;
    unsigned int m = 0, d = 0;
    std::cout << "Year:"; std::cin >> y;
    std::cout << "Month:"; std::cin >> m;
    std::cout << "Day:"; std::cin >> d;

    std::cout << "Calendar week:" << calendar_week(y, m, d) << std::endl;
    std::cout << "Day of year:" << day_of_year(y, m, d) << std::endl;
}
```

43. Meeting time for multiple time zones

To work with time zones, you must use the `tz.h` header of the `date` library. However, this needs the *IANA Time Zone Database* to be downloaded and uncompressed on your machine.

This is how to prepare the time zone database for the date library:

- Download the latest version of the database from `https://www.iana.org/time-zones`. Currently, the latest version is called `tzdata2017c.tar.gz`.
- Uncompress this to any location on your machine, in a subdirectory called `tzdata`. Let's suppose the parent directory is `c:\work\challenges\libs\date` (on a Windows machine); this will have a sub directory called `tzdata`.
- For Windows, you need to download a file called `windowsZones.xml`, containing mappings of Windows time zones to IANA time zones. This is available at `https://unicode.org/repos/cldr/trunk/common/supplemental/windowsZones.xml`. The file must be stored in the same `tzdata` sub directory created earlier.
- In your project settings, define a preprocessor macro called `INSTALL` that indicates the parent directory for the `tzdata` sub directory. For the example given here, you should have `INSTALL=c:\\work\\challenges\\libs\\date`. (Note that the double backslash is necessary because the macro is used to create a file path using stringification and concatenation, and would otherwise result in an incorrect path.)

To solve this problem, we will consider a user structure with minimal information, such as name and time zone. The time zone is created using the `date::locate_zone()` function:

```cpp
struct user
{
    std::string Name;
    date::time_zone const * Zone;

    explicit user(std::string_view name, std::string_view zone)
        : Name{name.data()}, Zone(date::locate_zone(zone.data()))
    {}
};
```

A function that displays a list of users and their local time for the start of a meeting should transform the given time from a reference zone to the time in their own zone. To do that, we can use a conversion constructor of the `date::zoned_time` class:

```cpp
template <class Duration, class TimeZonePtr>
void print_meeting_times(
    date::zoned_time<Duration, TimeZonePtr> const & time,
    std::vector<user> const & users)
{
    std::cout
        << std::left << std::setw(15) << std::setfill(' ')
        << "Local time: "
        << time << std::endl;

    for (auto const & user : users)
    {
        std::cout
            << std::left << std::setw(15) << std::setfill(' ')
            << user.Name
            << date::zoned_time<Duration, TimeZonePtr>(user.Zone, time)
            << std::endl;
    }
}
```

This function can be used as follows, where the given time (hour and minute) is represented in the current time zone:

```cpp
int main()
{
    std::vector<user> users{
        user{ "Ildiko", "Europe/Budapest" },
        user{ "Jens", "Europe/Berlin" },
        user{ "Jane", "America/New_York" }
    };
```

```
    unsigned int h, m;
    std::cout << "Hour:"; std::cin >> h;
    std::cout << "Minutes:"; std::cin >> m;

    date::year_month_day today =
        date::floor<date::days>(ch::system_clock::now());

    auto localtime = date::zoned_time<std::chrono::minutes>(
        date::current_zone(),
        static_cast<date::local_days>(today)+ch::hours{h}+ch::minutes{m});

    print_meeting_times(localtime, users);
}
```

44. Monthly calendar

Solving this task is actually partially based on the previous tasks. In order to print the days of the month as indicated in the problem, you should know:

- What weekday is the first day of the month. This can be determined using the `week_day()` function created for a previous problem.
- The number of days in the month. This can be determined using the `date::year_month_day_last` structure and retrieving the value of `day()`.

With this information determined first, you should:

- Print empty values for the first week before the first weekday
- Print the day number with the proper formatting from 1 to the last day of the month
- Break on a new line after every seven days (counting from day 1 of the first week, even though that could belong to the previous month)

The implementation of all this is shown here:

```
unsigned int week_day(int const y, unsigned int const m,
                      unsigned int const d)
{
    using namespace date;

    if(m < 1 || m > 12 || d < 1 || d > 31) return 0;

    auto const dt = date::year_month_day{year{ y }, month{ m }, day{ d }};
    auto const tiso = iso_week::year_weeknum_weekday{ dt };
```

```
      return (unsigned int)tiso.weekday();
   }

   void print_month_calendar(int const y, unsigned int m)
   {
      using namespace date;
      std::cout << "Mon Tue Wed Thu Fri Sat Sun" << std::endl;

      auto first_day_weekday = week_day(y, m, 1);
      auto last_day = (unsigned int)year_month_day_last(
         year{ y }, month_day_last{ month{ m } }).day();

      unsigned int index = 1;
      for (unsigned int day = 1; day < first_day_weekday; ++day, ++index)
      {
         std::cout << "    ";
      }

      for (unsigned int day = 1; day <= last_day; ++day)
      {
         std::cout << std::right << std::setfill(' ') << std::setw(3)
                  << day << ' ';
         if (index++ % 7 == 0) std::cout << std::endl;
      }

      std::cout << std::endl;
   }

   int main()
   {
      print_month_calendar(2017, 12);
   }
```

6
Algorithms and Data Structures

Problems

45. Priority queue

Write a data structure that represents a priority queue that provides constant time lookup for the largest element, but has logarithmic time complexity for adding and removing elements. A queue inserts new elements at the end and removes elements from the top. By default, the queue should use `operator<` to compare elements, but it should be possible for the user to provide a comparison function object that returns `true` if the first argument is less than the second. The implementation must provide at least the following operations:

- `push()` to add a new element
- `pop()` to remove the top element
- `top()` to provide access to the top element
- `size()` to indicate the number of elements in the queue
- `empty()` to indicate whether the queue is empty

46. Circular buffer

Create a data structure that represents a circular buffer of a fixed size. A circular buffer overwrites existing elements when the buffer is being filled beyond its fixed size. The class you must write should:

- Prohibit default construction
- Support the creation of objects with a specified size
- Allow checking of the buffer capacity and status
  (`empty()`, `full()`, `size()`, `capacity()`)
- Add a new element, an operation that could potentially overwrite the oldest element in the buffer
- Remove the oldest element from the buffer
- Support iteration through its elements

47. Double buffer

Write a class that represents a buffer that could be written and read at the same time without the two operations colliding. A read operation must provide access to the old data while a write operation is in progress. Newly written data must be available for reading upon completion of the write operation.

48. The most frequent element in a range

Write a function that, given a range, returns the most frequent element and the number of times it appears in the range. If more than one element appears the same maximum number of times then the function should return all the elements. For instance, for the range `{1,1,3,5,8,13,3,5,8,8,5}`, it should return `{5, 3}` and `{8, 3}`.

49. Text histogram

Write a program that, given a text, determines and prints a histogram with the frequency of each letter of the alphabet. The frequency is the percentage of the number of appearances of each letter from the total count of letters. The program should count only the appearances of letters and ignore digits, signs, and other possible characters. The frequency must be determined based on the count of letters and not the text size.

50. Filtering a list of phone numbers

Write a function that, given a list of phone numbers, returns only the numbers that are from a specified country. The country is indicated by its phone country code, such as 44 for Great Britain. Phone numbers may start with the country code, a + followed by the country code, or have no country code. The ones from this last category must be ignored.

51. Transforming a list of phone numbers

Write a function that, given a list of phone numbers, transforms them so they all start with a specified phone country code, preceded by the + sign. Any whitespaces from a phone number should also be removed. The following is a list of input and output examples:

```
07555 123456      => +447555123456
07555123456       => +447555123456
+44 7555 123456   => +447555123456
44 7555 123456    => +447555123456
7555 123456       => +447555123456
```

52. Generating all the permutations of a string

Write a function that, prints on the console all the possible permutations of a given string. You should provide two versions of this function: one that uses recursion, and one that does not.

53. Average rating of movies

Write a program that calculates and prints the average rating of a list of movies. Each movie has a list of ratings from 1 to 10 (where 1 is the lowest and 10 is the highest rating). In order to compute the rating, you must remove 5% of the highest and lowest ratings before computing their average. The result must be displayed with a single decimal point.

54. Pairwise algorithm

Write a general-purpose function that, given a range, returns a new range with pairs of consecutive elements from the input range. Should the input range have an odd number of elements, the last one must be ignored. For example, if the input range was `{1, 1, 3, 5, 8, 13, 21}`, the result must be `{ {1, 1}, {3, 5}, {8, 13}}`.

55. Zip algorithm

Write a function that, given two ranges, returns a new range with pairs of elements from the two ranges. Should the two ranges have different sizes, the result must contain as many elements as the smallest of the input ranges. For example, if the input ranges were { 1, 2, 3, 4, 5, 6, 7, 8, 9, 10 } and { 1, 1, 3, 5, 8, 13, 21 }, the result should be {{1,1}, {2,1}, {3,3}, {4,5}, {5,8}, {6,13}, {7,21}}.

56. Select algorithm

Write a function that, given a range of values and a projection function, transforms each value into a new one and returns a new range with the selected values. For instance, if you have a type book that has an id, title, and author, and have a range of such book values, it should be possible for the function to select only the title of the books. Here is an example of how the function should be used:

```cpp
struct book
{
    int         id;
    std::string title;
    std::string author;
};

std::vector<book> books{
    {101, "The C++ Programming Language", "Bjarne Stroustrup"},
    {203, "Effective Modern C++", "Scott Meyers"},
    {404, "The Modern C++ Programming Cookbook", "Marius Bancila"}};

auto titles = select(books, [](book const & b) {return b.title; });
```

57. Sort algorithm

Write a function that, given a pair of random-access iterators to define its lower and upper bounds, sorts the elements of the range using the quicksort algorithm. There should be two overloads of the sort function: one that uses `operator<` to compare the elements of the range and put them in ascending order, and one that uses a user-defined binary comparison function for comparing the elements.

58. The shortest path between nodes

Write a program that, given a network of nodes and the distances between them, computes and displays the shortest distance from a specified node to all the others, as well as the path between the start and end node. As input, consider the following undirected graph:

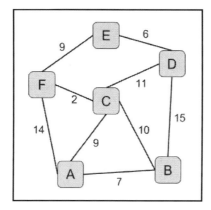

The program output for this graph should be the following:

```
A -> A : 0      A
A -> B : 7      A -> B
A -> C : 9      A -> C
A -> D : 20     A -> C -> D
A -> E : 20     A -> C -> F -> E
A -> F : 11     A -> C -> F
```

59. The Weasel program

Write a program that implements Richard Dawkins' weasel computer simulation, described in Dawkins' words as follows (*The Blind Watchmaker*, chapter 3):

> *We again use our computer monkey, but with a crucial difference in its program. It again begins by choosing a random sequence of 28 letters, just as before ... it duplicates it repeatedly, but with a certain chance of random error – 'mutation' – in the copying. The computer examines the mutant nonsense phrases, the 'progeny' of the original phrase, and chooses the one which, however slightly, most resembles the target phrase, METHINKS IT IS LIKE A WEASEL.*

60. The Game of Life

Write a program that implements the *Game of Life* cellular automaton proposed by *John Horton Conway*. The universe of this game is a grid of square cells that could have one of two states: dead or alive. Every cell interacts with its adjacent neighbors, with the following transactions occurring on every step:

- Any live cell with fewer than two live neighbors dies, as if caused by under-population
- Any live cell with two or three live neighbors lives on to the next generation
- Any live cell with more than three live neighbors dies, as if by overpopulation
- Any dead cell with exactly three live neighbors becomes a live cell, as if by reproduction

The status of the game on each iteration should be displayed on the console, and for convenience, you should pick a reasonable size, such as 20 rows x 50 columns.

Solutions

45. Priority queue

A priority queue is an abstract data type whose elements have a priority attached to them. Instead of working as a first-in-first-out container, a priority queue makes elements available in the order of their priority. This data structure is used in algorithms such as Dijkstra's shortest path, Prim's algorithm, heap sort, the A* search algorithm, in Huffman codes used for data compression, and others.

A very simple approach to implement a priority queue would be to use an `std::vector` as the underlying container of elements and always maintain it sorted. That means the maximum and minimum elements are always at the two ends. However, this approach does not provide the most efficient operations.

The most suitable data structure that can be used to implement a priority queue is a heap. This is a tree-based data structure that satisfies the following property: if P is a parent node of C, then the key (the value) of P is either greater than or equal to (in a max heap) or less than or equal to (in a min heap) the key of C.

The standard library provides several operations for working with heaps:

- `std::make_heap()`: This creates a max heap for the given range, using either `operator<` or a user-provided comparison function to order the elements
- `std::push_heap()`: This inserts a new element at the end of the max heap
- `std::pop_heap()`: This removes the first element of the heap (by swapping the values in the first and last position and making the sub-range `[first, last-1)` a max heap)

A priority queue implementation, that uses `std::vector` to hold data and the standard functions for heaps, can look as follows:

```
template <class T,
    class Compare = std::less<typename std::vector<T>::value_type>>
class priority_queue
{
    typedef typename std::vector<T>::value_type value_type;
    typedef typename std::vector<T>::size_type size_type;
    typedef typename std::vector<T>::reference reference;
    typedef typename std::vector<T>::const_reference const_reference;
public:
    bool empty() const noexcept { return data.empty(); }
```

```
      size_type size() const noexcept { return data.size(); }

      void push(value_type const & value)
      {
         data.push_back(value);
         std::push_heap(std::begin(data), std::end(data), comparer);
      }

      void pop()
      {
         std::pop_heap(std::begin(data), std::end(data), comparer);
         data.pop_back();
      }

      const_reference top() const { return data.front(); }
      void swap(priority_queue& other) noexcept
      {
         swap(data, other.data);
         swap(comparer, other.comparer);
      }
private:
   std::vector<T> data;
   Compare comparer;
};

template<class T, class Compare>
void swap(priority_queue<T, Compare>& lhs,
          priority_queue<T, Compare>& rhs)
noexcept(noexcept(lhs.swap(rhs)))
{
   lhs.swap(rhs);
}
```

This class can be used as follows:

```
int main()
{
   priority_queue<int> q;
   for (int i : {1, 5, 3, 1, 13, 21, 8})
   {
      q.push(i);
   }

   assert(!q.empty());
   assert(q.size() == 7);

   while (!q.empty())
   {
```

```
        std::cout << q.top() << ' ';
        q.pop();
    }
}
```

46. Circular buffer

A circular buffer is a fixed-size container that behaves as if its two ends were connected to form a virtual circular memory layout. Its main benefit is that you don't need a large amount of memory to retain data, as older entries are overwritten by newer ones. Circular buffers are used in I/O buffering, bounded logging (when you only want to retain the last messages), buffers for asynchronous processing, and others.

We can differentiate between two situations:

1. The number of elements added to the buffer has not reached its capacity (its user-defined fixed size). In this case, it behaves likes a regular container, such as a vector.
2. The number of elements added to the buffer has reached and exceeded its capacity. In this case, the buffer's memory is reused and older elements are being overwritten.

We could represent such a structure using:

- A regular container with a pre-allocated number of elements
- A head pointer to indicate the position of the last inserted element
- A size counter to indicate the number of elements in the container, which cannot exceed its capacity (since elements are being overwritten in this case)

The two main operations with a circular buffer are:

- Adding a new element to the buffer. We always insert at the next position of the head pointer (or index). This is the push() method shown below.
- Removing an existing element from the buffer. We always remove the oldest element. That element is at position head - size (this must account for the circular nature of the index). This is the pop() method shown below.

The implementation of such a data structure is shown here:

```cpp
template <class T>
class circular_buffer
{
   typedef circular_buffer_iterator<T> const_iterator;

   circular_buffer() = delete;
public:
   explicit circular_buffer(size_t const size) :data_(size)
   {}

   bool clear() noexcept { head_ = -1; size_ = 0; }
   bool empty() const noexcept { return size_ == 0; }
   bool full() const noexcept { return size_ == data_.size(); }
   size_t capacity() const noexcept { return data_.size(); }
   size_t size() const noexcept { return size_; }

   void push(T const item)
   {
      head_ = next_pos();
      data_[head_] = item;
      if (size_ < data_.size()) size_++;
   }

   T pop()
   {
      if (empty()) throw std::runtime_error("empty buffer");
      auto pos = first_pos();
      size_--;
      return data_[pos];
   }

   const_iterator begin() const
   {
      return const_iterator(*this, first_pos(), empty());
   }

   const_iterator end() const
   {
      return const_iterator(*this, next_pos(), true);
   }

private:
   std::vector<T> data_;
   size_t head_ = -1;
   size_t size_ = 0;
```

```
    size_t next_pos() const noexcept
    { return size_ == 0 ? 0 : (head_ + 1) % data_.size(); }
    size_t first_pos() const noexcept
    { return size_ == 0 ? 0 : (head_ + data_.size() - size_ + 1) %
                               data_.size(); }

    friend class circular_buffer_iterator<T>;
};
```

Because of the circular nature of the indexes mapped on a contiguous memory layout, the iterator type for this class cannot be a pointer type. The iterators must be able to point elements by applying modulo operations on the index. Here is a possible implementation for such an iterator:

```
template <class T>
class circular_buffer_iterator
{
    typedef circular_buffer_iterator        self_type;
    typedef T                               value_type;
    typedef T&                              reference;
    typedef T const&                        const_reference;
    typedef T*                              pointer;
    typedef std::random_access_iterator_tag iterator_category;
    typedef ptrdiff_t                       difference_type;
public:
    circular_buffer_iterator(circular_buffer<T> const & buf,
                        size_t const pos, bool const last) :
    buffer_(buf), index_(pos), last_(last)
    {}

    self_type & operator++ ()
    {
        if (last_)
           throw std::out_of_range("Iterator cannot be incremented past the
end of range.");
        index_ = (index_ + 1) % buffer_.data_.size();
        last_ = index_ == buffer_.next_pos();
        return *this;
    }

    self_type operator++ (int)
    {
        self_type tmp = *this;
        ++*this;
        return tmp;
    }
```

```
    bool operator== (self_type const & other) const
    {
        assert(compatible(other));
        return index_ == other.index_ && last_ == other.last_;
    }

    bool operator!= (self_type const & other) const
    {
        return !(*this == other);
    }

    const_reference operator* () const
    {
        return buffer_.data_[index_];
    }

    const_reference operator-> () const
    {
        return buffer_.data_[index_];
    }
private:
    bool compatible(self_type const & other) const
    {
        return &buffer_ == &other.buffer_;
    }

    circular_buffer<T> const & buffer_;
    size_t index_;
    bool last_;
};
```

With all these implemented, we could write code such as the following. Notice that in the comments, the first range shows the actual content of the internal vector, and the second range shows the logical content as exposed with iterator access:

```
int main()
{
    circular_buffer<int> cbuf(5); // {0, 0, 0, 0, 0} -> {}

    cbuf.push(1);                  // {1, 0, 0, 0, 0} -> {1}
    cbuf.push(2);                  // {1, 2, 0, 0, 0} -> {1, 2}
    cbuf.push(3);                  // {1, 2, 3, 0, 0} -> {1, 2, 3}

    auto item = cbuf.pop();        // {1, 2, 3, 0, 0} -> {2, 3}
    cbuf.push(4);                  // {1, 2, 3, 4, 0} -> {2, 3, 4}
    cbuf.push(5);                  // {1, 2, 3, 4, 5} -> {2, 3, 4, 5}
    cbuf.push(6);                  // {6, 2, 3, 4, 5} -> {2, 3, 4, 5, 6}
```

```
    cbuf.push(7);           // {6, 7, 3, 4, 5} -> {3, 4, 5, 6, 7}
    cbuf.push(8);           // {6, 7, 8, 4, 5} -> {4, 5, 6, 7, 8}

    item = cbuf.pop();      // {6, 7, 8, 4, 5} -> {5, 6, 7, 8}
    item = cbuf.pop();      // {6, 7, 8, 4, 5} -> {6, 7, 8}
    item = cbuf.pop();      // {6, 7, 8, 4, 5} -> {7, 8}

    item = cbuf.pop();      // {6, 7, 8, 4, 5} -> {8}
    item = cbuf.pop();      // {6, 7, 8, 4, 5} -> {}

    cbuf.push(9);           // {6, 7, 8, 9, 5} -> {9}
}
```

47. Double buffer

The problem described here is a typical double buffering situation. Double buffering is the most common case of multiple buffering, which is a technique that allows a reader to see a complete version of the data and not a partially updated version produced by a writer. This is a common technique – especially in computer graphics – for avoiding flickering.

In order to implement the requested functionality, the buffer class that we should write must have two internal buffers: one that contains temporary data being written, and another one that contains completed (or committed) data. Upon the completion of a write operation, the content of the temporary buffer is written in the primary buffer. For the internal buffers, the implementation below uses `std::vector`. When the write operation completes, instead of copying data from one buffer to the other, we just swap the content of the two, which is a much faster operation. Access to the completed data is provided with either the `read()` function, which copies the content of the read buffer into a designated output, or with direct element access (overloaded `operator[]`). Access to the read buffer is synchronized with an `std::mutex` to make it safe to read from one thread while another is writing to the buffer:

```
template <typename T>
class double_buffer
{
    typedef T            value_type;
    typedef T&           reference;
    typedef T const &    const_reference;
    typedef T*           pointer;
public:
    explicit double_buffer(size_t const size) :
        rdbuf(size), wrbuf(size)
    {}
```

```cpp
    size_t size() const noexcept { return rdbuf.size(); }

    void write(T const * const ptr, size_t const size)
    {
        std::unique_lock<std::mutex> lock(mt);
        auto length = std::min(size, wrbuf.size());
        std::copy(ptr, ptr + length, std::begin(wrbuf));
        wrbuf.swap(rdbuf);
    }

    template <class Output>
    void read(Output it) const
    {
        std::unique_lock<std::mutex> lock(mt);
        std::copy(std::cbegin(rdbuf), std::cend(rdbuf), it);
    }
    pointer data() const
    {
        std::unique_lock<std::mutex> lock(mt);
        return rdbuf.data();
    }

    reference operator[](size_t const pos)
    {
        std::unique_lock<std::mutex> lock(mt);
        return rdbuf[pos];
    }
    const_reference operator[](size_t const pos) const
    {
        std::unique_lock<std::mutex> lock(mt);
        return rdbuf[pos];
    }

    void swap(double_buffer other)
    {
        std::swap(rdbuf, other.rdbuf);
        std::swap(wrbuf, other.wrbuf);
    }

private:
    std::vector<T>    rdbuf;
    std::vector<T>    wrbuf;
    mutable std::mutex mt;
};
```

The following is an example of how this double buffer class can be used for both writing and reading by two different entities:

```cpp
template <typename T>
void print_buffer(double_buffer<T> const & buf)
{
   buf.read(std::ostream_iterator<T>(std::cout, " "));
   std::cout << std::endl;
}

int main()
{
   double_buffer<int> buf(10);

   std::thread t([&buf]() {
      for (int i = 1; i < 1000; i += 10)
      {
         int data[] = { i, i + 1, i + 2, i + 3, i + 4,
                        i + 5, i + 6,i + 7,i + 8,i + 9 };
         buf.write(data, 10);

         using namespace std::chrono_literals;
         std::this_thread::sleep_for(100ms);
      }
   });

   auto start = std::chrono::system_clock::now();
   do
   {
      print_buffer(buf);

      using namespace std::chrono_literals;
      std::this_thread::sleep_for(150ms);
   } while (std::chrono::duration_cast<std::chrono::seconds>(
            std::chrono::system_clock::now() - start).count() < 12);

   t.join();
}
```

48. The most frequent element in a range

In order to determine and return the most frequent element in a range you should do the following:

- Count the appearances of each element in an `std::map`. The key is the element and the value is its number of appearances.
- Determine the maximum element of the map using `std::max_element()`. The result is a map element, that is, a pair containing the element and its number of appearances.

- Copy all map elements that have the value (appearance count) equal to the maximum element's value and return that as the final result.

An implementation of the steps described previously is shown in the following listing:

```cpp
template <typename T>
std::vector<std::pair<T, size_t>> find_most_frequent(
    std::vector<T> const & range)
{
    std::map<T, size_t> counts;
    for (auto const & e : range) counts[e]++;

    auto maxelem = std::max_element(
        std::cbegin(counts), std::cend(counts),
        [](auto const & e1, auto const & e2) {
            return e1.second < e2.second;
    });

    std::vector<std::pair<T, size_t>> result;

    std::copy_if(
        std::begin(counts), std::end(counts),
        std::back_inserter(result),
        [maxelem](auto const & kvp) {
            return kvp.second == maxelem->second;
    });

    return result;
}
```

The `find_most_frequent()` function can be used as follows:

```
int main()
{
    auto range = std::vector<int>{1,1,3,5,8,13,3,5,8,8,5};
    auto result = find_most_frequent(range);

    for (auto const & e : result)
    {
        std::cout << e.first << " : " << e.second << std::endl;
    }
}
```

49. Text histogram

A histogram is a representation of the distribution of numerical data. Widely known histograms are the color and image histograms that are used in photography and image processing. A text histogram, as described here, is a representation of the frequency of letters in a given text. This problem is partially similar to the previous one, except that the range elements are characters now and we must determine the frequency of them all. To solve this problem you should:

- Count the appearances of each letter using a map. The key is the letter and the value is its appearance count.
- When counting, ignore all characters that are not letters. Uppercase and lowercase characters must be treated as identical, as they represent the same letter.
- Use `std::accumulate()` to count the total number of appearances of all the letters in the given text.
- Use `std::for_each()` or a range-based `for` loop to go through all the elements of the map and transform the appearance count into a frequency.

The following is a possible implementation of the problem:

```
std::map<char, double> analyze_text(std::string_view text)
{
    std::map<char, double> frequencies;
    for (char ch = 'a'; ch <= 'z'; ch++)
        frequencies[ch] = 0;

    for (auto ch : text)
    {
        if (isalpha(ch))
```

```
            frequencies[tolower(ch)]++;
    }

    auto total = std::accumulate(
        std::cbegin(frequencies), std::cend(frequencies),
        0ull,
        [](auto sum, auto const & kvp) {
            return sum + static_cast<unsigned long long>(kvp.second);
    });

    std::for_each(
        std::begin(frequencies), std::end(frequencies),
        [total](auto & kvp) {
            kvp.second = (100.0 * kvp.second) / total;
    });

    return frequencies;
}
```

The following program prints the frequency of the letters from a text on the console:

```
int main()
{
    auto result = analyze_text(R"(Lorem ipsum dolor sit amet, consectetur
        adipiscing elit, sed do eiusmod tempor incididunt ut labore et
        dolore magna aliqua.)");

    for (auto const & kvp : result)
    {
        std::cout << kvp.first << " : "
                  << std::fixed
                  << std::setw(5) << std::setfill(' ')
                  << std::setprecision(2) << kvp.second << std::endl;
    }
}
```

50. Filtering a list of phone numbers

The solution to this problem is relatively simple: you have to iterate through all the phone numbers and copy to a separate container (such as an `std::vector`) the phone numbers that start with the country code. If the specified country code is, for instance, 44, then you must check for both 44 and +44. Filtering the input range in this manner is possible using the `std::copy_if()` function. A solution to this problem is shown here:

```cpp
bool starts_with(std::string_view str, std::string_view prefix)
{
    return str.find(prefix) == 0;
}

template <typename InputIt>
std::vector<std::string> filter_numbers(InputIt begin, InputIt end,
                                        std::string const & countryCode)
{
    std::vector<std::string> result;
    std::copy_if(
        begin, end,
        std::back_inserter(result),
        [countryCode](auto const & number) {
            return starts_with(number, countryCode) ||
                    starts_with(number, "+" + countryCode);
    });
    return result;
}

std::vector<std::string> filter_numbers(
    std::vector<std::string> const & numbers,
    std::string const & countryCode)
{
    return filter_numbers(std::cbegin(numbers), std::cend(numbers),
                          countryCode);
}
```

This is how this function can be used:

```
int main()
{
    std::vector<std::string> numbers{
        "+40744909080",
        "44 7520 112233",
        "+44 7555 123456",
        "40 7200 123456",
        "7555 123456"
    };

    auto result = filter_numbers(numbers, "44");

    for (auto const & number : result)
    {
        std::cout << number << std::endl;
    }
}
```

51. Transforming a list of phone numbers

This problem is somewhat similar in some aspects to the previous one. However, instead of selecting phone numbers that start with a specified country code, we must transform each number so that they all start with that country code preceded by a +. There are several cases that must be considered:

- The phone number starts with a 0. That indicates a number without a country code. To modify the number to include the country code we must replace the 0 with the actual country code, preceded by +.
- The phone number starts with the country code. In this case, we just prepend + sign to the beginning.
- The phone number starts with + followed by the country code. In this case, the number is already in the expected format.
- None of these cases applies, therefore the result is obtained by concatenating the country code preceded by + and the phone number.

 For simplicity, we will ignore the possibility that the number is actually prefixed with another country code. You can take it as a further exercise to modify the implementation so that it can handle phone numbers with a different country prefix. These numbers should be removed from the list.

In all of the preceding cases, it is possible that the number could contain spaces. According to the requirements, these must be removed. The std::remove_if() and isspace() functions are used for this purpose.

The following is an implementation of the described solution:

```
bool starts_with(std::string_view str, std::string_view prefix)
{
    return str.find(prefix) == 0;
}

void normalize_phone_numbers(std::vector<std::string>& numbers,
                             std::string const & countryCode)
{
    std::transform(
        std::cbegin(numbers), std::cend(numbers),
        std::begin(numbers),
        [countryCode](std::string const & number) {
            std::string result;
            if (number.size() > 0)
            {
                if (number[0] == '0')
                    result = "+" + countryCode +
                             number.substr(1);
                else if (starts_with(number, countryCode))
                    result = "+" + number;
                else if (starts_with(number, "+" + countryCode))
                    result = number;
                else
                    result = "+" + countryCode + number;
            }

            result.erase(
                std::remove_if(std::begin(result), std::end(result),
                    [](const char ch) {return isspace(ch); }),
                std::end(result));
            return result;
        });
}
```

The following program normalizes a given list of phone numbers according to the requirement and prints them on the console:

```
int main()
{
    std::vector<std::string> numbers{
        "07555 123456",
        "07555123456",
        "+44 7555 123456",
        "44 7555 123456",
        "7555 123456"
    };

    normalize_phone_numbers(numbers, "44");

    for (auto const & number : numbers)
    {
        std::cout << number << std::endl;
    }
}
```

52. Generating all the permutations of a string

You can solve this problem by taking advantage of some general-purpose algorithms from the standard library. The simplest of the two required versions is the non-recursive one, at least when you use `std::next_permutation()`. This function transforms the input range (that is required to be sorted) into the next permutation from the set of all possible permutations, ordered lexicographically with `operator<` or the specified comparison function object. If such a permutation exists then it returns `true`, otherwise, it transforms the range into the first permutation and returns `false`. Therefore, a non-recursive implementation based on `std::next_permuation()` looks like this:

```
void print_permutations(std::string str)
{
    std::sort(std::begin(str), std::end(str));

    do
    {
        std::cout << str << std::endl;
    } while (std::next_permutation(std::begin(str), std::end(str)));
}
```

The recursive alternative is a little bit more complex. One way to implement it is to have an input and output string; initially, the input string is the string for which we want to generate permutations and the output string is empty. We take one character at a time from the input string and put it in the output string. When the input string becomes empty, the output string represents the next permutation. The recursive algorithm for doing this is the following:

- If the input string is empty, then print the output string and return
- Otherwise iterate through all the characters in the input string, and for each element:
    - Call the method recursively by removing the first character from the input string and concatenating it at the end of the output string
    - Rotate the input string so that the first character becomes the last, the second becomes the first, and so on

This algorithm is visually explained in the following diagram:

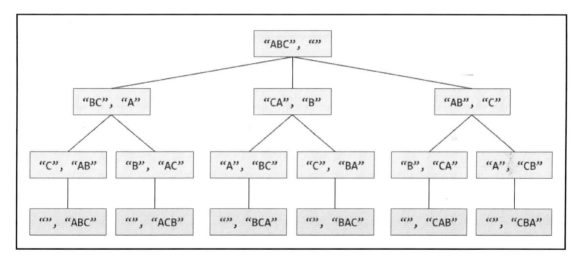

For rotating the input string, we could use the standard library function `std::rotate()`, which performs a left rotation on a range of elements. An implementation of the described recursive algorithm looks like this:

```
void next_permutation(std::string str, std::string perm)
{
    if (str.empty()) std::cout << perm << std::endl;
    else
    {
        for (size_t i = 0; i < str.size(); ++i)
        {
            next_permutation(str.substr(1), perm + str[0]);

            std::rotate(std::begin(str), std::begin(str) + 1, std::end(str));
        }
    }
}


void print_permutations_recursive(std::string str)
{
    next_permutation(str, "");
}
```

This is how both of these implementations can be used:

```
int main()
{
    std::cout << "non-recursive version" << std::endl;
    print_permutations("main");

    std::cout << "recursive version" << std::endl;
    print_permutations_recursive("main");
}
```

53. Average rating of movies

The problem requires the computing of a movie rating using a truncated mean. This is a statistical measure of a central tendency where the mean is calculated after discarding parts of a probability distribution or sample at the high and low ends. Typically, this is done by removing an equal amount of points at the two ends. For this problem, you are required to remove 5% of both the highest and lowest user ratings.

A function that calculates a truncated mean for a given range should do the following:

- Sort the range so that elements are ordered (either ascending or descending)
- Remove the required percentage of elements at both ends
- Count the sum of all remaining elements
- Compute the average by dividing the sum to the remaining count of elements

The `truncated_mean()` function shown here implements the described algorithm:

```
double truncated_mean(std::vector<int> values, double const percentage)
{
    std::sort(std::begin(values), std::end(values));
    auto remove_count = static_cast<size_t>(
                            values.size() * percentage + 0.5);

    values.erase(std::begin(values), std::begin(values) + remove_count);
    values.erase(std::end(values) - remove_count, std::end(values));

    auto total = std::accumulate(
        std::cbegin(values), std::cend(values),
        0ull,
        [](auto const sum, auto const e) {
            return sum + e; });
    return static_cast<double>(total) / values.size();
}
```

A program that uses this function in order to calculate and print movie average ratings may look like the following:

```
struct movie
{
    int             id;
    std::string     title;
    std::vector<int> ratings;
};

void print_movie_ratings(std::vector<movie> const & movies)
{
    for (auto const & m : movies)
    {
        std::cout << m.title << " : "
                  << std::fixed << std::setprecision(1)
                  << truncated_mean(m.ratings, 0.05) << std::endl;
    }
}
```

```
int main()
{
    std::vector<movie> movies
    {
        { 101, "The Matrix", {10, 9, 10, 9, 9, 8, 7, 10, 5, 9, 9, 8} },
        { 102, "Gladiator", {10, 5, 7, 8, 9, 8, 9, 10, 10, 5, 9, 8, 10} },
        { 103, "Interstellar", {10, 10, 10, 9, 3, 8, 8, 9, 6, 4, 7, 10} }
    };

    print_movie_ratings(movies);
}
```

54. Pairwise algorithm

The pairwise function proposed for this problem must pair adjacent elements of an input range and produce `std::pair` elements that are added to an output range. The following code listing provides two implementations:

- A general function template that takes iterators as arguments: a begin and end iterator define the input range, and an output iterator defines the position in the output range where the results are to be inserted
- An overload that takes an `std::vector<T>` as the input argument and returns an `std::vector<std::pair<T, T>>` as the result; this one simply calls the first overload:

```
template <typename Input, typename Output>
void pairwise(Input begin, Input end, Output result)
{
    auto it = begin;
    while (it != end)
    {
        auto v1 = *it++; if (it == end) break;
        auto v2 = *it++;
        result++ = std::make_pair(v1, v2);
    }
}
template <typename T>
std::vector<std::pair<T, T>> pairwise(std::vector<T> const & range)
{
    std::vector<std::pair<T, T>> result;
    pairwise(std::begin(range), std::end(range),
             std::back_inserter(result));
    return result;
}
```

The following program pairs the elements of a vector of integers and prints the pairs on the console:

```
int main()
{
    std::vector<int> v{ 1, 1, 3, 5, 8, 13, 21 };
    auto result = pairwise(v);

    for (auto const & p : result)
    {
        std::cout << '{' << p.first << ',' << p.second << '}' << std::endl;
    }
}
```

55. Zip algorithm

This problem is relatively similar to the previous one, although there are two input ranges instead of just one. The result is again a range of std::pair. However, the two input ranges may hold elements of different types. Again, the implementation shown here contains two overloads:

- A general-purpose function with iterators as arguments. A begin and end iterator for each input range define its bounds, and an output iterator defines the position in the output range where the result must be written.
- A function that takes two std::vector arguments, one that holds elements of type T and one that holds elements of type U and returns an std::vector<std::pair<T, U>>. This overload simply calls the previous one:

```
template <typename Input1, typename Input2, typename Output>
void zip(Input1 begin1, Input1 end1,
         Input2 begin2, Input1 end2,
         Output result)
{
```

```
    auto it1 = begin1;
    auto it2 = begin2;
    while (it1 != end1 && it2 != end2)
    {
        result++ = std::make_pair(*it1++, *it2++);
    }
}

template <typename T, typename U>
std::vector<std::pair<T, U>> zip(
    std::vector<T> const & range1,
    std::vector<U> const & range2)
{
    std::vector<std::pair<T, U>> result;

    zip(std::begin(range1), std::end(range1),
        std::begin(range2), std::end(range2),
        std::back_inserter(result));

    return result;
}
```

In the following listing, you can see two vectors of integers zipped together and the result printed on the console:

```
int main()
{
    std::vector<int> v1{ 1, 2, 3, 4, 5, 6, 7, 8, 9, 10 };
    std::vector<int> v2{ 1, 1, 3, 5, 8, 13, 21 };

    auto result = zip(v1, v2);
    for (auto const & p : result)
    {
        std::cout << '{' << p.first << ',' << p.second << '}' << std::endl;
    }
}
```

56. Select algorithm

The `select()` function that you have to implement takes an `std::vector<T>` as an input argument and a function of type `F` and returns a `std::vector<R>` as the result, where `R` is the result of applying `F` to `T`. We could use `std::result_of()` to deduce the return type of an invoke expression at compile time. Internally, the `select()` function should use `std::transform()` to iterate over the elements of the input vector, apply function `f` to each element, and insert the result in an output vector.

The following listing shows the implementation for this function:

```
template <
    typename T, typename A, typename F,
    typename R = typename std::decay<typename std::result_of<
                    typename std::decay<F>::type& (
                    typename std::vector<T, A>::const_reference)>::type>::type>
std::vector<R> select(std::vector<T, A> const & c, F&& f)
{
    std::vector<R> v;
    std::transform(std::cbegin(c), std::cend(c),
                    std::back_inserter(v),
                    std::forward<F>(f));
    return v;
}
```

This function can be used as follows:

```
int main()
{
    std::vector<book> books{
        {101, "The C++ Programming Language", "Bjarne Stroustrup"},
        {203, "Effective Modern C++", "Scott Meyers"},
        {404, "The Modern C++ Programming Cookbook", "Marius Bancila"}};

    auto titles = select(books, [](book const & b) {return b.title; });
    for (auto const & title : titles)
    {
        std::cout << title << std::endl;
    }
}
```

57. Sort algorithm

Quicksort is a comparison sorting algorithm for elements of an array for which a total order is defined. When implemented well, it is significantly faster than *merge sort* or *heap sort*.

Although in worst-case scenarios the algorithm makes $O(n^2)$ comparisons (when the range is already sorted), on average the complexity is only $O(n \cdot log(n))$. Quicksort is a divide and conquer algorithm; it partitions (divides) a large range into smaller ones and sorts them recursively. There are several partitioning schemes. In the implementation shown here, we use the original one developed by *Tony Hoare*. The algorithm for this scheme is described in pseudocode as follows:

```
algorithm quicksort(A, lo, hi) is
    if lo < hi then
        p := partition(A, lo, hi)
        quicksort(A, lo, p)
        quicksort(A, p + 1, hi)

algorithm partition(A, lo, hi) is
    pivot := A[lo]
    i := lo - 1
    j := hi + 1
    loop forever
        do
            i := i + 1
        while A[i] < pivot

        do
            j := j - 1
        while A[j] > pivot

        if i >= j then
            return j

        swap A[i] with A[j]
```

A general-purpose implementation of the algorithm should use iterators and not arrays and indexes. The requirement for the following implementation is that the iterators are random-access (so they could be moved to any element in constant time):

```cpp
template <class RandomIt>
RandomIt partition(RandomIt first, RandomIt last)
{
    auto pivot = *first;
    auto i = first + 1;
    auto j = last - 1;
    while (i <= j)
    {
        while (i <= j && *i <= pivot) i++;
        while (i <= j && *j > pivot) j--;
        if (i < j) std::iter_swap(i, j);
    }

    std::iter_swap(i - 1, first);

    return i - 1;
}

template <class RandomIt>
void quicksort(RandomIt first, RandomIt last)
{
    if (first < last)
    {
        auto p = partition(first, last);
        quicksort(first, p);
        quicksort(p + 1, last);
    }
}
```

The `quicksort()` function, shown as follows, can be used to sort various types of containers:

```cpp
int main()
{
    std::vector<int> v{ 1,5,3,8,6,2,9,7,4 };
    quicksort(std::begin(v), std::end(v));

    std::array<int, 9> a{ 1,2,3,4,5,6,7,8,9 };
    quicksort(std::begin(a), std::end(a));

    int a[]{ 9,8,7,6,5,4,3,2,1 };
    quicksort(std::begin(a), std::end(a));
}
```

The requirement was that the sorting algorithm must allow the specifying of a user-defined comparison function. The only change, in this case, is the partitioning function, where instead of using operator < and > to compare the current element with the pivot, we use the user-defined comparison function:

```
template <class RandomIt, class Compare>
RandomIt partitionc(RandomIt first, RandomIt last, Compare comp)
{
    auto pivot = *first;
    auto i = first + 1;
    auto j = last - 1;
    while (i <= j)
    {
        while (i <= j && comp(*i, pivot)) i++;
        while (i <= j && !comp(*j, pivot)) j--;
        if (i < j) std::iter_swap(i, j);
    }

    std::iter_swap(i - 1, first);

    return i - 1;
}

template <class RandomIt, class Compare>
void quicksort(RandomIt first, RandomIt last, Compare comp)
{
    if (first < last)
    {
        auto p = partitionc(first, last, comp);
        quicksort(first, p, comp);
        quicksort(p + 1, last, comp);
    }
}
```

With this overload we could sort a range in descending order, as shown in the following example:

```
int main()
{
    std::vector<int> v{ 1,5,3,8,6,2,9,7,4 };
    quicksort(std::begin(v), std::end(v), std::greater<>());
}
```

It is possible to implement an iterative version of the quicksort algorithm also. The performance of the iterative version is the same as for the recursive version $(O(n \cdot log(n))$ for most cases, but degrading to $O(n^2)$ in the worst case when the range is already sorted). Converting from the recursive version of the algorithm to an iterative one is relatively simple; it is done by using a stack to emulate the recursive calls and to store the bounds of the partitions. The following is an iterative implementation of the version that uses `operator<` to compare elements:

```cpp
template <class RandomIt>
void quicksorti(RandomIt first, RandomIt last)
{
    std::stack<std::pair<RandomIt, RandomIt>> st;
    st.push(std::make_pair(first, last));
    while (!st.empty())
    {
        auto iters = st.top();
        st.pop();

        if (iters.second - iters.first < 2) continue;

        auto p = partition(iters.first, iters.second);

        st.push(std::make_pair(iters.first, p));
        st.push(std::make_pair(p+1, iters.second));
    }
}
```

This iterative implementation can be used just like its recursive counterpart:

```cpp
int main()
{
    std::vector<int> v{ 1,5,3,8,6,2,9,7,4 };
    quicksorti(std::begin(v), std::end(v));
}
```

58. The shortest path between nodes

To solve the proposed problem you must use the Dijkstra algorithm for finding the shortest path in a graph. Although the original algorithm finds the shortest path between two given nodes, the requirement here is to find the shortest path between one specified node and all the others in the graph, which is another version of the algorithm.

An efficient way to implement the algorithm is using a priority queue. The pseudocode for the algorithm (see `https://en.wikipedia.org/wiki/Dijkstra%27s_algorithm`) is the following:

```
function Dijkstra(Graph, source):
    dist[source] ← 0                    // Initialization

    create vertex set Q
    for each vertex v in Graph:
        if v ≠ source
            dist[v] ← INFINITY          // Unknown distance from source to v
            prev[v] ← UNDEFINED         // Predecessor of v

        Q.add_with_priority(v, dist[v])

    while Q is not empty:                // The main loop
        u ← Q.extract_min()             // Remove and return best vertex
        for each neighbor v of u:       // only v that is still in Q
            alt ← dist[u] + length(u, v)
            if alt < dist[v]
                dist[v] ← alt
                prev[v] ← u
                Q.decrease_priority(v, alt)

    return dist[], prev[]
```

To represent the graph we could use the following data structure, which can be used for both directional or unidirectional graphs. The class provides support for adding new vertices and edges, and can return the list of vertices and the neighbors of a specified vertex (that is, both the nodes and the distance to them):

```cpp
template <typename Vertex = int, typename Weight = double>
class graph
{
public:
    typedef Vertex                      vertex_type;
    typedef Weight                      weight_type;
    typedef std::pair<Vertex, Weight>   neighbor_type;
    typedef std::vector<neighbor_type>  neighbor_list_type;
public:
    void add_edge(Vertex const source, Vertex const target,
                  Weight const weight, bool const bidirectional = true)
    {
        adjacency_list[source].push_back(std::make_pair(target, weight));
        adjacency_list[target].push_back(std::make_pair(source, weight));
    }
```

```
size_t vertex_count() const { return adjacency_list.size(); }
std::vector<Vertex> verteces() const
{
    std::vector<Vertex> keys;
    for (auto const & kvp : adjacency_list)
        keys.push_back(kvp.first);
    return keys;
}

neighbor_list_type const & neighbors(Vertex const & v) const
{
    auto pos = adjacency_list.find(v);
    if (pos == adjacency_list.end())
        throw std::runtime_error("vertex not found");
    return pos->second;
}

constexpr static Weight Infinity =
        std::numeric_limits<Weight>::infinity();
private:
    std::map<vertex_type, neighbor_list_type> adjacency_list;
};
```

The implementation of the shortest path algorithm as described in the preceding pseudocode could look like the following. An `std::set` (that is, a self-balancing binary search tree) is used instead of the priority queue. `std::set` has the same $O(log(n))$ complexity for adding and removing the top element as a binary heap (used for a priority queue). On the other hand, `std::set` also allows finding and removing any other element in $O(log(n))$, which is helpful in order to implement the decrease-key step in logarithmic time by removing and inserting again:

```
template <typename Vertex, typename Weight>
void shortest_path(
    graph<Vertex, Weight> const & g,
    Vertex const source,
    std::map<Vertex, Weight>& min_distance,
    std::map<Vertex, Vertex>& previous)
{
    auto const n = g.vertex_count();
    auto const verteces = g.verteces();

    min_distance.clear();
    for (auto const & v : verteces)
        min_distance[v] = graph<Vertex, Weight>::Infinity;
    min_distance[source] = 0;
```

```
    previous.clear();

    std::set<std::pair<Weight, Vertex> > vertex_queue;
    vertex_queue.insert(std::make_pair(min_distance[source], source));

    while (!vertex_queue.empty())
    {
        auto dist = vertex_queue.begin()->first;
        auto u = vertex_queue.begin()->second;

        vertex_queue.erase(std::begin(vertex_queue));

        auto const & neighbors = g.neighbors(u);
        for (auto const & neighbor : neighbors)
        {
            auto v = neighbor.first;
            auto w = neighbor.second;
            auto dist_via_u = dist + w;
            if (dist_via_u < min_distance[v])
            {
                vertex_queue.erase(std::make_pair(min_distance[v], v));

                min_distance[v] = dist_via_u;
                previous[v] = u;
                vertex_queue.insert(std::make_pair(min_distance[v], v));
            }
        }
    }
}
```

The following helper functions print the results in the specified format:

```
template <typename Vertex>
void build_path(
    std::map<Vertex, Vertex> const & prev, Vertex const v,
    std::vector<Vertex> & result)
{
    result.push_back(v);

    auto pos = prev.find(v);
    if (pos == std::end(prev)) return;

    build_path(prev, pos->second, result);
}

template <typename Vertex>
std::vector<Vertex> build_path(std::map<Vertex, Vertex> const & prev,
                               Vertex const v)
```

```
{
    std::vector<Vertex> result;
    build_path(prev, v, result);
    std::reverse(std::begin(result), std::end(result));
    return result;
}

template <typename Vertex>
void print_path(std::vector<Vertex> const & path)
{
    for (size_t i = 0; i < path.size(); ++i)
    {
        std::cout << path[i];
        if (i < path.size() - 1) std::cout << " -> ";
    }
}
```

The following program solves the given task:

```
int main()
{
    graph<char, double> g;
    g.add_edge('A', 'B', 7);
    g.add_edge('A', 'C', 9);
    g.add_edge('A', 'F', 14);
    g.add_edge('B', 'C', 10);
    g.add_edge('B', 'D', 15);
    g.add_edge('C', 'D', 11);
    g.add_edge('C', 'F', 2);
    g.add_edge('D', 'E', 6);
    g.add_edge('E', 'F', 9);

    char source = 'A';
    std::map<char, double> min_distance;
    std::map<char, char> previous;
    shortest_path(g, source, min_distance, previous);

    for (auto const & kvp : min_distance)
    {
        std::cout << source << " -> " << kvp.first << " : "
                  << kvp.second << '\t';

        print_path(build_path(previous, kvp.first));

        std::cout << std::endl;
    }
}
```

59. The Weasel program

The Weasel program is a thought experiment proposed by Richard Dawkins, intended to demonstrate how the accumulated small improvements (mutations that bring a benefit to the individual so that it is chosen by natural selection) produce fast results as opposed to the mainstream misinterpretation that evolution happens in big leaps. The algorithm for the Weasel simulation, as described on Wikipedia (see `https://en.wikipedia.org/wiki/Weasel_program`), is as follows:

1. Start with a random string of 28 characters.
2. Make 100 copies of this string, with a 5% chance per character of that character being replaced with a random character.
3. Compare each new string with the target METHINKS IT IS LIKE A WEASEL, and give each a score (the number of letters in the string that are correct and in the correct position).
4. If any of the new strings has a perfect score (28), then stop.
5. Otherwise, take the highest-scoring string and go to step 2.

A possible implementation is as follows. The `make_random()` function creates a random starting sequence of the same length as the target; the `fitness()` function computes the score of each mutated string (that is, resemblance with the target); the `mutate()` function produces a new string from a parent with a given chance for each character to mutate:

```
class weasel
{
    std::string target;
    std::uniform_int_distribution<> chardist;
    std::uniform_real_distribution<> ratedist;
    std::mt19937 mt;
    std::string const allowed_chars = "ABCDEFGHIJKLMNOPQRSTUVWXYZ ";
public:
    weasel(std::string_view t) :
        target(t), chardist(0, 26), ratedist(0, 100)
    {
        std::random_device rd;
        auto seed_data = std::array<int, std::mt19937::state_size> {};
        std::generate(std::begin(seed_data), std::end(seed_data),
        std::ref(rd));
        std::seed_seq seq(std::begin(seed_data), std::end(seed_data));
        mt.seed(seq);
    }
```

```
    void run(int const copies)
    {
        auto parent = make_random();
        int step = 1;
        std::cout << std::left << std::setw(5) << std::setfill(' ')
                  << step << parent << std::endl;

        do
        {
            std::vector<std::string> children;
            std::generate_n(std::back_inserter(children), copies,
                [parent, this]() {return mutate(parent, 5); });

            parent = *std::max_element(
                std::begin(children), std::end(children),
                [this](std::string_view c1, std::string_view c2) {
                    return fitness(c1) < fitness(c2); });

            std::cout << std::setw(5) << std::setfill(' ') << step
                      << parent << std::endl;

            step++;
        } while (parent != target);
    }
private:
    weasel() = delete;

    double fitness(std::string_view candidate) const
    {
        int score = 0;
        for (size_t i = 0; i < candidate.size(); ++i)
        {
            if (candidate[i] == target[i])
                score++;
        }
        return score;
    }

    std::string mutate(std::string_view parent, double const rate)
    {
        std::stringstream sstr;
        for (auto const c : parent)
        {
            auto nc = ratedist(mt) > rate ? c : allowed_chars[chardist(mt)];
            sstr << nc;
        }
        return sstr.str();
    }
```

```
    std::string make_random()
    {
        std::stringstream sstr;
        for (size_t i = 0; i < target.size(); ++i)
        {
            sstr << allowed_chars[chardist(mt)];
        }
        return sstr.str();
    }
};
```

This is how the class can be used:

```
int main()
{
    weasel w("METHINKS IT IS LIKE A WEASEL");
    w.run(100);
}
```

60. The Game of Life

The class `universe` presented below implements the game as described. There are several functions of interest:

- `initialize()` generates a starting layout; although the code accompanying the book contains more options, only two are listed here: `random`, which generates a random layout, and `ten_cell_row`, which represents a line of 10 cells in the middle of the grid.
- `reset()` sets all the cells as `dead`.
- `count_neighbors()` returns the number of alive neighbors. It uses a helper variadic function template `count_alive()`. Although this could be implemented with fold expressions, this is not yet supported in Visual C++ and therefore I have opted not to use it here.
- `next_generation()` produces a new state of the game based on the transition rules.
- `display()` shows the game status on the console; this uses a system call to erase the console, although you could use other means to do so, such as specific operating system APIs.

- `run()` initializes the starting layout and then produces a new generation at a user-specified interval, for a user-specified number of iterations, or indefinitely (if the number of iterations was set to 0).

```cpp
class universe
{
private:
   universe() = delete;
public:
   enum class seed
   {
      random, ten_cell_row
   };
public:
   universe(size_t const width, size_t const height):
      rows(height), columns(width),grid(width * height), dist(0, 4)
   {
      std::random_device rd;
      auto seed_data = std::array<int, std::mt19937::state_size> {};
      std::generate(std::begin(seed_data), std::end(seed_data),
      std::ref(rd));
      std::seed_seq seq(std::begin(seed_data), std::end(seed_data));
      mt.seed(seq);
   }

   void run(seed const s, int const generations,
            std::chrono::milliseconds const ms =
               std::chrono::milliseconds(100))
   {
      reset();
      initialize(s);
      display();

      int i = 0;
      do
      {
         next_generation();
         display();

         using namespace std::chrono_literals;
         std::this_thread::sleep_for(ms);
      } while (i++ < generations || generations == 0);
   }

private:
   void next_generation()
   {
```

```cpp
        std::vector<unsigned char> newgrid(grid.size());

        for (size_t r = 0; r < rows; ++r)
        {
            for (size_t c = 0; c < columns; ++c)
            {
                auto count = count_neighbors(r, c);

                if (cell(c, r) == alive)
                {
                    newgrid[r * columns + c] =
                        (count == 2 || count == 3) ? alive : dead;
                }
                else
                {
                    newgrid[r * columns + c] = (count == 3) ? alive : dead;
                }
            }
        }

        grid.swap(newgrid);
    }

    void reset_display()
    {
#ifdef WIN32
        system("cls");
#endif
    }

    void display()
    {
        reset_display();

        for (size_t r = 0; r < rows; ++r)
        {
            for (size_t c = 0; c < columns; ++c)
            {
                std::cout << (cell(c, r) ? '*' : ' ');
            }
            std::cout << std::endl;
        }
    }

    void initialize(seed const s)
    {
        if (s == seed::ten_cell_row)
        {
```

```
      for (size_t c = columns / 2 - 5; c < columns / 2 + 5; c++)
         cell(c, rows / 2) = alive;
   }
   else
   {
      for (size_t r = 0; r < rows; ++r)
      {
         for (size_t c = 0; c < columns; ++c)
         {
            cell(c, r) = dist(mt) == 0 ? alive : dead;
         }
      }
   }
}

void reset()
{
   for (size_t r = 0; r < rows; ++r)
   {
      for (size_t c = 0; c < columns; ++c)
      {
         cell(c, r) = dead;
      }
   }
}

int count_alive() { return 0; }

template<typename T1, typename... T>
auto count_alive(T1 s, T... ts) { return s + count_alive(ts...); }

int count_neighbors(size_t const row, size_t const col)
{
   if (row == 0 && col == 0)
      return count_alive(cell(1, 0), cell(1,1), cell(0, 1));
   if (row == 0 && col == columns - 1)
      return count_alive(cell(columns - 2, 0), cell(columns - 2, 1),
                         cell(columns - 1, 1));
   if (row == rows - 1 && col == 0)
      return count_alive(cell(0, rows - 2), cell(1, rows - 2),
                         cell(1, rows - 1));
   if (row == rows - 1 && col == columns - 1)
      return count_alive(cell(columns - 1, rows - 2),
                         cell(columns - 2, rows - 2),
                         cell(columns - 2, rows - 1));
```

```
        if (row == 0 && col > 0 && col < columns - 1)
            return count_alive(cell(col - 1, 0), cell(col - 1, 1),
                               cell(col, 1), cell(col + 1, 1),
                               cell(col + 1, 0));
        if (row == rows - 1 && col > 0 && col < columns - 1)
            return count_alive(cell(col - 1, row), cell(col - 1, row - 1),
                               cell(col, row - 1), cell(col + 1, row - 1),
                               cell(col + 1, row));
        if (col == 0 && row > 0 && row < rows - 1)
            return count_alive(cell(0, row - 1), cell(1, row - 1),
                               cell(1, row), cell(1, row + 1),
                               cell(0, row + 1));
        if (col == columns - 1 && row > 0 && row < rows - 1)
            return count_alive(cell(col, row - 1), cell(col - 1, row - 1),
                               cell(col - 1, row), cell(col - 1, row + 1),
                               cell(col, row + 1));

        return count_alive(cell(col - 1, row - 1), cell(col, row - 1),
                           cell(col + 1, row - 1), cell(col + 1, row),
                           cell(col + 1, row + 1), cell(col, row + 1),
                           cell(col - 1, row + 1), cell(col - 1, row));
    }

    unsigned char& cell(size_t const col, size_t const row)
    {
        return grid[row * columns + col];
    }

private:
    size_t rows;
    size_t columns;

    std::vector<unsigned char> grid;
    const unsigned char alive = 1;
    const unsigned char dead = 0;

    std::uniform_int_distribution<> dist;
    std::mt19937 mt;
};
```

This is how the game can be run for 100 iterations starting from a random state:

```
int main()
{
    using namespace std::chrono_literals;
    universe u(50, 20);
    u.run(universe::seed::random, 100, 100ms);
}
```

Here is an example of the program output (the screenshot represents a single iteration in the Game of Life's universe):

7 Concurrency

Problems

61. Parallel transform algorithm

Write a general-purpose algorithm that applies a given unary function to transform the elements of a range in parallel. The unary operation used to transform the range must not invalidate range iterators or modify the elements of the range. The level of parallelism, that is, the number of execution threads and the way it is achieved, is an implementation detail.

62. Parallel min and max element algorithms using threads

Implement general-purpose parallel algorithms that find the minimum value and, respectively, the maximum value in a given range. The parallelism should be implemented using threads, although the number of concurrent threads is an implementation detail.

63. Parallel min and max element algorithms using asynchronous functions

Implement general-purpose parallel algorithms that find the minimum value and, respectively, the maximum value in a given range. The parallelism should be implemented using asynchronous functions, although the number of concurrent functions is an implementation detail.

64. Parallel sort algorithm

Write a parallel version of the sort algorithm as defined for problem *53. Sort Algorithm*, in `Chapter 6`, *Algorithms and Data Structures*, which, given a pair of random access iterators to define its lower and upper bounds, sorts the elements of the range using the quicksort algorithm. The function should use the comparison operators for comparing the elements of the range. The level of parallelism and the way to achieve it is an implementation detail.

65. Thread-safe logging to the console

Write a class that enables components running in different threads to safely print log messages to the console by synchronizing access to the standard output stream to guarantee the integrity of the output. This logging component should have a method called `log()` with a string argument representing the message to be printed to the console.

66. Customer service system

Write a program that simulates the way customers are served in an office. The office has three desks where customers can be served at the same time. Customers can enter the office at any time. They take a ticket with a service number from a ticketing machine and wait until their number is next for service at one of the desks. Customers are served in the order they entered the office, or more precisely, in the order given by their ticket. Every time a service desk finishes serving a customer, the next customer in order is served. The simulation should stop after a particular number of customers have been issued tickets and served.

Solutions

61. Parallel transform algorithm

The general-purpose function `std::transform()` applies a given function to a range and stores the result in another (or the same) range. The requirement for this problem is implementing a parallel version of such a function. A general-purpose one would take iterators as arguments to define the first and one-past-last element of the range. Because the unary function is applied in the same manner to all the elements of the range, it is fairly simple to parallelize the operation. For this task, we will be using threads. Since it is not specified how many threads should be running at the same time, we could use `std::thread::hardware_concurrency()`. This function returns a hint for the number of concurrent threads supported by the implementation.

A parallel version of the algorithm performs better than a sequential implementation only if the size of the range exceeds a particular threshold, which may vary with compilation options, platform, or hardware. In the following implementation that threshold is set to 10,000 elements. As a further exercise, you could experiment with various thresholds and range sizes to see how the execution time changes.

The following function, `ptransform()`, implements the parallel transform algorithm as requested. It simply calls `std::transform()` if the range size does not exceed the defined threshold. Otherwise, it splits the range into several equal parts, one for each thread, and calls `std::transform()` on each thread for a particular subrange. In this case, the function blocks the calling thread until all the worker threads finish execution:

```
template <typename RandomAccessIterator, typename F>
void ptransform(RandomAccessIterator begin, RandomAccessIterator end,
                F&& f)
{
    auto size = std::distance(begin, end);
    if (size <= 10000)
    {
        std::transform(begin, end, begin, std::forward<F>(f));
    }
    else
    {
        std::vector<std::thread> threads;
        int thread_count = std::thread::hardware_concurrency();
        auto first = begin;
        auto last = first;
        size /= thread_count;
```

```
        for (int i = 0; i < thread_count; ++i)
        {
            first = last;
            if (i == thread_count - 1) last = end;
            else std::advance(last, size);

            threads.emplace_back([first, last, &f]() {
                std::transform(first, last, first, std::forward<F>(f));
            });
        }

        for (auto & t : threads) t.join();
    }
}
```

The function `palter()`, shown as follows, is a helper function that applies `ptransform()` to an `std::vector` and returns another `std::vector` with the result:

```
template <typename T, typename F>
std::vector<T> palter(std::vector<T> data, F&& f)
{
    ptransform(std::begin(data), std::end(data),
                std::forward<F>(f));
    return data;
}
```

The function can be used as follows (a complete example can be found in the source code accompanying this book):

```
int main()
{
    std::vector<int> data(1000000);
    // init data
    auto result = palter(data, [](int const e) {return e * e; });
}
```

In C++17, a series of standard general-purpose algorithms, including `std::transform()`, have overloads that implement a parallel version of the algorithm that can be executed according to a specified execution policy.

62. Parallel min and max element algorithms using threads

This problem, and its solution, is similar in most ways to the previous one. What is slightly different is that the function concurrently executing on each thread must return a value that represents the minimum or the maximum element in the subrange.

The `pprocess()` function template, shown as follows, is a higher-level function that implements the requested functionality generically, in the following way:

- Its arguments are the first and one-past-last iterators to the range and a function object that processes the range that we will call `f`.

- If the size of the range is smaller than a particular threshold, set to 10,000 elements here, it simply executes the function object `f` received as argument.

- Otherwise, it splits the input range into a number of subranges of equal size, one for each concurrent thread that could be executed. Each thread runs `f` for the selected subrange.

- The results of the parallel execution of `f` are collected in an `std::vector`, and after the execution of all threads is completed, `f` is used again to determine the overall result from the intermediate results:

```cpp
template <typename Iterator, typename F>
auto pprocess(Iterator begin, Iterator end, F&& f)
{
    auto size = std::distance(begin, end);
    if (size <= 10000)
    {
        return std::forward<F>(f)(begin, end);
    }
    else
    {
        int thread_count = std::thread::hardware_concurrency();
        std::vector<std::thread> threads;
        std::vector<typename std::
            iterator_traits<Iterator>::value_type>
        mins(thread_count);

        auto first = begin;
        auto last = first;
        size /= thread_count;
        for (int i = 0; i < thread_count; ++i)
        {
            first = last;
            if (i == thread_count - 1) last = end;
```

```
        else std::advance(last, size);

        threads.emplace_back([first, last, &f, &r=mins[i]]() {
        r = std::forward<F>(f)(first, last);
        });
    }

    for (auto & t : threads) t.join();

    return std::forward<F>(f)(std::begin(mins), std::end(mins));
    }
}
```

Two functions, called `pmin()` and `pmax()`, are provided to implement the required general-purpose min and max parallel algorithms. These two are in turn calling `pprocess()`, passing for the third argument a lambda that uses either the `std::min_element()` or the `std::max_element()` standard algorithm:

```
template <typename Iterator>
auto pmin(Iterator begin, Iterator end)
{
    return pprocess(begin, end,
                    [](auto b, auto e){return *std::min_element(b, e);});
}

template <typename Iterator>
auto pmax(Iterator begin, Iterator end)
{
    return pprocess(begin, end,
                    [](auto b, auto e){return *std::max_element(b, e);});
}
```

These functions can be used as follows:

```
int main()
{
    std::vector<int> data(count);
    // init data
    auto rmin = pmin(std::begin(data), std::end(data));
    auto rmax = pmin(std::begin(data), std::end(data));
}
```

You can take it as a further exercise to implement yet another general-purpose algorithm that computes the sum of all the elements of a range in parallel using threads.

63. Parallel min and max element algorithms using asynchronous functions

The only difference between this problem and the previous one is how the parallelism is achieved. For the previous problem, the use of threads was required. For this one, you must use asynchronous functions. A function can be executed asynchronously with `std::async()`. This function creates a *promise*, which is an asynchronous provider of the result of a function executed asynchronously. A promise has a shared state (which can store either the return value of a function or an exception that resulted from the execution of the function) and an associated *future* object that provides access to the shared state from a different thread. The promise-future pair defines a channel that enables communicating values across threads. `std::async()` returns the future associated with the promise it creates.

In the following implementation of `pprocess()`, the use of threads from the previous version has been replaced with calls to `std::async()`. Note that you must specify `std::launch::async` as the first parameter to `std::async()` to guarantee an asynchronous execution and not a lazy evaluation. The amount of changes from the previous implementation is very small and it should be easy to follow the code based on the description of the algorithm from the previous implementation:

```
template <typename Iterator, typename F>
auto pprocess(Iterator begin, Iterator end, F&& f)
{
    auto size = std::distance(begin, end);
    if (size <= 10000)
    {
        return std::forward<F>(f)(begin, end);
    }
    else
    {
        int task_count = std::thread::hardware_concurrency();
        std::vector<std::future<
            typename std::iterator_traits<Iterator>::value_type>> tasks;

        auto first = begin;
        auto last = first;
```

```
            size /= task_count;
            for (int i = 0; i < task_count; ++i)
            {
                first = last;
                if (i == task_count - 1) last = end;
                else std::advance(last, size);

                tasks.emplace_back(std::async(
                    std::launch::async,
                    [first, last, &f]() {
                        return std::forward<F>(f)(first, last);
                }));
            }

            std::vector<typename std::iterator_traits<Iterator>::value_type>
                mins;

            for (auto & t : tasks)
                mins.push_back(t.get());

            return std::forward<F>(f)(std::begin(mins), std::end(mins));
        }
    }

template <typename Iterator>
auto pmin(Iterator begin, Iterator end)
{
    return pprocess(begin, end,
                    [](auto b, auto e){return *std::min_element(b, e);});
}

template <typename Iterator>
auto pmax(Iterator begin, Iterator end)
{
    return pprocess(begin, end,
                    [](auto b, auto e){return *std::max_element(b, e);});
}
```

The following code shows how this function can be used:

```
int main()
{
    std::vector<int> data(count);
    // init data
    auto rmin = pmin(std::begin(data), std::end(data));
    auto rmax = pmax(std::begin(data), std::end(data));
}
```

You can again take it as a further exercise to implement a general-purpose algorithm that computes the sum of all the elements of a range in parallel using asynchronous functions.

64. Parallel sort algorithm

We saw a sequential implementation of the quicksort algorithm earlier. Quicksort is a divide and conquer algorithm that relies on partitioning the range to be sorted into two parts, one that contains only elements smaller than a selected element, called the pivot, and one that contains only elements greater than the pivot. It then proceeds to recursively apply the same algorithm on the two partitions, until the partitions have only one element or none. Because of the nature of the algorithm, quicksort can be easily parallelized to recursively apply the algorithm on the two partitions concurrently.

The pquicksort() function uses asynchronous functions for this purpose. However, parallelization is only efficient for larger ranges. There is a threshold under which the overhead with context switches for parallel execution is too large and the parallel execution time is greater than the sequential execution time. In the following implementation, this threshold is set to 100,000 elements, but as a further exercise, you could experiment with setting different values and see how the parallel version performs compared to the sequential one:

```
template <class RandomIt>
RandomIt partition(RandomIt first, RandomIt last)
{
    auto pivot = *first;
    auto i = first + 1;
    auto j = last - 1;
    while (i <= j)
    {
        while (i <= j && *i <= pivot) i++;
        while (i <= j && *j > pivot) j--;
        if (i < j) std::iter_swap(i, j);
    }

    std::iter_swap(i - 1, first);

    return i - 1;
}
```

```
template <class RandomIt>
void pquicksort(RandomIt first, RandomIt last)
{
   if (first < last)
   {
      auto p = partition(first, last);

      if(last - first <= 100000)
      {
         pquicksort(first, p);
         pquicksort(p + 1, last);
      }
      else
      {
         auto f1 = std::async(std::launch::async,
            [first, p](){ pquicksort(first, p);});
         auto f2 = std::async(std::launch::async,
            [last, p]() { pquicksort(p+1, last);});
         f1.wait();
         f2.wait();
      }
   }
}
```

The following code shows how a large vector of random integers (with values between 1 and 1000) can be sorted using the pquicksort() function:

```
int main()
{
   std::random_device rd;
   std::mt19937 mt;
   auto seed_data = std::array<int, std::mt19937::state_size> {};
   std::generate(std::begin(seed_data), std::end(seed_data),
                  std::ref(rd));
   std::seed_seq seq(std::begin(seed_data), std::end(seed_data));
   mt.seed(seq);
   std::uniform_int_distribution<> ud(1, 1000);

   const size_t count = 1000000;
   std::vector<int> data(count);
   std::generate_n(std::begin(data), count,
   [&mt, &ud]() {return ud(mt); });

   pquicksort(std::begin(data), std::end(data));
}
```

65. Thread-safe logging to the console

Although C++ does not have the concept of a console and uses streams to perform input and output operations on sequential media such as files, the `std::cout` and `std::wcout` global objects control the output to a stream buffer associated with the C output stream `stdout`. These global stream objects cannot be safely accessed from different threads. Should you need that, you must synchronize the access to them. That is exactly the purpose of the requested component for this problem.

The `logger` class, shown as follows, uses an `std::mutex` to synchronize access to the `std::cout` object in the `log()` method. The class is implemented as a thread-safe singleton. The static method `instance()` returns a reference to a local static object (that has storage duration). In C++11, initialization of a static object happens only once, even if several threads attempt to initialize the same static object at the same time. In such a case, concurrent threads are blocked until the initialization executed on the first calling thread completes. Therefore, there is no need for additional user-defined synchronization mechanisms:

```cpp
class logger
{
protected:
    logger() {}
public:
    static logger& instance()
    {
        static logger lg;
        return lg;
    }

    logger(logger const &) = delete;
    logger& operator=(logger const &) = delete;

    void log(std::string_view message)
    {
        std::lock_guard<std::mutex> lock(mt);
        std::cout << "LOG: " << message << std::endl;
    }

private:
    std::mutex mt;
};
```

The preceding `logger` class can be used to write console message from multiple threads:

```
int main()
{
    std::vector<std::thread> modules;

    for(int id = 1; id <= 5; ++id)
    {
        modules.emplace_back([id](){
            std::random_device rd;
            std::mt19937 mt(rd());
            std::uniform_int_distribution<> ud(100, 1000);

            logger::instance().log(
                "module " + std::to_string(id) + " started");

            std::this_thread::sleep_for(std::chrono::milliseconds(ud(mt)));

            logger::instance().log(
                "module " + std::to_string(id) + " finished");
        });
    }

    for(auto & m : modules) m.join();
}
```

66. Customer service system

In order to implement the simulation of the customer service office as required, we could use several helper classes. `ticketing_machine` is a class that models a very simple machine that issues incremental ticketing numbers, starting with an initial, user-specified seed. `customer` is a class that represents a customer that enters the store and receives a ticket from the ticketing machine. `operator<` is overloaded for this class in order to store customers in a priority queue from which they should be taken in the order given by their ticket number. In addition, the `logger` class from the previous problem is used to print messages to the console:

```
class ticketing_machine
{
public:
    ticketing_machine(int const start) :
        last_ticket(start), first_ticket(start)
    {}
```

```
    int next() { return last_ticket++; }
    int last() const { return last_ticket - 1; }
    void reset() { last_ticket = first_ticket; }
private:
    int first_ticket;
    int last_ticket;
};

class customer
{
public:
    customer(int const no) : number(no) {}

    int ticket_number() const noexcept { return number; }
private:
    int number;
    friend bool operator<(customer const & l, customer const & r);
};

bool operator<(customer const & l, customer const & r)
{
    return l.number > r.number;
}
```

Each desk from the office is modeled using a different thread. Customers entering the store and queuing after getting a ticket are modeled using a separate thread. In the following simulation, a new customer enters the store every 200-500 milliseconds, gets a ticket and is placed in a priority queue. The execution of the store thread finishes after 25 customers enter the store and are placed in the queue. An `std::condition_variable` is used to communicate between threads to notify that a new customer has been placed in the queue or that an existing customer has been removed from the queue (which happens when a customer moves to an open desk). The threads that represent the office desk are running until a flag indicating the office is opened is reset but not before all customers that are in the queue are served. In this simulation, each customer spends 2,000 to 3,000 milliseconds at a desk:

```
int main()
{
    std::priority_queue<customer> customers;
    bool office_open = true;
    std::mutex mt;
    std::condition_variable cv;

    std::vector<std::thread> desks;
    for (int i = 1; i <= 3; ++i)
    {
```

```
    desks.emplace_back([i, &office_open, &mt, &cv, &customers]() {
        std::random_device rd;
        auto seed_data = std::array<int, std::mt19937::state_size> {};
        std::generate(std::begin(seed_data), std::end(seed_data),
                      std::ref(rd));
        std::seed_seq seq(std::begin(seed_data), std::end(seed_data));
        std::mt19937 eng(seq);
        std::uniform_int_distribution<> ud(2000, 3000);

        logger::instance().log("desk " + std::to_string(i) + " open");

        while (office_open || !customers.empty())
        {
            std::unique_lock<std::mutex> locker(mt);

            cv.wait_for(locker, std::chrono::seconds(1),
                [&customers]() {return !customers.empty(); });

            if (!customers.empty())
            {
                auto const c = customers.top();
                customers.pop();

                logger::instance().log(
                    "[-] desk " + std::to_string(i) + " handling customer "
                    + std::to_string(c.ticket_number()));

                logger::instance().log(
                    "[=] queue size: " + std::to_string(customers.size()));

                locker.unlock();
                cv.notify_one();

                std::this_thread::sleep_for(
                    std::chrono::milliseconds(ud(eng)));

                logger::instance().log(
                    "[ ] desk " + std::to_string(i) + " done with customer "
                    + std::to_string(c.ticket_number()));
            }
        }

        logger::instance().log("desk " + std::to_string(i) + " closed");
    });
}

std::thread store([&office_open, &customers, &mt, &cv]() {
    ticketing_machine tm(100);
```

```
std::random_device rd;
auto seed_data = std::array<int, std::mt19937::state_size> {};
std::generate(std::begin(seed_data), std::end(seed_data),
            std::ref(rd));
std::seed_seq seq(std::begin(seed_data), std::end(seed_data));
std::mt19937 eng(seq);
std::uniform_int_distribution<> ud(200, 500);

for (int i = 1; i <= 25; ++i)
{
    customer c(tm.next());
    customers.push(c);

    logger::instance().log("[+] new customer with ticket " +
        std::to_string(c.ticket_number()));
    logger::instance().log("[=] queue size: " +
        std::to_string(customers.size()));

    cv.notify_one();

    std::this_thread::sleep_for(std::chrono::milliseconds(ud(eng)));
}

office_open = false;
});

store.join();
for (auto & desk : desks) desk.join();
}
```

Here is a snippet of the output of an execution of this problem:

```
LOG: desk 1 open
LOG: desk 2 open
LOG: desk 3 open
LOG: [+] new customer with ticket 100
LOG: [-] desk 2 handling customer 100
LOG: [=] queue size: 0
LOG: [=] queue size: 0
LOG: [+] new customer with ticket 101
LOG: [=] queue size: 1
LOG: [-] desk 3 handling customer 101
LOG: [=] queue size: 0
LOG: [+] new customer with ticket 102
LOG: [=] queue size: 1
LOG: [-] desk 1 handling customer 102
LOG: [=] queue size: 0
LOG: [+] new customer with ticket 103
```

```
LOG: [=] queue size: 1
. . .
LOG: [+] new customer with ticket 112
LOG: [=] queue size: 7
LOG: [+] new customer with ticket 113
LOG: [=] queue size: 8
LOG: [ ] desk 2 done with customer 103
LOG: [-] desk 2 handling customer 106
LOG: [=] queue size: 7
. . .
LOG: [ ] desk 1 done with customer 120
LOG: [-] desk 1 handling customer 123
LOG: [=] queue size: 1
LOG: [ ] desk 2 done with customer 121
LOG: [-] desk 2 handling customer 124
LOG: [=] queue size: 0
LOG: [ ] desk 3 done with customer 122
LOG: desk 3 closed
LOG: [ ] desk 1 done with customer 123
LOG: desk 1 closed
LOG: [ ] desk 2 done with customer 124
LOG: desk 2 closed
```

As a further exercise, you can try to change the intervals at which the customers enter the store, how many customers are allowed to get a ticket before the office closes, how long it takes to serve them, or how many desks are opened in the office.

8
Design Patterns

Problems

67. Validating passwords

Write a program that validates password strength based on predefined rules, which may then be selected in various combinations. At a minimum, every password must meet a minimum length requirement. In addition, other rules could be enforced, such as the presence of at least one symbol, digit, uppercase and lowercase letter, and so on.

68. Generating random passwords

Write a program that can generate random passwords according to some predefined rules. Every password must have a configurable minimum length. In addition, it should be possible to include in the generation rules such as the presence of at least one digit, symbol, lower or uppercase character, and so on. These additional rules must be configurable and composable.

69. Generating social security numbers

Write a program that can generate social security numbers for two countries, Northeria and Southeria, that have different but similar formats for the numbers:

- In Northeria, the numbers have the format SYYYYMMDDNNNNNC, where S is a digit representing the sex, 9 for females and 7 for males, YYYYMMDD is the birth date, NNNNN is a five-digit random number, unique for a day (meaning that the same number can appear twice for two different dates, but not the same date), and C is a digit picked so that the checksum computed as described later is a multiple of 11.
- In Southeria, the numbers have the format SYYYYMMDDNNNNC, where S is a digit representing the sex, 1 for females and 2 for males, YYYYMMDD is the birth date, NNNN is a four-digit random number, unique for a day, and C is a digit picked so that the checksum computed as described below is a multiple of 10.

The checksum in both cases is a sum of all the digits, each multiplied by its weight (the position from the most significant digit to the least). For example, the checksum for the Southerian number 12017120134895 is computed as follows:

```
crc = 14*1 + 13*2 + 12*0 + 11*1 + 10*7 + 9*1 + 8*2 + 7*0 + 6*1 + 5*3
        +  4*4 +  3*8 +  2*9 +  1*5
    = 230 = 23 * 10
```

70. Approval system

Write a program for a purchasing department of a company that allows employees to approve new purchases (or expenses). However, based on their position, each employee may only approve expenses up to a predefined limit. For instance, regular employees can approve expenses up to 1,000 currency units, team managers up to 10,000, and the department manager up to 100,000. Any expense greater than that must be explicitly approved by the company president.

71. Observable vector container

Write a class template that behaves like a vector but can notify registered parties of internal state changes. The class must provide at least the following operations:

- Various constructors for creating new instances of the class
- `operator=` to assign values to the container
- `push_back()` to add a new element at the end of the container
- `pop_back()` to remove the last element from the container
- `clear()` to remove all the elements from the container
- `size()` to return the number of elements from the container
- `empty()` to indicate whether the container is empty or has elements

`operator=`, `push_back()`, `pop_back()`, and `clear()` must notify others of the state changes. The notification should include the type of the change, and, when the case, the index of the element that was changed (such as added or removed).

72. Computing order price with discounts

A retail store sells a variety of goods and can offer various types of discount, for selected customers, articles, or per order. The following types of discount could be available:

- A fixed discount, such as 5%, regardless of the article or the quantity that is purchased.
- A volume discount, such as 10%, for each article when buying more than a particular quantity of that article.
- A price discount per total order of an article, that is, a discount for an article when a customer buys a quantity of that article so that the total cost exceeds a particular amount. For instance, a 15% discount for an article when the total cost of that article exceeds $100. If the article costs $5, and the customer buys 30 units, the total cost is $150; therefore, a 15% discount applies to the order of that article.
- A price discount per entire order (regardless what articles and in which quantity they were ordered).

Write a program that can calculate the final price of a particular order. It is possible to compute the final price in different ways; for instance, all discounts could be cumulative, or on the other hand, if an article has a discount, a customer or total order discount might not be considered.

Solutions

67. Validating passwords

The problem described here is a typical case for the *decorator* pattern. This design pattern allows adding behavior to an object without affecting other objects of the same type. This is achieved by wrapping an object within another object. Multiple decorators could be stacked on top of each other, each time adding new functionality. In our case, the functionality would be validating that a given password meets a particular requirement.

The following class diagram describes the pattern for validating passwords:

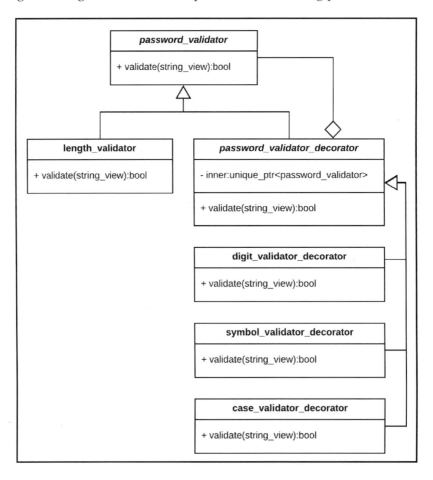

The implementation of the pattern, as described in the diagram, is as follows:

```
class password_validator
{
public:
   virtual bool validate(std::string_view password) = 0;
   virtual ~password_validator() {}
};

class length_validator final : public password_validator
{
public:
   length_validator(unsigned int min_length): length(min_length)
   {}

   virtual bool validate(std::string_view password) override
   {
      return password.length() >= length;
   }

private:
   unsigned int length;
};

class password_validator_decorator : public password_validator
{
public:
   explicit password_validator_decorator(
      std::unique_ptr<password_validator> validator):
         inner(std::move(validator))
   {
   }

   virtual bool validate(std::string_view password) override
   {
      return inner->validate(password);
   }

private:
   std::unique_ptr<password_validator> inner;
};

class digit_password_validator final : public password_validator_decorator
{
public:
   explicit digit_password_validator(
      std::unique_ptr<password_validator> validator):
         password_validator_decorator(std::move(validator))
```

```
        {
        }

        virtual bool validate(std::string_view password) override
        {
            if(!password_validator_decorator::validate(password))
                return false;

            return password.find_first_of("0123456789") != std::string::npos;
        }
};

class case_password_validator final : public password_validator_decorator
{
public:
    explicit case_password_validator(
        std::unique_ptr<password_validator> validator):
            password_validator_decorator(std::move(validator))
        {
        }

        virtual bool validate(std::string_view password) override
        {
            if(!password_validator_decorator::validate(password))
                return false;

            bool haslower = false;
            bool hasupper = false;

            for(size_t i = 0; i < password.length() && !(hasupper && haslower);
                ++i)
            {
                if(islower(password[i])) haslower = true;
                else if(isupper(password[i])) hasupper = true;
            }

            return haslower && hasupper;
        }
};

class symbol_password_validator final : public password_validator_decorator
{
public:
    explicit symbol_password_validator(
        std::unique_ptr<password_validator> validator):
            password_validator_decorator(std::move(validator))
        {
        }
```

```
        virtual bool validate(std::string_view password) override
        {
            if(!password_validator_decorator::validate(password))
                return false;

            return password.find_first_of("!@#$%^&*(){}[]?<>") !=
                std::string::npos;
        }
    };
```

`password_validator` is the base class and has a single virtual method called `validate()` with a string argument representing the password. `length_validator` is derived from this class and implements the mandatory password requirement for a minimum length.

`password_validator_decorator` is also derived from `password_validator` and contains an inner `password_validator` component. Its `validate()` implementation simply resolves to calling `inner->validate()`. The other classes, `digit_password_validator`, `symbol_password_validator`, and `case_password_validator`, are derived from it and implement the other individual password strength requirements.

The following are examples of how these classes could be composed to create various password validators:

```
int main()
{
    auto validator1 = std::make_unique<digit_password_validator>(
        std::make_unique<length_validator>(8));

    assert(validator1->validate("abc123!@#"));
    assert(!validator1->validate("abcde!@#"));

    auto validator2 =
        std::make_unique<symbol_password_validator>(
            std::make_unique<case_password_validator>(
                std::make_unique<digit_password_validator>(
                    std::make_unique<length_validator>(8))));

    assert(validator2->validate("Abc123!@#"));
    assert(!validator2->validate("Abc123567"));
}
```

68. Generating random passwords

This problem could be solved using the *composite* pattern or a variation of the pattern. This design pattern composes objects into tree hierarchies and enables treating groups (or trees) of objects the same way as individual objects of the same type. The following class diagram shows a hierarchy of classes that can be used for generating passwords:

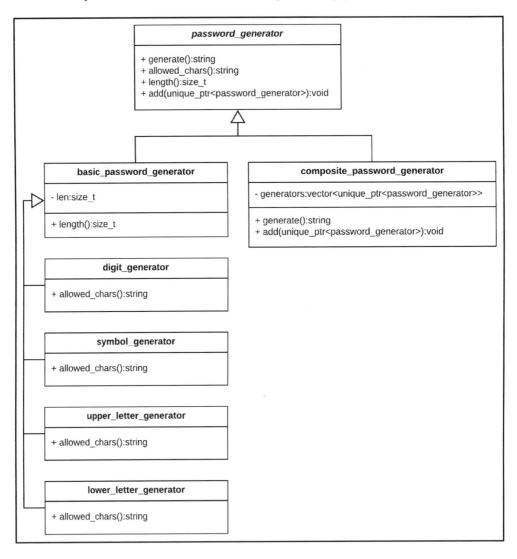

`password_generator` is the base class and has several virtual methods: `generate()` returns a new random string, `length()` specifies the length of the strings it generates, `allowed_chars()` returns a string with all the characters it uses for generating passwords, and `add()` adds a new child component to a composite generator. `basic_password_generator` is derived from this base class and defines a generator with a minimum length. `digit_generator`, `symbol_generator`, `upper_letter_generator`, and `lower_letter_generator` are derived from `basic_password_generator` and override `allowed_chars()` to define subsets of characters used to generate random texts.

`composite_password_generator` is also derived from `password_generator` and has a collection of `password_generator` objects that it uses to compose a random text. This is done in the overridden `generate()` method, which concatenates all the strings generated by the child components and then randomly shuffles them to produce a final string representing a password:

```
class password_generator
{
public:
    virtual std::string generate() = 0;

    virtual std::string allowed_chars() const = 0;
    virtual size_t length() const = 0;
    virtual void add(std::unique_ptr<password_generator> generator) = 0;

    virtual ~password_generator(){}
};

class basic_password_generator : public password_generator
{
    size_t len;
public:
    explicit basic_password_generator(size_t const len) noexcept : len(len)
    {}

    virtual std::string generate() override
    { throw std::runtime_error("not implemented"); }

    virtual void add(std::unique_ptr<password_generator>) override
    { throw std::runtime_error("not implemented"); }

    virtual size_t length() const override final
    {return len;}
};
```

```cpp
class digit_generator : public basic_password_generator
{
public:
   explicit digit_generator(size_t const len) noexcept
   : basic_password_generator(len) {}

   virtual std::string allowed_chars() const override
   {return "0123456789";}
};

class symbol_generator : public basic_password_generator
{
public:
   explicit symbol_generator(size_t const len) noexcept
   : basic_password_generator(len) {}

   virtual std::string allowed_chars() const override
   {return "!@#$%^&*(){}[]?<>";}
};

class upper_letter_generator : public basic_password_generator
{
public:
   explicit upper_letter_generator(size_t const len) noexcept
   : basic_password_generator(len) {}

   virtual std::string allowed_chars() const override
   {return "ABCDEFGHIJKLMNOPQRSTUVXYWZ";}
};

class lower_letter_generator : public basic_password_generator
{
public:
   explicit lower_letter_generator(size_t const len) noexcept
   : basic_password_generator(len) {}

   virtual std::string allowed_chars() const override
   {return "abcdefghijklmnopqrstuvxywz";}
};

class composite_password_generator : public password_generator
{
   virtual std::string allowed_chars() const override
   { throw std::runtime_error("not implemented"); };
   virtual size_t length() const override
   { throw std::runtime_error("not implemented"); };
public:
   composite_password_generator()
```

```
    {
        auto seed_data = std::array<int, std::mt19937::state_size> {};
        std::generate(std::begin(seed_data), std::end(seed_data),
                    std::ref(rd));
        std::seed_seq seq(std::begin(seed_data), std::end(seed_data));
        eng.seed(seq);
    }

    virtual std::string generate() override
    {
        std::string password;
        for(auto & generator : generators)
        {
            std::string chars = generator->allowed_chars();
            std::uniform_int_distribution<> ud(
                0, static_cast<int>(chars.length() - 1));

            for(size_t i = 0; i < generator->length(); ++i)
                password += chars[ud(eng)];
        }

        std::shuffle(std::begin(password), std::end(password), eng);

        return password;
    }

    virtual void add(std::unique_ptr<password_generator> generator) override
    {
        generators.push_back(std::move(generator));
    }

private:
    std::random_device rd;
    std::mt19937 eng;
    std::vector<std::unique_ptr<password_generator>> generators;
};
```

The preceding code can be used to generate passwords in the following manner:

```
int main()
{
    composite_password_generator generator;
    generator.add(std::make_unique<symbol_generator>(2));
    generator.add(std::make_unique<digit_generator>(2));
    generator.add(std::make_unique<upper_letter_generator>(2));
    generator.add(std::make_unique<lower_letter_generator>(4));

    auto password = generator.generate();
}
```

You could use the password validator we wrote for the previous problem to make sure the passwords generated in this way do indeed meet the expected requirements.

69. Generating social security numbers

The formats for both countries are very similar, although several details are different:

- The value of the digit for the sex
- The length of the random part, and therefore the length of the entire number
- The number the checksum must be a multiple of

This problem can be solved using the *template method* design pattern, which defines the skeleton of an algorithm and lets subclasses redefine particular steps:

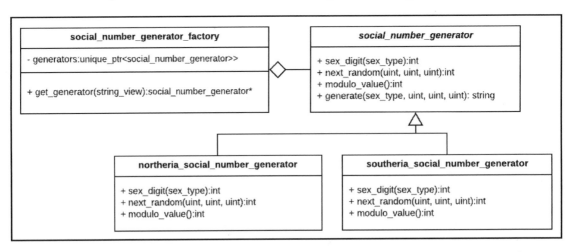

social_number_generator is a base class that has a public method called generate() that produces a new social security number for a specified sex and birth date. This method internally calls several protected virtual methods, sex_digit(), next_random(), and modulo_value(). These virtual methods are overridden in the two derived classes, northeria_social_number_generator and southeria_social_number_generator. In addition, a factory class holds instances of these social number generators and makes them available to the calling clients:

```cpp
enum class sex_type {female, male};

class social_number_generator
{
protected:
    virtual int sex_digit(sex_type const sex) const noexcept = 0;
    virtual int next_random(unsigned const year, unsigned const month,
                            unsigned const day) = 0;
    virtual int modulo_value() const noexcept = 0;

    social_number_generator(int const min, int const max):ud(min, max)
    {
        std::random_device rd;
        auto seed_data = std::array<int, std::mt19937::state_size> {};
        std::generate(std::begin(seed_data), std::end(seed_data),
                    std::ref(rd));
        std::seed_seq seq(std::begin(seed_data), std::end(seed_data));
        eng.seed(seq);
    }

public:
    std::string generate(
        sex_type const sex,
        unsigned const year, unsigned const month, unsigned const day)
    {
        std::stringstream snumber;

        snumber << sex_digit(sex);

        snumber << year << month << day;

        snumber << next_random(year, month, day);

        auto number = snumber.str();

        auto index = number.length();
        auto sum = std::accumulate(std::begin(number), std::end(number), 0,
            [&index](int const s, char const c) {
```

```
                return s + index-- * (c-'0');});

        auto rest = sum % modulo_value();
        snumber << modulo_value() - rest;

        return snumber.str();
    }

    virtual ~social_number_generator() {}

protected:
    std::map<unsigned, int> cache;
    std::mt19937 eng;
    std::uniform_int_distribution<> ud;
};

class southeria_social_number_generator final :
    public social_number_generator
{
public:
    southeria_social_number_generator():
        social_number_generator(1000, 9999)
    {
    }

protected:
    virtual int sex_digit(sex_type const sex) const noexcept override
    {
        if(sex == sex_type::female) return 1;
        else return 2;
    }

    virtual int next_random(unsigned const year, unsigned const month,
                            unsigned const day) override
    {
        auto key = year * 10000 + month * 100 + day;
        while(true)
        {
            auto number = ud(eng);
            auto pos = cache.find(number);
            if(pos == std::end(cache))
            {
                cache[key] = number;
                return number;
            }
        }
    }
```

```
      virtual int modulo_value() const noexcept override
      {
         return 11;
      }
};

class northeria_social_number_generator final :
   public social_number_generator
{
public:
   northeria_social_number_generator():
      social_number_generator(10000, 99999)
      {
      }

protected:
   virtual int sex_digit(sex_type const sex) const noexcept override
   {
      if(sex == sex_type::female) return 9;
      else return 7;
   }

   virtual int next_random(unsigned const year, unsigned const month,
                           unsigned const day) override
   {
      auto key = year * 10000 + month * 100 + day;
      while(true)
      {
         auto number = ud(eng);
         auto pos = cache.find(number);
         if(pos == std::end(cache))
         {
            cache[key] = number;
            return number;
         }
      }
   }

   virtual int modulo_value() const noexcept override
   {
      return 11;
   }
};

class social_number_generator_factory
{
public:
   social_number_generator_factory()
```

```
    {
        generators["northeria"] =
        std::make_unique<northeria_social_number_generator>();
        generators["southeria"] =
            std::make_unique<southeria_social_number_generator>();
    }

    social_number_generator* get_generator(std::string_view country) const
    {
        auto it = generators.find(country.data());
        if(it != std::end(generators))
        return it->second.get();

        throw std::runtime_error("invalid country");
    }

private:
    std::map<std::string,
    std::unique_ptr<social_number_generator>> generators;
};
```

Using this code, social security numbers can be generated as follows:

```
int main()
{
    social_number_generator_factory factory;

    auto sn1 = factory.get_generator("northeria")->generate(
                sex_type::female, 2017, 12, 25);
    auto sn2 = factory.get_generator("northeria")->generate(
                sex_type::female, 2017, 12, 25);
    auto sn3 = factory.get_generator("northeria")->generate(
                sex_type::male, 2017, 12, 25);

    auto sss1 = factory.get_generator("southeria")->generate(
                sex_type::female, 2017, 12, 25);
    auto ss2 = factory.get_generator("southeria")->generate(
                sex_type::female, 2017, 12, 25);
    auto ss3 = factory.get_generator("southeria")->generate(
                sex_type::male, 2017, 12, 25);
}
```

70. Approval system

The problem described can be expressed in a series of `if ... else if ... else ... endif` statements. An object-oriented version of this idiom is the *chain of responsibility* design pattern. This pattern defines a chain of receiver objects that have the responsibility of either handling a request or passing it to the next receiver in the chain if one exists. The following class diagram shows a possible implementation of the pattern for this problem:

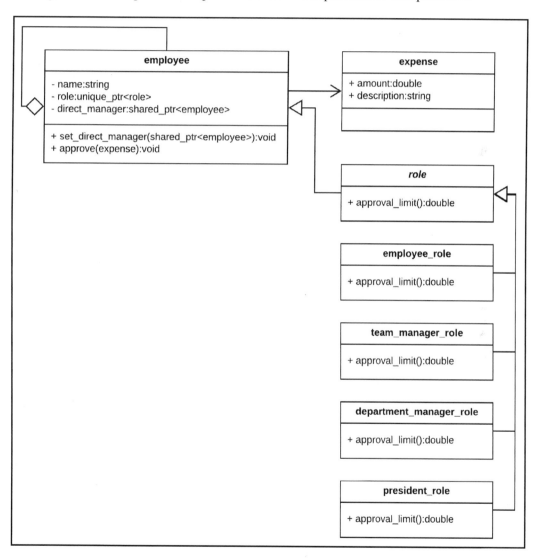

`employee` is a class that represents an employee in the company. An employee may have a direct manager that is set with a call to the `set_direct_manager()` method. Every employee has a name and a role that defines their responsibilities and permissions. `role` is an abstract base class for possible roles and has a pure virtual method, `approval_limit()`, that derived classes such as `employee_role`, `team_manager_role`, `department_manager_role`, and `president_role` override to indicate the limit up to which an employee can approve expenses. The `approve()` method from the `employee` class is used to let an employee approve an expense. If the role of the employee allows them to approve an expense, they do so; otherwise, the request is passed to their direct manager, if any is defined:

```
class role
{
public:
    virtual double approval_limit() const noexcept = 0;
    virtual ~role() {}
};

class employee_role : public role
{
public:
    virtual double approval_limit() const noexcept override
    {
        return 1000;
    }
};

class team_manager_role : public role
{
public:
    virtual double approval_limit() const noexcept override
    {
        return 10000;
    }
};

class department_manager_role : public role
{
public:
    virtual double approval_limit() const noexcept override
    {
        return 100000;
    }
};
```

```cpp
class president_role : public role
{
public:
   virtual double approval_limit() const noexcept override
   {
      return std::numeric_limits<double>::max();
   }
};

struct expense
{
   double amount;
   std::string description;

   expense(double const amount, std::string_view desc):
      amount(amount), description(desc)
   {
   }
};

class employee
{
public:
   explicit employee(std::string_view name, std::unique_ptr<role> ownrole)
      : name(name), own_role(std::move(ownrole))
   {
   }

   void set_direct_manager(std::shared_ptr<employee> manager)
   {
      direct_manager = manager;
   }

   void approve(expense const & e)
   {
      if(e.amount <= own_role->approval_limit())
         std::cout << name << " approved expense '" << e.description
                   << "', cost=" << e.amount << std::endl;
      else if(direct_manager != nullptr)
         direct_manager->approve(e);
  }

private:
   std::string            name;
   std::unique_ptr<role>      own_role;
   std::shared_ptr<employee> direct_manager;
};
```

The following example shows how this code can be used to approve expenses:

```
int main()
{
    auto john = std::make_shared<employee>("john smith",
                    std::make_unique<employee_role>());

    auto robert = std::make_shared<employee>("robert booth",
                    std::make_unique<team_manager_role>());

    auto david = std::make_shared<employee>("david jones",
                    std::make_unique<department_manager_role>());

    auto cecil = std::make_shared<employee>("cecil williamson",
                    std::make_unique<president_role>());

    john->set_direct_manager(robert);
    robert->set_direct_manager(david);
    david->set_direct_manager(cecil);

    john->approve(expense{500, "magazins"});
    john->approve(expense{5000, "hotel accomodation"});
    john->approve(expense{50000, "conference costs"});
    john->approve(expense{200000, "new lorry"});
}
```

71. Observable vector container

The observable vector described in this problem is a typical example of a subject in the design pattern called observer. This pattern describes an object, called the **subject**, that maintains a list of dependent objects, called **observers**, and notifies them of any state changes by calling one of their methods. The class diagram shown here describes a possible pattern implementation for the proposed problem:

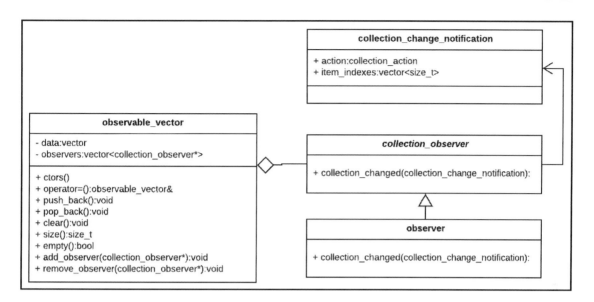

observable_vector is a class that wraps an std::vector and exposes the required operations. It also maintains a list of pointers to collection_observer objects. This is a base class for objects that want to be informed of any state changes in the observable_vector. It has a virtual method called collection_changed() with an argument of type collection_changed_notification that contains information about the change. When any change in the internal state of observable_vector occurs, it calls this method on all the registered observers. Observers can be added to the vector with the add_observer() method, or removed from the vector by calling the remove_observer() method:

```
enum class collection_action
{
    add,
    remove,
    clear,
    assign
};

std::string to_string(collection_action const action)
{
    switch(action)
    {
        case collection_action::add:    return "add";
        case collection_action::remove: return "remove";
        case collection_action::clear:  return "clear";
        case collection_action::assign: return "assign";
```

```
      }
   }

   struct collection_change_notification
   {
      collection_action action;
      std::vector<size_t> item_indexes;
   };

   class collection_observer
   {
   public:
      virtual void collection_changed(
         collection_change_notification notification) = 0;
      virtual ~collection_observer() {}
   };

   template <typename T, class Allocator = std::allocator<T>>
   class observable_vector final
   {
      typedef typename std::vector<T, Allocator>::size_type size_type;
   public:
      observable_vector() noexcept(noexcept(Allocator()))
         : observable_vector( Allocator() ) {}
      explicit observable_vector( const Allocator& alloc ) noexcept
         : data(alloc){}
      observable_vector( size_type count, const T& value,
                         const Allocator& alloc = Allocator())
         : data(count, value, alloc){}
      explicit observable_vector( size_type count,
                                  const Allocator& alloc = Allocator() )
         :data(count, alloc){}
      observable_vector(observable_vector&& other) noexcept
         :data(other.data){}
      observable_vector(observable_vector&& other,
                        const Allocator& alloc)
         :data(other.data, alloc){}
      observable_vector(std::initializer_list<T> init,
         const Allocator& alloc = Allocator())
         :data(init, alloc){}
      template<class InputIt>
      observable_vector(InputIt first, InputIt last, const
                        Allocator& alloc = Allocator())
         :data(first, last, alloc){}

      observable_vector& operator=(observable_vector const & other)
      {
         if(this != &other)
```

```
   {
      data = other.data;

      for(auto o : observers)
      {
         if(o != nullptr)
         {
            o->collection_changed({
               collection_action::assign,
               std::vector<size_t> {}
            });
         }
      }
   }

   return *this;
}

observable_vector& operator=(observable_vector&& other)
{
   if(this != &other)
   {
      data = std::move(other.data);

      for(auto o : observers)
      {
         if(o != nullptr)
         {
            o->collection_changed({
               collection_action::assign,
               std::vector<size_t> {}
            });
         }
      }
   }

   return *this;
}

void push_back(T&& value)
{
   data.push_back(value);

   for(auto o : observers)
   {
      if(o != nullptr)
      {
         o->collection_changed({
```

```
                    collection_action::add,
                    std::vector<size_t> {data.size()-1}
            });
        }
    }
}

void pop_back()
{
    data.pop_back();

    for(auto o : observers)
    {
        if(o != nullptr)
        {
            o->collection_changed({
                collection_action::remove,
                std::vector<size_t> {data.size()+1}
            });
        }
    }
}

void clear() noexcept
{
    data.clear();

    for(auto o : observers)
    {
        if(o != nullptr)
        {
            o->collection_changed({
                collection_action::clear,
                std::vector<size_t> {}
            });
        }
    }
}

size_type size() const noexcept
{
    return data.size();
}

[[nodiscard]] bool empty() const noexcept
{
    return data.empty();
}
```

```
    void add_observer(collection_observer * const o)
    {
       observers.push_back(o);
    }

    void remove_observer(collection_observer const * const o)
    {
       observers.erase(std::remove(std::begin(observers),
                                   std::end(observers), o),
                       std::end(observers));
    }

private:
    std::vector<T, Allocator> data;
    std::vector<collection_observer*> observers;
};

class observer : public collection_observer
{
public:
    virtual void collection_changed(
       collection_change_notification notification) override
    {
       std::cout << "action: " << to_string(notification.action);
       if(!notification.item_indexes.empty())
       {
          std::cout << ", indexes: ";
          for(auto i : notification.item_indexes)
             std::cout << i << ' ';
       }
       std::cout << std::endl;
    }
};
```

The following are examples of using the observable_vector class and getting notifications of the changes in its internal state:

```
int main()
{
   observable_vector<int> v;
   observer o;

   v.add_observer(&o);

   v.push_back(1);
   v.push_back(2);
   v.pop_back();
```

```
            v.clear();

            v.remove_observer(&o);

            v.push_back(3);
            v.push_back(4);

            v.add_observer(&o);

          observable_vector<int> v2 {1,2,3};
          v = v2;
          v = observable_vector<int> {7,8,9};
        }
```

You can take it as a further exercise to add more functionality to `observable_vector`, such as providing access to the elements using iterators.

72. Computing order price with discounts

The problem proposed here can be solved with the *strategy* pattern. This design pattern defines a family of algorithms and makes them interchangeable within the family. In this particular problem, both the discounts and the final order price calculators could be implemented based on the strategy pattern. The following diagram describes the hierarchy of discount types and their interchangeable use within the other classes, `customer`, `article`, `order_line`, and `order`:

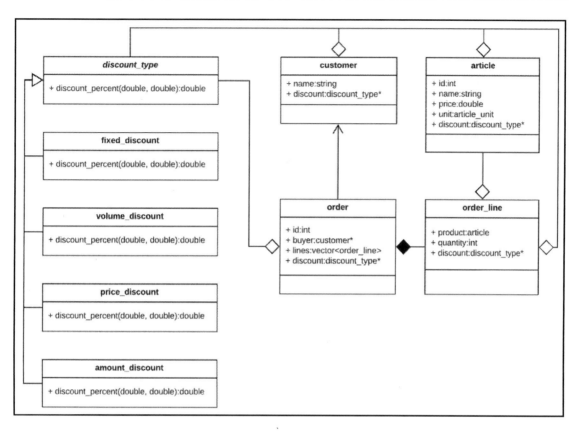

The implementation of the discount types is shown here:

```
struct discount_type
{
   virtual double discount_percent(
      double const price, double const quantity) const noexcept = 0;
   virtual ~discount_type() {}
};

struct fixed_discount final : public discount_type
{
   explicit fixed_discount(double const discount) noexcept
      : discount(discount) {}
   virtual double discount_percent(
      double const, double const) const noexcept
   {return discount;}

private:
   double discount;
```

```
};

struct volume_discount final : public discount_type
{
   explicit volume_discount(double const quantity,
                            double const discount) noexcept
     : discount(discount), min_quantity(quantity) {}
   virtual double discount_percent(
      double const, double const quantity) const noexcept
   {return quantity >= min_quantity ? discount : 0;}

private:
   double discount;
   double min_quantity;
};

struct price_discount : public discount_type
{
   explicit price_discount(double const price,
                           double const discount) noexcept
     : discount(discount), min_total_price(price) {}
   virtual double discount_percent(
      double const price, double const quantity) const noexcept
   {return price*quantity >= min_total_price ? discount : 0;}

private:
   double discount;
   double min_total_price;
};

struct amount_discount : public discount_type
{
   explicit amount_discount(double const price,
                            double const discount) noexcept
     : discount(discount), min_total_price(price) {}
   virtual double discount_percent(
      double const price, double const) const noexcept
   {return price >= min_total_price ? discount : 0;}

private:
   double discount;
   double min_total_price;
};
```

The classes that model customers, articles, and orders have only a minimum structure, in order to keep the solution simple. They are shown here:

```
struct customer
{
    std::string    name;
    discount_type* discount;
};

enum class article_unit
{
    piece, kg, meter, sqmeter, cmeter, liter
};

struct article
{
    int            id;
    std::string    name;
    double         price;
    article_unit   unit;
    discount_type* discount;
};

struct order_line
{
    article        product;
    int            quantity;
    discount_type* discount;
};

struct order
{
    int                     id;
    customer*               buyer;
    std::vector<order_line> lines;
    discount_type*          discount;
};
```

For computing the final price of an order, we could use various types of calculator. This is yet another instantiation of the strategy pattern:

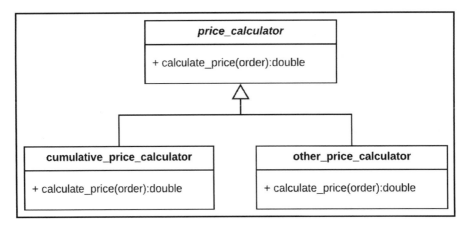

`price_calculator` is an abstract base class that has a pure virtual method, `calculate_price()`. The classes derived from `price_calculator`, such as `cumulative_price_calculator`, provide the actual algorithm implementation by overriding the `calculate_price()` method. For simplicity, in this implementation only one concrete strategy for price calculation is provided. As a further exercise, you can implement others:

```
struct price_calculator
{
    virtual double calculate_price(order const & o) = 0;
};

struct cumulative_price_calculator : public price_calculator
{
    virtual double calculate_price(order const & o) override
    {
        double price = 0;

        for(auto ol : o.lines)
        {
            double line_price = ol.product.price * ol.quantity;

            if(ol.product.discount != nullptr)
                line_price *= (1.0 - ol.product.discount->discount_percent(
                    ol.product.price, ol.quantity));

            if(ol.discount != nullptr)
```

```
            line_price *= (1.0 - ol.discount->discount_percent(
                ol.product.price, ol.quantity));

        if(o.buyer != nullptr && o.buyer->discount != nullptr)
            line_price *= (1.0 - o.buyer->discount->discount_percent(
                ol.product.price, ol.quantity));

        price += line_price;
    }

    if(o.discount != nullptr)
        price *= (1.0 - o.discount->discount_percent(price, 0));

    return price;
    }
};
```

Here are examples of how to compute the final order price using
`cumulative_price_calculator`:

```
inline bool are_equal(double const d1, double const d2,
                      double const diff = 0.001)
{
    return std::abs(d1 - d2) <= diff;
}

int()
{
    fixed_discount   d1(0.1);
    volume_discount  d2(10, 0.15);
    price_discount   d3(100, 0.05);
    amount_discount  d4(100, 0.05);

    customer c1 {"default", nullptr};
    customer c2 {"john", &d1};
    customer c3 {"joane", &d3};

    article a1 {1, "pen", 5, article_unit::piece, nullptr};
    article a2 {2, "expensive pen", 15, article_unit::piece, &d1};
    article a3 {3, "scissors", 10, article_unit::piece, &d2};

    cumulative_price_calculator calc;

    order o1 {101, &c1, {{a1, 1, nullptr}}, nullptr};
    assert(are_equal(calc.calculate_price(o1), 5));
```

```
    order o3 {103, &c1, {{a2, 1, nullptr}}, nullptr};
    assert(are_equal(calc.calculate_price(o3), 13.5));

    order o6 {106, &c1, {{a3, 15, nullptr}}, nullptr};
    assert(are_equal(calc.calculate_price(o6), 127.5));

    order o9 {109, &c3, {{a2, 20, &d1}}, &d4};
    assert(are_equal(calc.calculate_price(o9), 219.3075));
}
```

9
Data Serialization

Problems

73. Serializing and deserializing data to/from XML

Write a program that can serialize a list of movies to an XML file, and deserialize an XML file with a list of movies. Each movie has a numerical identifier, title, release year, length in minutes, a list of directors, a list of writers, and a list of casting roles with actor name and character name. Such an XML may look like the following:

```xml
<?xml version="1.0"?>
<movies>
  <movie id="9871" title="Forrest Gump" year="1994" length="202">
    <cast>
      <role star="Tom Hanks" name="Forrest Gump" />
      <role star="Sally Field" name="Mrs. Gump" />
      <role star="Robin Wright" name="Jenny Curran" />
      <role star="Mykelti Williamson" name="Bubba Blue" />
    </cast>
    <directors>
      <director name="Robert Zemeckis" />
    </directors>
    <writers>
      <writer name="Winston Groom" />
      <writer name="Eric Roth" />
    </writers>
  </movie>
  <!-- more movie elements -->
</movies>
```

74. Selecting data from XML using XPath

Consider an XML file with a list of movies as described for the previous problem. Write a program that can select and print the following:

- The title of all the movies released after a given year
- The name of the last actor in the casting list for each movie in the file

75. Serializing data to JSON

Write a program that can serialize a list of movies, as defined for the previous problems, to a JSON file. Each movie has a numerical identifier, title, release year, length in minutes, a list of directors, a list of writers, and a list of casting roles with actor name and character name. The following is an example of the expected JSON format:

```json
{
  "movies": [{
    "id": 9871,
    "title": "Forrest Gump",
    "year": 1994,
    "length": 202,
    "cast": [{
        "star": "Tom Hanks",
        "name": "Forrest Gump"
      },
      {
        "star": "Sally Field",
        "name": "Mrs. Gump"
      },
      {
        "star": "Robin Wright",
        "name": "Jenny Curran"
      },
      {
        "star": "Mykelti Williamson",
        "name": "Bubba Blue"
      }
    ],
    "directors": ["Robert Zemeckis"],
    "writers": ["Winston Groom", "Eric Roth"]
  }]
}
```

76. Deserializing data from JSON

Consider a JSON file with a list of movies as shown in the previous problem. Write a program that can deserialize its content.

77. Printing a list of movies to a PDF

Write a program that can print to a PDF file a list of movies in a tabular form, with the following requirements:

- There must be a heading to the list with the content *List of movies*. This must appear only on the first page of the document.
- For each movie, it should display the title, the release year, and the length.
- The title, followed by the release year in parentheses, must be left-aligned.
- The length, in hours and minutes (for example, 2:12), must be right-aligned.
- There must be a line above and below the movie listing on each page.

Here is an example of such a PDF output:

List of movies	
The Matrix (1999)	2:16
Forrest Gump (1994)	2:22
The Truman Show (1998)	1:43
The Pursuit of Happyness (2006)	1:57
Fight Club (1999)	2:19

78. Creating a PDF from a collection of images

Write a program that can create a PDF document that contains images from a user-specified directory. The images must be displayed one after another. If an image does not fit on the remainder of a page, it must be placed on the next page.

The following is an example of such a PDF file, created from several images of Albert Einstein (these pictures are featured along with the source code accompanying the book):

Solutions

73. Serializing and deserializing data to/from XML

The C++ standard library does not have any support for XML, but there are multiple open source, cross-platform libraries that you can use. Some libraries are lightweight, supporting a set of basic XML features, while others are more complex and rich in functionality. It is up to you to decide which is most suitable for a particular project.

The list of libraries you may want to consider should include *Xerces-C++*, *libxml++*, *tinyxml* or *tinyxml2*, *pugixml*, *gSOAP*, and *RapidXml*. For solving this particular task I will choose *pugixml*. This is a cross-platform, lightweight library, with a fast, although non-validating, XML parser. It has a DOM-like interface with rich traversal/modification capabilities, with support for Unicode and XPath 1.0. On the limitations of the library, it should be mentioned that it lacks support for schema validation. The pugixml library is available at `https://pugixml.org/`.

To represent the movies, as described in the problem, we shall use the following structures:

```cpp
struct casting_role
{
   std::string actor;
   std::string role;
};

struct movie
{
   unsigned int              id;
   std::string               title;
   unsigned int              year;
   unsigned int              length;
   std::vector<casting_role> cast;
   std::vector<std::string>  directors;
   std::vector<std::string>  writers;
};

using movie_list = std::vector<movie>;
```

To create an XML document you must use the `pugi::xml_document` class. After constructing the DOM tree you can save it to a file by calling `save_file()`. Nodes can be added by calling `append_child()`, and attributes with `append_attribute()`. The following method serializes a list of movies in the requested format:

```cpp
void serialize(movie_list const & movies, std::string_view filepath)
{
    pugi::xml_document doc;
    auto root = doc.append_child("movies");

    for (auto const & m : movies)
    {
        auto movie_node = root.append_child("movie");

        movie_node.append_attribute("id").set_value(m.id);
        movie_node.append_attribute("title").set_value(m.title.c_str());
        movie_node.append_attribute("year").set_value(m.year);
        movie_node.append_attribute("length").set_value(m.length);

        auto cast_node = movie_node.append_child("cast");
        for (auto const & c : m.cast)
        {
            auto node = cast_node.append_child("role");
            node.append_attribute("star").set_value(c.actor.c_str());
            node.append_attribute("name").set_value(c.role.c_str());
        }

        auto directors_node = movie_node.append_child("directors");
        for (auto const & director : m.directors)
        {
            directors_node.append_child("director")
                          .append_attribute("name")
                          .set_value(director.c_str());
        }

        auto writers_node = movie_node.append_child("writers");
        for (auto const & writer : m.writers)
        {
            writers_node.append_child("writer")
                        .append_attribute("name")
                        .set_value(writer.c_str());
        }
    }

    doc.save_file(filepath.data());
}
```

For the opposite operation, you can load the content of the XML file into a `pugi::xml_document` by calling its `load_file()` method. You can access nodes by calling methods such as `child()` and `next_sibling()`, and attributes by calling `attribute()`. The `deserialize()` method, shown as follows, reads the DOM tree and constructs a list of movies:

```cpp
movie_list deserialize(std::string_view filepath)
{
    pugi::xml_document doc;
    movie_list movies;

    auto result = doc.load_file(filepath.data());
    if (result)
    {
        auto root = doc.child("movies");
        for (auto movie_node = root.child("movie");
            movie_node;
            movie_node = movie_node.next_sibling("movie"))
        {
            movie m;
            m.id = movie_node.attribute("id").as_uint();
            m.title = movie_node.attribute("title").as_string();
            m.year = movie_node.attribute("year").as_uint();
            m.length = movie_node.attribute("length").as_uint();

            for (auto role_node :
                movie_node.child("cast").children("role"))
            {
                m.cast.push_back(casting_role{
                    role_node.attribute("star").as_string(),
                    role_node.attribute("name").as_string() });
            }

            for (auto director_node :
                movie_node.child("directors").children("director"))
            {
                m.directors.push_back(
                    director_node.attribute("name").as_string());
            }

            for (auto writer_node :
                movie_node.child("writers").children("writer"))
            {
                m.writers.push_back(
                    writer_node.attribute("name").as_string());
            }
```

```
            movies.push_back(m);
        }
    }

    return movies;
}
```

An example of how these functions can be used is shown in the following listing:

```
int main()
{
    movie_list movies
    {
        {
            11001, "The Matrix",1999, 196,
            { {"Keanu Reeves", "Neo"},
              {"Laurence Fishburne", "Morpheus"},
              {"Carrie-Anne Moss", "Trinity"},
              {"Hugo Weaving", "Agent Smith"} },
            {"Lana Wachowski", "Lilly Wachowski"},
            {"Lana Wachowski", "Lilly Wachowski"},
        },
        {
            9871, "Forrest Gump", 1994, 202,
            { {"Tom Hanks", "Forrest Gump"},
              {"Sally Field", "Mrs. Gump"},
              {"Robin Wright","Jenny Curran"},
              {"Mykelti Williamson","Bubba Blue"} },
            {"Robert Zemeckis"},
            {"Winston Groom", "Eric Roth"},
        }
    };

    serialize(movies, "movies.xml");
    auto result = deserialize("movíes.xml");

    assert(result.size() == 2);
    assert(result[0].title == "The Matrix");
    assert(result[1].title == "Forrest Gump");
}
```

74. Selecting data from XML using XPath

Navigation through the elements and attributes of an XML file can be done with *XPath*. XPath uses XPath expressions for that purpose and there is a long list of built-in functions for that. *pugixml* supports XPath expressions and you can use the `select_nodes()` method from the `xml_document` class for that purpose. Note that, if an error occurs during the XPath selection, an `xpath_exception` is thrown. The following XPath expressions can be used for selecting the nodes according to the problem requirements:

- For all movies released after a given year (in this example that year is 1995):
  `/movies/movie[@year>1995]`
- For the last casting role of each movie: `/movies/movie/cast/role[last()]`

The following program loads an XML document from a string buffer and then performs node selection using the XPath expressions listed earlier. The XML document is defined as follows:

```
std::string text = R"(
<?xml version="1.0"?>
<movies>
  <movie id="11001" title="The Matrix" year="1999" length="196">
    <cast>
      <role star="Keanu Reeves" name="Neo" />
      <role star="Laurence Fishburne" name="Morpheus" />
      <role star="Carrie-Anne Moss" name="Trinity" />
      <role star="Hugo Weaving" name=" Agent Smith" />
    </cast>
    <directors>
      <director name="Lana Wachowski" />
      <director name="Lilly Wachowski" />
    </directors>
    <writers>
      <writer name="Lana Wachowski" />
      <writer name="Lilly Wachowski" />
    </writers>
  </movie>
  <movie id="9871" title="Forrest Gump" year="1994" length="202">
    <cast>
      <role star="Tom Hanks" name="Forrest Gump" />
      <role star="Sally Field" name="Mrs. Gump" />
      <role star="Robin Wright" name="Jenny Curran" />
      <role star="Mykelti Williamson" name="Bubba Blue" />
    </cast>
    <directors>
      <director name="Robert Zemeckis" />
```

```
        </directors>
        <writers>
          <writer name="Winston Groom" />
          <writer name="Eric Roth" />
        </writers>
      </movie>
  </movies>
)";
```

The selection of the requested data can be done in the following manner:

```cpp
pugi::xml_document doc;
if (doc.load_string(text.c_str()))
{
    try
    {
        auto titles = doc.select_nodes("/movies/movie[@year>1995]");

        for (auto it : titles)
        {
            std::cout << it.node().attribute("title").as_string()
                      << std::endl;
        }
    }
    catch (pugi::xpath_exception const & e)
    {
        std::cout << e.result().description() << std::endl;
    }

    try
    {
        auto titles = doc.select_nodes("/movies/movie/cast/role[last()]");

        for (auto it : titles)
        {
            std::cout << it.node().attribute("star").as_string()
                      << std::endl;
        }
    }
    catch (pugi::xpath_exception const & e)
    {
        std::cout << e.result().description() << std::endl;
    }
}
```

75. Serializing data to JSON

As with XML, no standard support for JSON exists. However, there are a large number of cross-platform libraries for this purpose. At the time of writing, the *nativejson-benchmark* project, available at `https://github.com/miloyip/nativejson-benchmark`, lists more than 40 libraries. This project is a benchmark that evaluates the conformance and performance (speed, memory, and code size) of open source C/C++ libraries with JSON parsing/generation capabilities. This makes it perhaps a bit hard to choose the right library, although top contenders may include `RapidJSON`, `NLohmann`, `taocpp/json`, `Configuru`, `json_spirit`, `jsoncpp`. For solving this task we will use here the `nlohmann/json` library. It is a cross-platform, header only library for C++11, with an intuitive syntax and good documentation. This library is available at `https://github.com/nlohmann/json`.

We will use the same data structures to represent movies that we used for the problem *Serializing and deserializing data to/from XML*. The `nlohmann` library uses `nlohmann::json` as its main data type for representing JSON objects. Although you can create JSON values with a more explicit syntax, there are also implicit conversions to and from scalar types and standard containers. In addition, you can also enable this implicit conversion to and from your custom types by providing a `to_json()` and `from_json()` method in the namespace of the type to be converted. There are some requirements for these functions that you can read about in the documentation.

In the following code, this is the chosen approach. Since the `movie` and `casting_role` types were defined in the global namespace, the `to_json()` overloads that serialize these types are also defined in the global namespace. On the other hand, the type `movie_list` is actually a type alias for `std::vector<movie>` and can be serialized and deserialized directly because, as mentioned earlier, the library supports implicit conversion to and from standard containers:

```
using json = nlohmann::json;

void to_json(json& j, casting_role const & c)
{
    j = json{ {"star", c.actor}, {"name", c.role} };
}

void to_json(json& j, movie const & m)
{
    j = json::object({
        {"id", m.id},
        {"title", m.title},
        {"year", m.year},
        {"length", m.length},
```

```cpp
            {"cast", m.cast },
            {"directors", m.directors},
            {"writers", m.writers}
        });
    }

    void serialize(movie_list const & movies, std::string_view filepath)
    {
        json jdata{ { "movies", movies } };

        std::ofstream ofile(filepath.data());
        if (ofile.is_open())
        {
            ofile << std::setw(2) << jdata << std::endl;
        }
    }
```

The function `serialize()` can be used as shown in the following example:

```cpp
    int main()
    {
        movie_list movies
        {
            {
                11001, "The Matrix", 1999, 196,
                { {"Keanu Reeves", "Neo"},
                  {"Laurence Fishburne", "Morpheus"},
                  {"Carrie-Anne Moss", "Trinity"},
                  {"Hugo Weaving", "Agent Smith"} },
                {"Lana Wachowski", "Lilly Wachowski"},
                {"Lana Wachowski", "Lilly Wachowski"},
            },
            {
                9871, "Forrest Gump", 1994, 202,
                { {"Tom Hanks", "Forrest Gump"},
                  {"Sally Field", "Mrs. Gump"},
                  {"Robin Wright","Jenny Curran"},
                  {"Mykelti Williamson","Bubba Blue"} },
                {"Robert Zemeckis"},
                {"Winston Groom", "Eric Roth"},
            }
        };

        serialize(movies, "movies.json");
    }
```

76. Deserializing data from JSON

For solving this task we will use the `nlohmann/json` library again. Instead of writing `from_json()` functions, as was mentioned in the solution to the previous problem, we will take a more explicit approach. The content of a JSON file can be loaded into an `nlohmann::json` object using the overloaded `operator>>`. To access the object values, you should use the `at()` method rather than `operator[]`, because the former throws an exception if the key does not exist (an exception that you can handle), while the latter exhibits undefined behavior. To retrieve an object value as a particular `T` object, use the `get<T>()` method. However, this requires the type `T` to be default constructible.

The `deserialize()` function shown here returns an `std::vector<movie>` constructed from the content of a specified JSON file:

```
using json = nlohmann::json;

movie_list deserialize(std::string_view filepath)
{
    movie_list movies;

    std::ifstream ifile(filepath.data());
    if (ifile.is_open())
    {
        json jdata;

        try
        {
            ifile >> jdata;

            if (jdata.is_object())
            {
                for (auto & element : jdata.at("movies"))
                {
                    movie m;

                    m.id = element.at("id").get<unsigned int>();
                    m.title = element.at("title").get<std::string>();
                    m.year = element.at("year").get<unsigned int>();
                    m.length = element.at("length").get<unsigned int>();

                    for (auto & role : element.at("cast"))
                    {
                        m.cast.push_back(casting_role{
                            role.at("star").get<std::string>(),
                            role.at("name").get<std::string>() });
```

```
            }

            for (auto & director : element.at("directors"))
            {
                m.directors.push_back(director);
            }

            for (auto & writer : element.at("writers"))
            {
                m.writers.push_back(writer);
            }

            movies.push_back(m);
        }
    }
}
catch (std::exception const & ex)
{
    std::cout << ex.what() << std::endl;
}
}

return movies;
}
```

This deserialization function can be used as follows:

```
int main()
{
    auto movies = deserialize("movies.json");

    assert(movies.size() == 2);
    assert(movies[0].title == "The Matrix");
    assert(movies[1].title == "Forrest Gump");
}
```

77. Printing a list of movies to a PDF

There are various C++ libraries for working with PDF files. *HaHu, PoDoFo, JagPDF,* and *PDF-Writer* (also known as *Hummus*) are some of the open source and cross-platform libraries that you could use for this purpose. In this book, I will use *PDF-Writer*, available at `https://github.com/galkahana/PDF-Writer`. This is a free, fast, and extensible library with a basic feature set that includes support for text, images, and shapes with both PDF operators and higher-level functions (which I will use for the solution to this problem).

The function `print_pdf()`, shown as follows, implements the following algorithm:

- Start a new PDF document with `PDFWriter::StartPDF()`.
- Print at most 25 movies on each page. Each page is represented by a `PDFPage()` object and has a `PageContentContext` object, which is created with `PDFPage::StartPageContentContext()` and used to draw items on the page.
- On the first page, put a heading with the content *List of movies*. Text is written on the page using `PageContentContext::WriteText()`.
- Movie information is written using different fonts.
- Lines are drawn on the top and bottom of the movie list on each page using `PageContentContext::DrawPath()`.
- `PDFWriter::EndPageContentContext()` and `PDFWriter::WritePageAndRelease()` must be called after finishing writing content to a page.
- `PDFWriter::EndPDF()` must be called when finishing writing the PDF document:

> For information about the types and methods used in the following code, as well as more information about creating PDF documents and working with text, shapes, and images, see the project documentation available at `https://github.com/galkahana/PDF-Writer/wiki`.

```cpp
#ifdef _WIN32
static const std::string fonts_dir = R"(c:\windows\fonts\)";
#elif defined (__APPLE__)
static const std::string fonts_dir = R"(/Library/Fonts/)";
#else
static const std::string fonts_dir = R"(/usr/share/fonts)";
#endif

void print_pdf(movie_list const & movies,
               std::string_view path)
{
    const int height = 842;
    const int width = 595;
    const int left = 60;
    const int top = 770;
    const int right = 535;
    const int bottom = 60;
    const int line_height = 28;
```

```
PDFWriter pdf;
pdf.StartPDF(path.data(), ePDFVersion13);
auto font = pdf.GetFontForFile(fonts_dir + "arial.ttf");

AbstractContentContext::GraphicOptions pathStrokeOptions(
    AbstractContentContext::eStroke,
    AbstractContentContext::eRGB,
    0xff000000,
    1);

PDFPage* page = nullptr;
PageContentContext* context = nullptr;
int index = 0;
for (size_t i = 0; i < movies.size(); ++i)
{
    index = i % 25;
    if (index == 0)
    {
        if (page != nullptr)
        {
            DoubleAndDoublePairList pathPoints;
            pathPoints.push_back(DoubleAndDoublePair(left, bottom));
            pathPoints.push_back(DoubleAndDoublePair(right, bottom));
            context->DrawPath(pathPoints, pathStrokeOptions);

            pdf.EndPageContentContext(context);
            pdf.WritePageAndRelease(page);
        }

        page = new PDFPage();
        page->SetMediaBox(PDFRectangle(0, 0, width, height));
        context = pdf.StartPageContentContext(page);

        {
            DoubleAndDoublePairList pathPoints;
            pathPoints.push_back(DoubleAndDoublePair(left, top));
            pathPoints.push_back(DoubleAndDoublePair(right, top));
            context->DrawPath(pathPoints, pathStrokeOptions);
        }
    }

    if (i == 0)
    {
        AbstractContentContext::TextOptions const textOptions(
            font, 26, AbstractContentContext::eGray, 0);
```

```
            context->WriteText(left, top + 15,
                                "List of movies", textOptions);
    }

    auto textw = 0;
    {
        AbstractContentContext::TextOptions const textOptions(
            font, 20, AbstractContentContext::eGray, 0);

        context->WriteText(left, top - 20 - line_height * index,
                                movies[i].title, textOptions);
        auto textDimensions = font->CalculateTextDimensions(
                                movies[i].title, 20);
        textw = textDimensions.width;
    }


    {
        AbstractContentContext::TextOptions const textOptions(
            font, 16, AbstractContentContext::eGray, 0);

        context->WriteText(left + textw + 5,
                                top - 20 - line_height * index,
                                " (" + std::to_string(movies[i].year) + ")",
                                textOptions);

        std::stringstream s;
        s << movies[i].length / 60 << ':' << std::setw(2)
          << std::setfill('0') << movies[i].length % 60;

        context->WriteText(right - 30, top - 20 - line_height * index,
            s.str(),
            textOptions);
    }
}

DoubleAndDoublePairList pathPoints;
pathPoints.push_back(
    DoubleAndDoublePair(left, top - line_height * (index + 1)));
pathPoints.push_back(
    DoubleAndDoublePair(right, top - line_height * (index + 1)));
context->DrawPath(pathPoints, pathStrokeOptions);

if (page != nullptr)
{
```

```
            pdf.EndPageContentContext(context);
            pdf.WritePageAndRelease(page);
        }

    pdf.EndPDF();
}
```

The `print_pdf()` function can be used as follows:

```
int main()
{
    movie_list movies
    {
        { 1, "The Matrix", 1999, 136},
        { 2, "Forrest Gump", 1994, 142},
        // .. other movies
        { 28, "L.A. Confidential", 1997, 138},
        { 29, "Shutter Island", 2010, 138},
    };

    print_pdf(movies, "movies.pdf");
}
```

78. Creating a PDF from a collection of images

To solve this problem we will use the same *PDF-Writer* library we used for the previous problem. I recommend that you look at and implement the previous problem first, if you have not done that already, before continuing with this one.

The following `get_images()` function returns a vector of strings that represent the path of all JPG images from a specified directory:

```
namespace fs = std::experimental::filesystem;

std::vector<std::string> get_images(fs::path const & dirpath)
{
    std::vector<std::string> paths;

    for (auto const & p : fs::directory_iterator(dirpath))
    {
```

```
        if (p.path().extension() == ".jpg")
            paths.push_back(p.path().string());
    }

    return paths;
}
```

The `print_pdf()` function creates a PDF document with all the JPG images from a specified directory. It implements the following algorithm:

- Create a new PDF document with `PDFWriter::StartPDF()`
- Create a page and its content and put as many images as can fit on the page, arranged vertically one after the other
- When a new image does not fit in the current page, close the page with `PDFWriter::EndPageContentContext()` and `PDFWriter::SavePageAndRelease()` and start a new page
- Write images on the page content using `PageContentContext::DrawImage()`
- End the document by calling `PDFWriter::EndPDF()`

```
void print_pdf(fs::path const & pdfpath,
               fs::path const & dirpath)
{
    const int height = 842;
    const int width = 595;
    const int margin = 20;

    auto image_paths = get_images(dirpath);

    PDFWriter pdf;
    pdf.StartPDF(pdfpath.string(), ePDFVersion13);

    PDFPage* page = nullptr;
    PageContentContext* context = nullptr;

    auto top = height - margin;
    for (size_t i = 0; i < image_paths.size(); ++i)
    {
        auto dims = pdf.GetImageDimensions(image_paths[i]);

        if (i == 0 || top - dims.second < margin)
        {
            if (page != nullptr)
            {
```

```
                pdf.EndPageContentContext(context);
                pdf.WritePageAndRelease(page);
            }

            page = new PDFPage();
            page->SetMediaBox(PDFRectangle(0, 0, width, height));
            context = pdf.StartPageContentContext(page);

            top = height - margin;
        }

        context->DrawImage(margin, top - dims.second, image_paths[i]);

        top -= dims.second + margin;
    }

    if (page != nullptr)
    {
        pdf.EndPageContentContext(context);
        pdf.WritePageAndRelease(page);
    }

    pdf.EndPDF();
}
```

The print_pdf() can be used as in the following example, where sample.pdf is the name of the output, and res is the name of the folder that contains the images:

```
int main()
{
    print_pdf("sample.pdf", "res");
}
```

10
Archives, Images, and Databases

Problems

79. Finding files in a ZIP archive

Write a program that can search for and print all the files in a ZIP archive whose name matches a user-provided regular expression (for instance, use ^.*\.jpg$ to find all files with the extension .jpg).

80. Compressing and decompressing files to/from a ZIP archive

Write a program that can do the following:

- Compress either a file or the contents of a user-specified directory, recursively, to a ZIP archive
- Decompress the contents of a ZIP archive to a user-specified destination directory

81. Compressing and decompressing files to/from a ZIP archive with a password

Write a program that can do the following:

- Compress either a file or the contents of a user-specified directory, recursively, to a password-protected ZIP archive
- Decompress the content of a password-protected ZIP archive to a user-specified destination directory

82. Creating a PNG that represents a national flag

Write a program that generates a PNG file that represents the national flag of Romania, shown here. The size of the image in pixels, as well as the path to the destination file, should be provided by the user:

83. Creating verification text PNG images

Write a program that can create Captcha-like PNG images for verifying human users to a system. Such an image should have:

- A gradient-colored background
- A series of random letters displayed at different angles both to the right and left
- Several random lines of different colors across the image (on top of the text)

Here is an example of such an image:

84. EAN-13 barcode generator

Write a program that can generate a PNG image with an EAN-13 barcode for any international article number in version 13 of the standard. For simplicity, the image should only contain the barcode and can skip the EAN-13 number printed under the barcode. Here is an example of the expected output for the number 5901234123457:

85. Reading movies from an SQLite database

Write a program that reads movies from an SQLite database and displays them on the console. Each movie must have a numerical identifier, a title, release year, length in minutes, list of directors, list of writers, and a cast that includes both the actor and the character names. The following is a diagram of the database that should be used for this purpose:

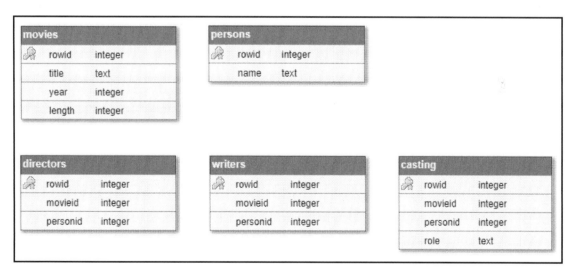

86. Inserting movies into an SQLite database transactionally

Extended the program written for the previous problem so that it can add new movies to the database. The movies could be read from the console, or alternatively from a text file. The insertion of movie data into several tables in the database must be performed transactionally.

87. Handling movie images in an SQLite database

Modify the program written for the previous problem to support adding media files (such as images, but also videos) to a movie. These files must be stored in a separate table in the database and have a unique numerical identifier, the movie identifier, a name (typically the filename), an optional description, and the actual media content, stored as a blob. The following is a diagram with the structure of the table that must be added to the existing database:

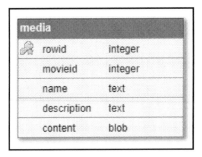

The program written for this problem must support several commands:

- Listing all movies that match a search criterion (notably the title)
- Listing information about all existing media files for a movie
- Adding a new media file for a movie
- Deleting an existing media file

Solutions

79. Finding files in a ZIP archive

There are a variety of libraries that provide support for working with ZIP archives. Among the ones available for free, the most used ones include *ZipLib*, *Info-Zip*, *MiniZip*, and *LZMA SDK* from 7z. And then, there are also commercial implementations. For the problems regarding ZIP archives in this book, I have chosen `ZipLib`. This is a lightweight, open source cross-platform C++11 library built around standard library streams, with no additional dependencies. The library, along with its documentation, is available at `https:/ /bitbucket.org/wbenny/ziplib`.

To implement the required functionality, you have to:

- Open the ZIP archive using `ZipFile::Open()`
- Enumerate all the entries in the archive using `ZipArchive::GetEntry()` and `ZipArchive::GetEntryCount()`
- For all entries that represent files, check that the name matches the provided regular expression using `ZipArchiveEntry::GetName()`
- For all entries that match the regular expression, add the full name to the list of results using `ZipArchiveEntry::GetFullName()`

The `find_in_archive()` function here is an implementation of the described algorithm:

```
namespace fs = std::experimental::filesystem;

std::vector<std::string> find_in_archive(
   fs::path const & archivepath,
   std::string_view pattern)
{
   std::vector<std::string> results;

   if (fs::exists(archivepath))
   {
      try
      {
         auto archive = ZipFile::Open(archivepath.string());

         for (size_t i = 0; i < archive->GetEntriesCount(); ++i)
         {
            auto entry = archive->GetEntry(i);
            if (entry)
```

```
                {
                    if (!entry->IsDirectory())
                    {
                        auto name = entry->GetName();
                        if (std::regex_match(name,
                                std::regex{ pattern.data() }))
                        {
                            results.push_back(entry->GetFullName());
                        }
                    }
                }
            }
        }
        catch (std::exception const & ex)
        {
            std::cout << ex.what() << std::endl;
        }
    }

    return results;
}
```

The following example shows how to search for all the files with the extension .jpg in a ZIP archive called sample79.zip. This file is available for testing together with the source code for the book:

```
int main()
{
    auto results = find_in_archive("sample79.zip", R"(^.*\.jpg$)"));
    for(auto const & name : results)
    {
        std::cout << name << std::endl;
    }
}
```

80. Compressing and decompressing files to/from a ZIP archive

To solve this two-part problem, we will use the same ZipLib library we saw for the solution of the previous problem. The solution to this problem consists of two functions, one that is able to perform the compression to a ZIP archive and one that is able to perform decompression from a ZIP archive.

In order to perform the requested compression, we should do the following:

- If the source path represents a regular file, then add that file to the ZIP archive using `ZipFile::AddFile()`
- If the source path represents a recursive directory, then:
  - Iterate recursively through all the entries in the directory
  - If an entry is a directory, then create a directory entry in the ZIP archive with that name using `ZipArchive::CreateEntry()`
  - If an entry is a regular file, then add that file to the ZIP archive using `ZipFile::AddFile()`

The `compress()` function shown in the following snippet implements this algorithm. It has three parameters: the first is the path of the file or folder to compress, the second is the path to the destination ZIP archive, and the third is a function object that is used to report the progress of the operation (such as a function that prints a message to the console):

```cpp
namespace fs = std::experimental::filesystem;

void compress(fs::path const & source,
              fs::path const & archive,
              std::function<void(std::string_view)> reporter)
{
    if (fs::is_regular_file(source))
    {
        if (reporter) reporter("Compressing " + source.string());
        ZipFile::AddFile(archive.string(), source.string(),
                         LzmaMethod::Create());
    }
    else
    {
        for (auto const & p : fs::recursive_directory_iterator(source))
        {
            if (reporter) reporter("Compressing " + p.path().string());

            if (fs::is_directory(p))
            {
                auto zipArchive = ZipFile::Open(archive.string());
                auto entry = zipArchive->CreateEntry(p.path().string());
                entry->SetAttributes(ZipArchiveEntry::Attributes::Directory);
                ZipFile::SaveAndClose(zipArchive, archive.string());
            }
            else if (fs::is_regular_file(p))
            {
                ZipFile::AddFile(archive.string(), p.path().string(),
                                 LzmaMethod::Create());
```

```
            }
         }
      }
   }
```

To implement the opposite operation, decompression, we must do the following:

- Open the ZIP archive using `ZipFile::Open()`
- Iterate through all the entries in the archive using `ZipArchive::GetEntriesCount()` and `ZipArchive::GetEntry()`
- If the entry is a directory, create it recursively in the destination path
- If the entry is a file, create a corresponding file in the destination and copy the content of the compressed file using `ZipArchiveEntry::GetDecompressionStream()`

The `decompress()` function shown here implements the preceding algorithm. Its parameters are similar to those of the `compress()` method: the first is the path to a destination directory, the second is the path to the ZIP archive to decompress, and the third is a function object used to report the progress of the operation:

```cpp
void decompress(fs::path const & destination,
                fs::path const & archive,
                std::function<void(std::string_view)> reporter)
{
    ensure_directory_exists(destination);

    auto zipArchive = ZipFile::Open(archive.string());

    for (int i = 0; i < zipArchive->GetEntriesCount(); ++i)
    {
        auto entry = zipArchive->GetEntry(i);
        if (entry)
        {
            auto filepath = destination / fs::path{
                entry->GetFullName() }.relative_path();
            if (reporter) reporter("Creating " + filepath.string());

            if (entry->IsDirectory())
            {
                ensure_directory_exists(filepath);
            }
            else
            {
                ensure_directory_exists(filepath.parent_path());
```

```
            std::ofstream destFile;
            destFile.open(filepath.string().c_str(),
                        std::ios::binary | std::ios::trunc);

            if (!destFile.is_open())
            {
                if(reporter)
                    reporter("Cannot create destination file!");
            }

            auto dataStream = entry->GetDecompressionStream();
            if (dataStream)
            {
                utils::stream::copy(*dataStream, destFile);
            }
        }
    }
}
}
```

This function uses `ensure_directory_exists()` to create a directory path recursively if it does not already exist. The implementation of this function is as follows:

```
void ensure_directory_exists(fs::path const & dir)
{
    if (!fs::exists(dir))
    {
        std::error_code err;
        fs::create_directories(dir, err);
    }
}
```

The following program allows the user to select the command to execute, either compression or decompression, as well as the path of the source and destination. It uses the `compress()` and `decompress()` functions shown above, providing them with a lambda function to be called for displaying the progress to the console:

```
int main()
{
    char option = 0;
    std::cout << "Select [c]ompress/[d]ecompress?";
    std::cin >> option;

    if (option == 'c')
    {
        std::string archivepath;
        std::string inputpath;
```

```
            std::cout << "Enter file or dir to compress:";
            std::cin >> inputpath;
            std::cout << "Enter archive path:";
            std::cin >> archivepath;

            compress(inputpath, archivepath,
                    [](std::string_view message) {
                        std::cout << message << std::endl; });
        }
        else if (option == 'd')
        {
            std::string archivepath;
            std::string outputpath;
            std::cout << "Enter dir to decompress:";
            std::cin >> outputpath;
            std::cout << "Enter archive path:";
            std::cin >> archivepath;

            decompress(outputpath, archivepath,
                    [](std::string_view message) {
                        std::cout << message << std::endl; });
        }
        else
        {
            std::cout << "invalid option" << std::endl;
        }
    }
```

81. Compressing and decompressing files to/from a ZIP archive with password

This problem is very similar to the previous one with the addition that the files must be encrypted. The `ZipLib` library supports PKWare encryption only. Should you need to use another method for encryption, then you have to use another library. The `compress()` and `decompress()` functions, shown in the following, are similar to the implementation from the previous problem, but have a few differences, apart from the extra parameter that represents the password for the encryption/decryption of files:

- Adding encrypted files to the archive is done with `ZipFile::AddEncryptedFile()` instead of `ZipFile::AddFile()`
- When decompressing, the password must be set with `ZipArchiveEntry::SetPassword()` if the entry is password-protected

The `compress()` function, with the aforementioned changes, is implemented as follows:

```cpp
namespace fs = std::experimental::filesystem;

void compress(fs::path const & source,
              fs::path const & archive,
              std::string_view password,
              std::function<void(std::string_view)> reporter)
{
   if (fs::is_regular_file(source))
   {
      if (reporter) reporter("Compressing " + source.string());
      ZipFile::AddEncryptedFile(
         archive.string(),
         source.string(),
         source.filename().string(),
         password.data(),
         LzmaMethod::Create());
   }
   else
   {
      for (auto const & p : fs::recursive_directory_iterator(source))
      {
         if (reporter) reporter("Compressing " + p.path().string());

         if (fs::is_directory(p))
         {
            auto zipArchive = ZipFile::Open(archive.string());
            auto entry = zipArchive->CreateEntry(p.path().string());
            entry->SetAttributes(ZipArchiveEntry::Attributes::Directory);
            ZipFile::SaveAndClose(zipArchive, archive.string());
         }
         else if (fs::is_regular_file(p))
         {
            ZipFile::AddEncryptedFile(
               archive.string(),
               p.path().string(),
               p.path().filename().string(),
               password.data(),
               LzmaMethod::Create());
         }
      }
   }
}
```

The decompress() function must set the password on each archive entry before using the decompression stream to copy the content of the file to the destination. You can find the function in the following listing:

```
void decompress(fs::path const & destination,
                fs::path const & archive,
                std::string_view password,
                std::function<void(std::string_view)> reporter)
{
    ensure_directory_exists(destination);

    auto zipArchive = ZipFile::Open(archive.string());

    for (size_t i = 0; i < zipArchive->GetEntriesCount(); ++i)
    {
        auto entry = zipArchive->GetEntry(i);
        if (entry)
        {
            auto filepath = destination / fs::path{
            entry->GetFullName() }.relative_path();
            if (reporter) reporter("Creating " + filepath.string());

            if(entry->IsPasswordProtected())
            entry->SetPassword(password.data());

            if (entry->IsDirectory())
            {
                ensure_directory_exists(filepath);
            }
            else
            {
                ensure_directory_exists(filepath.parent_path());

                std::ofstream destFile;
                destFile.open(filepath.string().c_str(),
                        std::ios::binary | std::ios::trunc);

                if (!destFile.is_open())
                {
                    if (reporter)
                        reporter("Cannot create destination file!");
                }

                auto dataStream = entry->GetDecompressionStream();
                if (dataStream)
                {
                    utils::stream::copy(*dataStream, destFile);
```

```
                }
              }
            }
          }
        }
```

The `ensure_directory_exists()` helper function is identical to the one with the same name from the previous problem and will not be listed again.

You can use these functions just like in the previous problem, except that you have to pass the password as well.

82. Creating a PNG that represents a national flag

The most feature-rich library for working with PNG files is *libpng*, a platform-independent, open source library written in C. There are also C++ libraries, some of which are wrappers for *libpng*, such as *png++*, *lodepng*, or *PNGWriter*. For the problems in this book, we will use the last one, *PNGWriter*. It is an open source library that works on Linux, Unix, macOS, and Windows. Its supported features include opening existing PNG images; plotting and reading pixels in the RGB, HSV, and CMYK color spaces; basic shapes; scaling; bilinear interpolation; full TrueType antialiased and rotated text support; and Bezier curves. It is a wrapper for *libpng* and also requires the `FreeType2` library for text support.

The library source code, along with documentation, can be found at `https://github.com/pngwriter/pngwriter`. Follow the installation instructions there to install the library.

The `pngwriter` class represents a PNG image. Its constructor allows us to set the width and height in pixels, a background color, and the path to the file where the image should be saved. There is a multitude of member functions that can write pixels, shapes, or text. For this problem, we need to fill three rectangles with different colors. For that, we can use the `filledsquare()` function. When we are done writing the image in memory, we have to call the `close()` method to save it to a disk file.

The following function creates a three-color flag with the size and destination file path provided as arguments:

```cpp
void create_flag(int const width, int const height,
                 std::string_view filepath)
{
   pngwriter flag { width, height, 0, filepath.data() };

   int const size = width / 3;
   // red rectangle
```

```
        flag.filledsquare(0, 0, size, 2 * size, 65535, 0, 0);
        // yellow rectangle
        flag.filledsquare(size, 0, 2 * size, 2 * size, 65535, 65535, 0);
        // blue rectangle
        flag.filledsquare(2 * size, 0, 3 * size, 2 * size, 0, 0, 65535);

        flag.close();
    }
```

This following program allows the user to enter the width and height of the image as well as the path to the output file, and uses `create_flag()` to generate the PNG image:

```
int main()
{
    int width = 0, height = 0;
    std::string filepath;

    std::cout << "Width: ";
    std::cin >> width;

    std::cout << "Heigh: ";
    std::cin >> height;

    std::cout << "Output: ";
    std::cin >> filepath;

    create_flag(width, height, filepath);
}
```

83. Creating verification text PNG images

This problem can be solved in a similar manner to the previous one with the national flag. If you haven't done that one first, I recommend that you do so before continuing with this one.

There are basically three elements that the image must have:

- A gradient-color background. This can be achieved by drawing lines (vertically or horizontally) of a different color from one side to the other of the image. Drawing lines can be done with the `pngwriter::line()` function. There are several overloads available; the one used in the following code takes the start and end position and three values for the red, green, and blue channels of the RGB color space.

- A random text with letters displayed at various random angles, both towards the left and right. Writing text is done with the pngwriter::plot_text() functions. This requires a dependency on the FreeType2 library. The overloaded function used here allows the specifying of the font file and its size, the position where the text should be written, the angle in radians, the text, and the color.
- Random lines across the image plotted on top of the text. Again, these are written using the pngwritter::line() function.

In order to display random text, colors, and line positions, the following code uses an std::mt19937 pseudo-random number generator and several uniform integer distributions:

```
void create_image(int const width, int const height,
                  std::string_view font, int const font_size,
                  std::string_view filepath)
{
    pngwriter image { width, height, 0, filepath.data() };

    std::random_device rd;
    std::mt19937 mt;
    auto seed_data = std::array<int, std::mt19937::state_size> {};
    std::generate(std::begin(seed_data), std::end(seed_data),
                  std::ref(rd));
    std::seed_seq seq(std::begin(seed_data), std::end(seed_data));
    mt.seed(seq);
    std::uniform_int_distribution<> udx(0, width);
    std::uniform_int_distribution<> udy(0, height);
    std::uniform_int_distribution<> udc(0, 65535);
    std::uniform_int_distribution<> udt(0, 25);

    // gradient background
    for (int iter = 0; iter < width; iter++)
    {
        image.line(
            iter, 0, iter, height,
            65535 - int(65535 * ((double)iter) / (width)),
            int(65535 * ((double)iter) / (width)),
            65535);
    }

    // random text
    std::string font_family = font.data();
    for (int i = 0; i < 6; ++i)
    {
        image.plot_text(
            // font
```

```
                    font_family.data(), font_size,
                    // position
                    i*width / 6 + 10, height / 2 - 10,
                    // angle
                    (i % 2 == 0 ? -1 : 1)*(udt(mt) * 3.14) / 180,
                    // text
                    std::string(1, char('A' + udt(mt))).data(),
                    // color
                    0, 0, 0);
        }

        // random lines
        for (int i = 0; i < 4; ++i)
        {
            image.line(udx(mt), 0, udx(mt), height,
                        udc(mt), udc(mt), udc(mt));

            image.line(0, udy(mt), width, udy(mt),
                        udc(mt), udc(mt), udc(mt));
        }

        image.close();
    }
```

This function can be used as in the following example. Note that the path to the font file (Arial in this case) is hard coded for Windows and Apple systems, but must be provided by the user for other platforms:

```
    int main()
    {
        std::string font_path;

#ifdef WIN32
        font_path = R"(c:\windows\fonts\arial.ttf)";
#elif defined (__APPLE__)
        font_path = R"(/Library/Fonts/Arial.ttf)";
#else
        std::cout << "Font path: ";
        std::cin >> font_path;
#endif

        create_image(200, 50,
                    font_path, 18,
                    "validation.png");
    }
```

The color scheme for the background in the `create_image()` function always produces the same gradient for images of equal width. You can take it as a further exercise to modify the function to randomize the gradient colors, as well as text colors.

84. EAN-13 barcode generator

The *International Article Number* (aka *European Article Number* or *EAN*), as described on Wikipedia, is a standard describing a barcode symbology and numbering system that is used in global trade to identify a specific retail product type, in a specific packaging configuration, from a specific manufacturer. The most commonly used EAN standard is the 13-digit EAN-13. A description of the standard, including information on how the barcode should be generated, can be found on Wikipedia at `https://en.wikipedia.org/wiki/International_Article_Number` and will not be detailed in this book. The following is the EAN-13 barcode for the number 5901234123457, given as an example in the problem's description (source: Wikipedia):

The `ean13` class that is shown in the following code represents a number in the EAN-13 standard. It can be created from a string or an `unsigned long long` and can be converted back to a string or an array of digits. It can either compute the 13th digit, representing the checksum if the provided constructor argument has 12 digits, or it can validate that the 13th digit is the correct checksum of the number if the provided argument has 13 digits. The checksum is the number that must be added to the weighted sum of the first 12 digits in order to make it a multiple of 10:

```
struct ean13
{
public:
    ean13(std::string_view code)
    {
        if (code.length() == 13)
        {
            if (code[12] != '0' + get_crc(code.substr(0,12)))
                throw std::runtime_error("Not an EAN-13 format.");
```

```
                number = code;
        }
        else if (code.length() == 12)
        {
            number = code.data() + std::string(1, '0' + get_crc(code));
        }
    }

    ean13(unsigned long long code) :ean13(std::to_string(code))
    { }

    std::array<unsigned char, 13> to_array() const
    {
        std::array<unsigned char, 13> result;
        for (int i = 0; i < 13; ++i)
            result[i] = static_cast<unsigned char>(number[i] - '0');
        return result;
    }

    std::string to_string() const noexcept { return number; }

private:
    unsigned char get_crc(std::string_view code)
    {
        unsigned char weights[12] = { 1,3,1,3,1,3,1,3,1,3,1,3 };
        size_t index = 0;
        auto sum = std::accumulate(
            std::begin(code), std::end(code), 0,
            [&weights, &index](int const total, char const c) {
                return total + weights[index++] * (c - '0'); });
        return 10 - sum % 10;
    }

    std::string number;
};
```

As described on Wikipedia, the barcode consists of 95 equally spaced areas, which are, from left to right:

- Three areas for the start marker.
- 42 areas for the left group of six digits. These 42 areas can be divided into six groups of seven areas, encoding the digits 2-7. These encodings can have even or odd parity and these parities together encode the first digit of EAN-13.
- 5 areas for the center marker.

- 42 areas for the right group of six digits. These 42 areas can be divided into six groups of seven areas, encoding the digits 8-13. These digits are all encoded with even parity. Digit 13 is the check digit.
- 3 areas for the end marker.

The following tables, taken as they are from Wikipedia, show the encoding of the two groups of six digits (the first table), as well as the encoding of the digits themselves, based on the value of the first digit (the second table):

First digit	First group of 6 digits	Last group of 6 digits
0	LLLLLL	RRRRRR
1	LLGLGG	RRRRRR
2	LLGGLG	RRRRRR
3	LLGGGL	RRRRRR
4	LGLLGG	RRRRRR
5	LGGLLG	RRRRRR
6	LGGGLL	RRRRRR
7	LGLGLG	RRRRRR
8	LGLGGL	RRRRRR
9	LGGLGL	RRRRRR

Digit	L-code	G-code	R-code
0	0001101	0100111	1110010
1	0011001	0110011	1100110
2	0010011	0011011	1101100
3	0111101	0100001	1000010
4	0100011	0011101	1011100
5	0110001	0111001	1001110
6	0101111	0000101	1010000
7	0111011	0010001	1000100
8	0110111	0001001	1001000
9	0001011	0010111	1110100

The `ean13_barcode_generator` class encapsulates the functionality for creating an EAN-13 barcode PNG from an `ean13` number representation and saving it to a disk file. There are several members of this class:

- `create()` is the only public function of the class. Its arguments are the EAN-13 number, the path of the output file, the width in pixels of each bit, the height of the barcode bar, and the margins for the barcode area. It draws, in order, the start marker, the first six digits, the center marker, the last six digits, and the end marker, and then saves the image to a file.
- `draw_digit()` is a private helper function that draws the seven-bit digits and the start, center, and end markers using the `pngwriter::filledsquare()` method.
- The encoding tables, as well as the marker values, are defined in the private member variables `encodings`, `eandigits`, `marker_start`, `marker_end`, and `marker_center`.

The `ean13_barcode_generator` class is shown in the following listing:

```
struct ean13_barcode_generator
{
    void create(ean13 const & code,
                std::string_view filename,
                int const digit_width = 3,
                int const height = 50,
                int const margin = 10);
private:
    int draw_digit(unsigned char code, unsigned int size,
                   pngwriter& image,
                   int const x, int const y,
                   int const digit_width, int const height)
    {
        std::bitset<7> bits(code);
        int pos = x;
        for (int i = size - 1; i >= 0; --i)
        {
            if (bits[i])
            {
                image.filledsquare(pos, y, pos + digit_width, y + height,
                                   0, 0, 0);
            }

            pos += digit_width;
        }

        return pos;
```

```
    }

    unsigned char encodings[10][3] =
    {
        { 0b0001101, 0b0100111, 0b1110010 },
        { 0b0011001, 0b0110011, 0b1100110 },
        { 0b0010011, 0b0011011, 0b1101100 },
        { 0b0111101, 0b0100001, 0b1000010 },
        { 0b0100011, 0b0011101, 0b1011100 },
        { 0b0110001, 0b0111001, 0b1001110 },
        { 0b0101111, 0b0000101, 0b1010000 },
        { 0b0111011, 0b0010001, 0b1000100 },
        { 0b0110111, 0b0001001, 0b1001000 },
        { 0b0001011, 0b0010111, 0b1110100 },
    };

    unsigned char eandigits[10][6] =
    {
        { 0,0,0,0,0,0 },
        { 0,0,1,0,1,1 },
        { 0,0,1,1,0,1 },
        { 0,0,1,1,1,0 },
        { 0,1,0,0,1,1 },
        { 0,1,1,0,0,1 },
        { 0,1,1,1,0,0 },
        { 0,1,0,1,0,1 },
        { 0,1,0,1,1,0 },
        { 0,1,1,0,1,0 },
    };

    unsigned char marker_start  = 0b101;
    unsigned char marker_end    = 0b101;
    unsigned char marker_center = 0b01010;
};
```

The `create()` method is implemented as follows:

```
void ean13_barcode_generator::create(ean13 const & code,
            std::string_view filename,
            int const digit_width = 3,
            int const height = 50,
            int const margin = 10)
{
    pngwriter image(
        margin * 2 + 95 * digit_width,
        height + margin * 2,
        65535,
        filename.data());
```

```cpp
std::array<unsigned char, 13> digits = code.to_array();

int x = margin;
x = draw_digit(marker_start, 3, image, x, margin,
               digit_width, height);

for (int i = 0; i < 6; ++i)
{
    int code = encodings[digits[1 + i]][eandigits[digits[0]][i]];
    x = draw_digit(code, 7, image, x, margin, digit_width, height);
}

x = draw_digit(marker_center, 5, image, x, margin,
               digit_width, height);

for (int i = 0; i < 6; ++i)
{
    int code = encodings[digits[7 + i]][2];
    x = draw_digit(code, 7, image, x, margin, digit_width, height);
}

x = draw_digit(marker_end, 3, image, x, margin,
               digit_width, height);

    image.close();
}
```

This class can be used as in the following example:

```cpp
int main()
{
    ean13_barcode_generator generator;

    generator.create(ean13("5901234123457"), "5901234123457.png",
                      5, 150, 30);
}
```

 You can take it as a further exercise to print the EAN-13 number below the generated barcode.

85. Reading movies from an SQLite database

SQLite is an in-process relational database management library written in C (although a large number of programming languages provide bindings to it). SQLite is not a client-server database engine, but one embedded into the application. The entire database, including tables, indexes, triggers, and views, is contained within a single disk file. Because accessing the database means accessing a local disk file, without any inter-process communication, SQLite has a better performance compared to other relational database engines. SQLite, as the name implies, uses SQL, although it does not implement all the features (such as `RIGHT OUTER JOIN`). SQLite is used in not just web browsers (several major ones allow storing and retrieving data to and from an SQLite database using the *Web SQL Database* technology), web frameworks (such as Bugzilla, Django, Drupal, or Ruby on Rails), and operating systems (included by default in Android, Windows 10, FreeBSD, OpenBSD, Symbian OS, and others), but also in mobile applications and games. SQLite has limitations too, with the most notable being the lack of any user management. A third party extension called SQLCipher provides transparent 256-bit AES encryption for an SQLite database. The library is available at `https://www.sqlite.org/`.

The `SQLite` library contains a lot of source files and scripts, but also provides a compact version of these, called an amalgamation, which is the actual version of the library that is recommended for use in all applications. The amalgamation contains only two files, `sqlite3.h` and `sqlite3.c`, that can be compiled with the application. The amalgamation package, as well as other library packages, including tools, can be downloaded from `https://www.sqlite.org/download.html`.

As mentioned earlier, the library is written in C. However, there are a variety of libraries that provide C++ wrappers, including `SQLiteCPP`, `CppSQLite`, `sqlite3cc`, and `sqlite_modern_cpp`. In this book, we will use the latter, `sqlite_modern_cpp`, because it is a lightweight wrapper, written in modern C++, with support for C++17 features but also for SQLCipher. The library is available at `https://github.com/SqliteModernCpp/sqlite_modern_cpp`. To use this library, you must include the `sqlite_modern_cpp.h` header in your sources.

Before we start writing the code to solve the proposed problem, we should create a database. The structure of the database is indicated in the problem description and we can use the SQLite command-line tool called `sqlite3` to do this. To create a new database, or open an existing one, you must execute the following command:

```
sqlite3 <filename>
```

In the source code accompanying this book, you can find an already created database called `cppchallenger85.db`. However, you can create the database yourself, by opening a new database file and then running the following commands:

```
create table movies(title text not null,
                     year integer not null,
                     length integer not null);

create table persons(name text not null);

create table directors(movieid integer not null,
                        personid integer not null);

create table writers(movieid integer not null,
                      personid integer not null);

create table casting(movieid integer not null,
                      personid integer not null,
                      role text not null);
```

Note that, apart from the columns defined here, SQLite adds an implicit column called `rowid`, which is an autoincremented 64-bit signed integer that uniquely identifies a row within the table. The `cppchallenger85.db` database contains several movies that have already been added using the following commands:

```
insert into movies values ('The Matrix', 1999, 196);
insert into movies values ('Forrest Gump', 1994, 202);

insert into persons values('Keanu Reeves');
insert into persons values('Laurence Fishburne');
insert into persons values('Carrie-Anne Moss');
insert into persons values('Hugo Weaving');
insert into persons values('Lana Wachowski');
insert into persons values('Lilly Wachowski');
insert into persons values('Tom Hanks');
insert into persons values('Sally Field');
insert into persons values('Robin Wright');
insert into persons values('Mykelti Williamson');
insert into persons values('Robert Zemeckis');
insert into persons values('Winston Groom');
insert into persons values('Eric Roth');

insert into directors values(1, 5);
insert into directors values(1, 6);
insert into directors values(2, 11);
```

```
insert into writers values(1, 5);
insert into writers values(1, 6);
insert into writers values(2, 12);
insert into writers values(2, 13);

insert into casting values(1, 1, 'Neo');
insert into casting values(1, 2, 'Morpheus');
insert into casting values(1, 3, 'Trinity');
insert into casting values(1, 4, 'Agent Smith');
insert into casting values(2, 7, 'Forrest Gump');
insert into casting values(2, 8, 'Mrs. Gump');
insert into casting values(2, 9, 'Jenny Curran');
insert into casting values(2, 10, 'Bubba Blue');
```

With the database created and populated with data, we can move on to the next phase of solving the problem. The following classes will be used for this problem and the next ones to represent a movie:

```
struct casting_role
{
    std::string actor;
    std::string role;
};

struct movie
{
    unsigned int                id;
    std::string                 title;
    int                         year;
    unsigned int                length;
    std::vector<casting_role>   cast;
    std::vector<std::string>    directors;
    std::vector<std::string>    writers;
};

using movie_list = std::vector<movie>;
```

The main class from the `sqlite_modern_cpp` library that we will work with is `sqlite::database`. It provides functionalities such as connecting to a database, preparing and executing statements, binding parameters and callbacks, and handling transactions. You can simply open a database by providing its file path to the `sqlite::database` constructor. Should any exceptions occur during an SQLite operation, an `sqlite::sqlite_exception` object is thrown. The following code shows the `main()` function of the program, which connects to a database file called `cppchallenger85.db` (from the current folder). If the connection is successful, it proceeds to fetch all the movies from the database and display them:

```cpp
int main()
{
    try
    {
        sqlite::database db(R"(cppchallenger85.db)");

        auto movies = get_movies(db);
        for (auto const & m : movies)
            print_movie(m);
    }
    catch (sqlite::sqlite_exception const & e)
    {
        std::cerr << e.get_code() << ": " << e.what() << " during "
                << e.get_sql() << std::endl;
    }
    catch (std::exception const & e)
    {
        std::cerr << e.what() << std::endl;
    }
}
```

The `print_movie()` function, shown as follows, displays a movie on the console:

```cpp
void print_movie(movie const & m)
{
    std::cout << "[" << m.id << "] "
                << m.title << " (" << m.year << ") "
                << m.length << "min" << std::endl;
    std::cout << " directed by: ";
    for (auto const & d : m.directors) std::cout << d << ",";
    std::cout << std::endl;
    std::cout << " written by: ";
    for (auto const & w : m.writers) std::cout << w << ",";
    std::cout << std::endl;
    std::cout << " cast: ";
    for (auto const & r : m.cast)
```

```
        std::cout << r.actor << " (" << r.role << "),";
    std::cout << std::endl << std::endl;
}
```

The `sqlite::database` class has the overloaded operators `<<` and `>>`, the former to prepare statements and bind parameters and perform other input operations on the database, and the latter to retrieve data from the database. To bind a parameter, you use the symbol `?` for the parameter name in the SQL statement and then input the parameter value with the overloaded `operator <<`. Parameters are bound in the order they are written to the `sqlite::database` object. For each row that results from the evaluation of the SQL statement, a callback function is invoked. In `sqlite_modern_cpp`, you define a lambda function that has a parameter (with the appropriate type) for each column in a row. For columns that can have null values, you can use either `std::unique_ptr<T>` or `std::optional<T>` if your compiler supports this C++17 feature.

The following function, called `get_directors()`, reads all the directors of a movie from the `directors` and `persons` tables. Note that in the following SQL statement, and the next ones, we use the implicitly added `rowid` column:

```cpp
std::vector<std::string> get_directors(sqlite3_int64 const movie_id,
                                        sqlite::database & db)
{
    std::vector<std::string> result;
    db << R"(select p.name from directors as d
            join persons as p on d.personid = p.rowid
            where d.movieid = ?;)"
        << movie_id
        >> [&result](std::string const name)
        {
            result.emplace_back(name);
        };

    return result;
}
```

In a very similar manner, `get_writers()` reads the movie writers from the `writers` table, as shown in the following listing:

```cpp
std::vector<std::string> get_writers(sqlite3_int64 const movie_id,
                                     sqlite::database & db)
{
    std::vector<std::string> result;
    db << R"(select p.name from writers as w
            join persons as p on w.personid = p.rowid
            where w.movieid = ?;)"
```

```
        << movie_id
        >> [&result](std::string const name)
           {
               result.emplace_back(name);
           };

    return result;
}
```

The movie cast is fetched from the `casting` table using the `get_cast()` function, as follows:

```
std::vector<casting_role> get_cast(sqlite3_int64 const movie_id,
                                   sqlite::database & db)
{
    std::vector<casting_role> result;
    db << R"(select p.name, c.role from casting as c
        join persons as p on c.personid = p.rowid
        where c.movieid = ?;)"
        << movie_id
        >> [&result](std::string const name, std::string role)
           {
               result.emplace_back(casting_role{ name, role });
           };

    return result;
}
```

All these functions are used in the `get_movies()` function, which returns a list of all the movies from the database. This function can be implemented as follows:

```
movie_list get_movies(sqlite::database & db)
{
    movie_list movies;

    db << R"(select rowid, * from movies;)"
        >> [&movies, &db](sqlite3_int64 const rowid,
                          std::string const & title,
                          int const year, int const length)
           {
               movies.emplace_back(movie{
                   static_cast<unsigned int>(rowid),
                   title,
                   year,
                   static_cast<unsigned int>(length),
                   get_cast(rowid, db),
                   get_directors(rowid, db),
```

```
            get_directors(rowid, db)
        });
    };

return movies;
}
```

With all these implemented, the solution is now complete. The following screenshot shows the output of the program with the data added as seen in the preceding code:

```
C:\WINDOWS\system32\cmd.exe                                          —     □     ×
[1] The Matrix (1999) 136min
 directed by: Lana Wachowski,Lilly Wachowski,
 written by: Lana Wachowski,Lilly Wachowski,
 cast: Keanu Reeves (Neo),Laurence Fishburne (Morpheus),Carrie-Anne Moss (Trinity),
Hugo Weaving (Agent Smith),

[2] Forrest Gump (1994) 142min
 directed by: Robert Zemeckis,
 written by: Winston Groom,Eric Roth,
 cast: Tom Hanks (Forrest Gump),Sally Field (Mrs. Gump),Robin Wright (Jenny Curran)
,Mykelti Williamson (Bubba Blue),

Press any key to continue . . .
```

86. Inserting movies into an SQLite database

The solution to this problem builds upon the previous one. You must solve that one before continuing here. Also, the function `split()` that is used in the code here is the same from problem 27, *Splitting a string into tokens with a list of possible delimiters*, from Chapter 3, *Strings and Regular Expressions*. For this reason, it will not be listed here again. In the source code for this book, you will find a database file called `cppchallenger86.db` that is prepared with several records for this problem.

The following function, `read_movie()`, reads information about a movie from the console (title, release year, length in minutes, directors, writers, and cast), creates a `movie` object, and returns it. The cast is expected to be provided as a comma-separated list of elements of the form *actor name=role name*. For example, the cast for the movie *The Matrix*, as already seen in previous problems, must be entered as a single line in the form `Keanu Reeves=Neo`, `Laurence Fishburne=Morpheus`, `Carrie-Anne Moss=Trinity`, `Hugo Weaving=Agent Smith`. In order to read lines of text that contain whitespaces, we must use the `std::getline()` function; reading using the `std::cin` object would limit the input to the first whitespace:

```
movie read_movie()
{
    movie m;

    std::cout << "Enter movie" << std::endl;
    std::cout << "Title: ";
    std::getline(std::cin, m.title);
    std::cout << "Year: "; std::cin >> m.year;
    std::cout << "Length: "; std::cin >> m.length;
    std::cin.ignore();
    std::string directors;
    std::cout << "Directors: ";
    std::getline(std::cin, directors);
    m.directors = split(directors, ',');
    std::string writers;
    std::cout << "Writers: ";
    std::getline(std::cin, writers);
    m.writers = split(writers, ',');
    std::string cast;
    std::cout << "Cast: ";
    std::getline(std::cin, cast);
    auto roles = split(cast, ',');
    for (auto const & r : roles)
    {
        auto pos = r.find_first_of('=');
        casting_role cr;
        cr.actor = r.substr(0, pos);
        cr.role = r.substr(pos + 1, r.size() - pos - 1);
        m.cast.push_back(cr);
    }

    return m;
}
```

The following function, `get_person_id()`, returns the numerical identifier of a person, which is the `rowid` autoincremented field added automatically by SQLite when you create a table (unless specified otherwise). The type of `rowid` column is `sqlite_int64`, which is a 64-bit signed integer:

```
sqlite_int64 get_person_id(std::string const & name, sqlite::database & db)
{
    sqlite_int64 id = 0;
    db << "select rowid from persons where name=?;"
        << name
        >> [&id](sqlite_int64 const rowid) {id = rowid; };

    return id;
}
```

The functions `insert_person()`, `insert_directors()`, `insert_writers()`, and `insert_cast()` are inserting new records in the tables `persons`, `directors`, `writers`, and `casting`. To do so, we are using a `sqlite::database` object passed as an argument from `main()`, as will be seen later on. When inserting a director, writer, or actor, we first check if the person already exists in the database, and if not, we add it:

```
sqlite_int64 insert_person(std::string_view name, sqlite::database & db)
{
    db << "insert into persons values(?);"
        << name.data();
    return db.last_insert_rowid();
}

void insert_directors(sqlite_int64 const movie_id,
                      std::vector<std::string> const & directors,
                      sqlite::database & db)
{
    for (auto const & director : directors)
    {
        auto id = get_person_id(director, db);

        if (id == 0)
            id = insert_person(director, db);

        db << "insert into directors values(?, ?);"
            << movie_id
            << id;
    }
}
```

```
void insert_writers(sqlite_int64 const movie_id,
                    std::vector<std::string> const & writers,
                    sqlite::database & db)
{
    for (auto const & writer : writers)
    {
        auto id = get_person_id(writer, db);

        if (id == 0)
            id = insert_person(writer, db);

        db << "insert into writers values(?, ?);"
            << movie_id
            << id;
    }
}

void insert_cast(sqlite_int64 const movie_id,
                 std::vector<casting_role> const & cast,
                 sqlite::database & db)
{
    for (auto const & cr : cast)
    {
        auto id = get_person_id(cr.actor, db);

        if (id == 0)
            id = insert_person(cr.actor, db);

        db << "insert into casting values(?,?,?);"
            << movie_id
            << id
            << cr.role;
    }
}
```

The function `insert_movie()` inserts a new record in the `movies` table and then calls the previously considered functions to also insert the movie directors, writers, and cast. All these operations are performed in a single transaction. Transactions are handled by the `sqlite::database` object using the `begin;`, `commit;`, and `rollback;` commands (note the semicolon at the end of each command). These commands are executed with the overloaded `operator<<` for the `sqlite::database` class. A transaction is started at the beginning of the function and committed at the end. If any exception occurs during the execution of the SQL commands, the transaction is rolled back:

```
void insert_movie(movie& m, sqlite::database & db)
{
   try
   {
      db << "begin;";

      db << "insert into movies values(?,?,?);"
         << m.title
         << m.year
         << m.length;

      auto movieid = db.last_insert_rowid();

      insert_directors(movieid, m.directors, db);
      insert_writers(movieid, m.writers, db);
      insert_cast(movieid, m.cast, db);

      m.id = static_cast<unsigned int>(movieid);

      db << "commit;";
   }
   catch (std::exception const &)
   {
      db << "rollback;";
   }
}
```

With all of these defined, we can write the following program that opens the SQLite database called cppchallenger86.db, reads a movie from the console, inserts it into the database, and then prints the entire list of movies to the console:

```
int main()
{
   try
   {
      sqlite::database db(R"(cppchallenger86.db)");

      auto movie = read_movie();
      insert_movie(movie, db);

      auto movies = get_movies(db);
      for (auto const & m : movies)
         print_movie(m);
   }
   catch (sqlite::sqlite_exception const & e)
   {
      std::cerr << e.get_code() << ": " << e.what() << " during "
```

```
                    << e.get_sql() << std::endl;
    }
    catch (std::exception const & e)
    {
        std::cerr << e.what() << std::endl;
    }
}
```

87. Handling movie images in an SQLite database

If you have not done so already, you must complete the previous two problems before continuing with this one. For this problem, we must extend the database model with an additional table to store images and possibly other media files, such as videos. The actual content of the media files must be stored in a blob field, but other attributes, such as description and filename, should also be stored.

When you are using large objects you have two options: either store them directly in the database as blobs or keep them in separate files and store only the file paths in the database. According to the tests performed by the developers of SQLite, for objects smaller than 100KB, reads are faster when they are stored directly in the database. For objects bigger than 100KB, reads are faster when the objects are stored in separate files. You should take this aspect into consideration when designing your database model. In this book, however, we will ignore these performance aspects and preserve the media files inside the database.

To create the additional tables for media files (which we will simply call media), open the database file in the command-line tool sqlite3 as shown for problem 85, and then run the following command. Note that in the code provided with this book you can find a database file called cppchallenger87.db that already contains the extended database model:

```
create table media(movieid integer not null,
                   name text not null,
                   description text,
                   content blob not null);
```

The field description can contain null values. With sqlite_modern_cpp you can use std::optional<T> if your compiler supports this C++17 feature. However, to do so, you must define the macro MODERN_SQLITE_STD_OPTIONAL_SUPPORT. Otherwise, you can use std::unique_ptr<T> instead.

To handle objects from the `media` table, we will use the types shown as follows. Although the type of the `rowid` field is `sqlite3_int64`, here we are using `unsigned int` only for the purpose of being consistent with the `movie` type seen in the previous two solutions and used for several other problems throughout this book:

```
struct media
{
    unsigned int                id;
    unsigned int                movie_id;
    std::string                 name;
    std::optional<std::string>  text;
    std::vector<char>           blob;
};

using media_list = std::vector<media>;
```

The functions `add_media()`, `get_media()`, and `delete_media()` add, retrieve, and delete media files for a movie. They should be simple to follow based on the experience with the `sqlite_modern_cpp` API accumulated from the previous problems. One important thing to note is that when selecting fields from a table—the `media` table, in this case—the `rowid` field must be explicitly specified, because it is not included by using `*` to select all the table fields:

```
bool add_media(sqlite_int64 const movieid,
               std::string_view name,
               std::string_view description,
               std::vector<char> content,
               sqlite::database & db)
{
    try
    {
        db << "insert into media values(?,?,?,?)"
            << movieid
            << name.data()
            << description.data()
            << content;
        return true;
    }
    catch (...) { return false; }
}

media_list get_media(sqlite_int64 const movieid,
                     sqlite::database & db)
{
    media_list list;
```

```
        db << "select rowid, * from media where movieid = ?;"
            << movieid
            >> [&list](sqlite_int64 const rowid,
                    sqlite_int64 const movieid,
                    std::string const & name,
                    std::optional<std::string> const text,
                    std::vector<char> const & blob
                )
                {
                    list.emplace_back(media{
                        static_cast<unsigned int>(rowid),
                        static_cast<unsigned int>(movieid),
                        name,
                        text,
                        blob});
                };

        return list;
    }

    bool delete_media(sqlite_int64 const mediaid,
                      sqlite::database & db)
    {
        try
        {
            db << "delete from media where rowid = ?;"
                << mediaid;

            return true;
        }
        catch (...) { return false; }
    }
```

The media files are associated with a movie by specifying the movie identifier. To find the identifier of a movie specified by its title, we use the function get_movies(), shown as follows. This retrieves a list of all the movies that match a specified title. If there is more than one, we can select which of the movies we want to add the media file to:

```
    movie_list get_movies(std::string_view title, sqlite::database & db)
    {
        movie_list movies;

        db << R"(select rowid, * from movies where title=?;)"
            << title.data()
            >> [&movies, &db](sqlite3_int64 const rowid,
                              std::string const & title,
                              int const year, int const length)
```

```
        {
            movies.emplace_back(movie{
                static_cast<unsigned int>(rowid),
                title,
                year,
                static_cast<unsigned int>(length),
                {},
                {},
                {}
                });
        };

    return movies;
}
```

The main program will be implemented as a small utility that accepts commands and prints the result of their execution to the console. The commands include finding movies and adding, listing, and deleting media files for a movie. The function `print_commands()`, shown as follows, displays the available supported commands:

```
void print_commands()
{
    std::cout
        << "find <title>                        finds a movie ID\n"
        << "list <movieid>                      lists the images of a movie\n"
        << "add <movieid>,<path>,<description> adds a new image\n"
        << "del <imageid>                       delete an image\n"
        << "help                                shows available commands\n"
        << "exit                                exists the application\n";
}
```

The implementation of the function `main()` is listed in the following code. We start by opening an SQLite database called `cppchallenger87.db`. Then we loop indefinitely on reading user input to the console and executing the command. The loop, and the main program implicitly, ends when the user inputs the command `exit`:

```
int main()
{
    try
    {
        sqlite::database db(R"(cppchallenger87.db)");

        while (true)
        {
            std::string line;
            std::getline(std::cin, line);
```

```
            if (line == "help") print_commands();
            else if (line == "exit") break;
            else
            {
                if (starts_with(line, "find"))
                    run_find(line, db);
                else if (starts_with(line, "list"))
                    run_list(line, db);
                else if (starts_with(line, "add"))
                    run_add(line, db);
                else if (starts_with(line, "del"))
                    run_del(line, db);
                else
                    std::cout << "unknown command" << std::endl;
            }

            std::cout << std::endl;
        }
    }
    catch (sqlite::sqlite_exception const & e)
    {
        std::cerr << e.get_code() << ": " << e.what() << " during "
                  << e.get_sql() << std::endl;
    }
    catch (std::exception const & e)
    {
        std::cerr << e.what() << std::endl;
    }
}
```

Each of the supported commands is implemented in a separate function. `run_find()`, `run_list()`, `run_add()`, and `run_del()` parse the user input, call the appropriate function for database access that we have seen earlier, and print the results to the console. These functions do not perform thorough checks on user input. The commands are case-sensitive and must be entered in lowercase.

The function `run_find()` extracts a movie title from the user input, calls `get_movie()` to retrieve the list of all the movies with that title, and prints the result to the console:

```
void run_find(std::string_view line, sqlite::database & db)
{
    auto title = trim(line.substr(5));

    auto movies = get_movies(title, db);
    if(movies.empty())
        std::cout << "empty" << std::endl;
    else
```

```
    {
        for (auto const m : movies)
        {
            std::cout << m.id << " | "
                        << m.title << " | "
                        << m.year << " | "
                        << m.length << "min"
                        << std::endl;
        }
    }
}
```

The function `run_list()` extracts a movie's numerical identifier from the user input, calls `get_media()` to retrieve the list of all the media files for that movie, and prints them to the console. This function only prints the length of the blob field and not the entire object:

```
void run_list(std::string_view line, sqlite::database & db)
{
    auto movieid = std::stoi(trim(line.substr(5)));
    if (movieid > 0)
    {
        auto list = get_media(movieid, db);
        if (list.empty())
        {
            std::cout << "empty" << std::endl;
        }
        else
        {
            for (auto const & m : list)
            {
                std::cout
                    << m.id << " | "
                    << m.movie_id << " | "
                    << m.name << " | "
                    << m.text.value_or("(null)") << " | "
                    << m.blob.size() << " bytes"
                    << std::endl;
            }
        }
    }
    else
        std::cout << "input error" << std::endl;
}
```

Adding a file to a movie is done with `run_add()`. This function extracts the movie identifier, the file path, and its description from the comma-separated format in the user input (as in add `<movieid>`,`<path>`,`<description>`), loads the content of the file from disk using the helper function `load_image()`, and then adds it as a new record to the `media` table. The implementation seen here does not do any checks on the file type, which makes it possible to actually add any file, not just images or videos, to a movie. You can take it as a further exercise to add additional validation to the program:

```cpp
std::vector<char> load_image(std::string_view filepath)
{
    std::vector<char> data;

    std::ifstream ifile(filepath.data(), std::ios::binary | std::ios::ate);
    if (ifile.is_open())
    {
        auto size = ifile.tellg();
        ifile.seekg(0, std::ios::beg);

        data.resize(static_cast<size_t>(size));
        ifile.read(reinterpret_cast<char*>(data.data()), size);
    }

    return data;
}

void run_add(std::string_view line, sqlite::database & db)
{
    auto parts = split(trim(line.substr(4)), ',');
    if (parts.size() == 3)
    {
        auto movieid = std::stoi(parts[0]);
        auto path = std::experimental::filesystem::path{parts[1]};
        auto desc = parts[2];

        auto content = load_image(parts[1]);
        auto name = path.filename().string();

        auto success = add_media(movieid, name, desc, content, db);
        if (success)
            std::cout << "added" << std::endl;
        else
            std::cout << "failed" << std::endl;
    }
    else
        std::cout << "input error" << std::endl;
}
```

The last command left to implement is deleting a media file. The function `run_del()` takes the identifier of the record in the media table that is supposed to be deleted and calls `delete_media()` to remove it from the table:

```
void run_del(std::string_view line, sqlite::database & db)
{
    auto mediaid = std::stoi(trim(line.substr(4)));
    if (mediaid > 0)
    {
        auto success = delete_media(mediaid, db);
        if (success)
            std::cout << "deleted" << std::endl;
        else
            std::cout << "failed" << std::endl;
    }
    else
        std::cout << "input error" << std::endl;
}
```

In the preceding code, there are several helper functions: `split()`, which splits a text into tokens separated by a specified delimiter character; `starts_with()`, which checks whether a given string starts with a specified sub string; and `trim()`, which removes all the spaces at the beginning and the end of a string. These functions are as follows:

```
std::vector<std::string> split(std::string text, char const delimiter)
{
    auto sstr = std::stringstream{ text };
    auto tokens = std::vector<std::string>{};
    auto token = std::string{};
    while (std::getline(sstr, token, delimiter))
    {
        if (!token.empty()) tokens.push_back(token);
    }
    return tokens;
}

inline bool starts_with(std::string_view text, std::string_view part)
{
    return text.find(part) == 0;
}

inline std::string trim(std::string_view text)
{
    auto first{ text.find_first_not_of(' ') };
    auto last{ text.find_last_not_of(' ') };
    return text.substr(first, (last - first + 1)).data();
}
```

The following is a listing of running several commands, as described previously. We start by displaying all movies called *The Matrix*, although only one is found. Then we list the media files for this movie, but none exist at this point. After that, we add a file called *the_matrix.jpg* from the *res* folder and print the list of media files again. Lastly, we delete the recently added media file and display the files again to make sure the list is empty:

```
find The Matrix
1 | The Matrix | 1999 | 196min

list 1
empty

add 1,.\res\the_matrix.jpg,Main poster
added

list 1
1 | 1 | the_matrix.jpg | Main poster | 193906 bytes

del 1
deleted

list 1
empty
```

11 Cryptography

Problems

88. Caesar cipher

Write a program that can encrypt and decrypt messages using a Caesar cipher with a right rotation and any shift value. For simplicity, the program should consider only uppercase text messages and only encode letters, ignoring digits, symbols, and other types of characters.

89. Vigenère cipher

Write a program that can encrypt and decrypt messages using the Vigenère cipher. For simplicity, the input plain-text messages for encryption should consist of only uppercase letters.

90. Base64 encoding and decoding

Write a program that can encode and decode binary data using the base64 encoding scheme. You must implement the encoding and decoding functions yourself and not use a 3rd party library. The table used for encoding should be the one from the MIME specification.

91. Validating user credentials

Write a program that simulates the way users authenticate to a secured system. In order to log in, a user must be already registered with the system. The user enters a username and a password and the program checks if it matches any of its registered users; if it does, the user is granted access, otherwise, the operation fails. For security reasons, the system must not record the password but use an SHA hash instead.

92. Computing file hashes

Write a program that, given a path to a file, computes and prints to the console the SHA1, SHA256, and MD5 hash values for the content of the file.

93. Encrypting and decrypting files

Write a program that can encrypt and decrypt files using the **Advanced Encryption Standard** (**AES** or **Rijndael**). It should be possible to specify both a source file and a destination file path, as well as a password.

94. File signing

Write a program that is able to sign files and verify that a signed file has not been tampered with, using RSA cryptography. When signing a file, the signature should be written to a separate file and used later for the verification process. The program should provide at least two functions: one that signs a file (taking as arguments the path to the file, the path to the RSA private key, and the path to the file where the signature will be written) and one that verifies a file (taking as arguments the path to the file, the path to the RSA public key, and the path to the signature file).

Solutions

88. Caesar cipher

A *Caesar cipher*, also known as *Caesar's cipher*, *Caesar's code*, *Caesar shift*, or *shift cipher*, is a very old, simple, and widely known encryption technique that substitutes each letter in the plain-text with a letter some fixed number of positions down the alphabet. This method was used by Julius Caesar to protect messages of military importance. He used a shift of three letters, therefore replacing A with D, B with E, and so on. In this encoding, the text CPPCHALLENGER becomes FSSFKDOOHQJHU. The cipher is described in detail on Wikipedia at `https://en.wikipedia.org/wiki/Caesar_cipher`.

Although the Caesar cipher has no place in modern cryptography since it is trivial to break, it is still used on online forums or newsgroups as a way to scramble text to hide spoilers, offensive words, puzzle solutions, and so on. This problem is intended only as a simple exercise along these lines. You should not use such a simple substitution cipher for any cryptographic purposes.

In order to solve the proposed problem, we must implement two functions: one that performs the encryption of a plain-text and one that decrypts an encrypted text. In the code listed as follows:

- `caesar_encrypt()` is a function that takes a `string_view` representing the plain-text and a shift value that indicates how many letters down the alphabet the substitution should occur. This function accounts for and substitutes only uppercase letters and leaves the other characters from the plain-text unmodified. The alphabet is modeled in a circular sequence, so that, in the case of a right shift of 3, X becomes A, Y becomes B, and Z becomes C.
- `caesar_decrypt()` is a function that takes a `string_view` representing a Caesar-encrypted text and a shift value that indicates how many letters down the alphabet (that is, a right rotation) the substitution occurred for the encryption. Like its encryption counterpart, this function only transforms uppercase letters and leaves the others untouched.

```
std::string caesar_encrypt(std::string_view text, int const shift)
{
    std::string str;
    str.reserve(text.length());
    for (auto const c : text)
    {
```

```
            if (isalpha(c) && isupper(c))
                str += 'A' + (c - 'A' + shift) % 26;
            else
                str += c;
        }

        return str;
    }

    std::string caesar_decrypt(std::string_view text, int const shift)
    {
        std::string str;
        str.reserve(text.length());
        for (auto const c : text)
        {
            if (isalpha(c) && isupper(c))
                str += 'A' + (26 + c - 'A' - shift) % 26;
            else
                str += c;
        }

        return str;
    }
```

The following is an example of how these functions can be used. The plain-text to be encrypted is actually the entire English alphabet, and the encryption/decryption is executed for every possible shift value:

```
    int main()
    {
        auto text = "ABCDEFGHIJKLMNOPQRSTUVWXYZ";
        for (int i = 1; i <= 26; ++i)
        {
            auto enc = caesar_encrypt(text, i);
            auto dec = caesar_decrypt(enc, i);
            assert(text == dec);
        }
    }
```

89. Vigenère cipher

The Vigenère cipher is an encryption technique that uses a series of interwoven Caesar ciphers. Although described in 1553 by Giovan Battista Ballaso, it was misattributed in the 19th century to Blaise de Vigenère and ended up being named after him. The cipher is described in detail on Wikipedia at `https://en.wikipedia.org/wiki/Vigen%C3%A8re_cipher`. Only a short summary is presented here.

 Although the Vigenère cipher took three centuries to be broken, it is nowadays trivial to break, just as in the case of the Caesar cipher, on which it is based. Like the previous problem, this one is proposed only as a fun and simple exercise and not as an argument in favor of using this cipher for cryptographic purposes.

The technique uses a table called **tabula recta** or a **Vigenère table**. For the English alphabet, this table has 26 rows and 26 columns, where each row is the entire alphabet shifted cyclically using a Caesar cipher. The following image, from the Wikipedia article listed above, shows the content of this table:

	A	B	C	D	E	F	G	H	I	J	K	L	M	N	O	P	Q	R	S	T	U	V	W	X	Y	Z
A	A	B	C	D	E	F	G	H	I	J	K	L	M	N	O	P	Q	R	S	T	U	V	W	X	Y	Z
B	B	C	D	E	F	G	H	I	J	K	L	M	N	O	P	Q	R	S	T	U	V	W	X	Y	Z	A
C	C	D	E	F	G	H	I	J	K	L	M	N	O	P	Q	R	S	T	U	V	W	X	Y	Z	A	B
D	D	E	F	G	H	I	J	K	L	M	N	O	P	Q	R	S	T	U	V	W	X	Y	Z	A	B	C
E	E	F	G	H	I	J	K	L	M	N	O	P	Q	R	S	T	U	V	W	X	Y	Z	A	B	C	D
F	F	G	H	I	J	K	L	M	N	O	P	Q	R	S	T	U	V	W	X	Y	Z	A	B	C	D	E
G	G	H	I	J	K	L	M	N	O	P	Q	R	S	T	U	V	W	X	Y	Z	A	B	C	D	E	F
H	H	I	J	K	L	M	N	O	P	Q	R	S	T	U	V	W	X	Y	Z	A	B	C	D	E	F	G
I	I	J	K	L	M	N	O	P	Q	R	S	T	U	V	W	X	Y	Z	A	B	C	D	E	F	G	H
J	J	K	L	M	N	O	P	Q	R	S	T	U	V	W	X	Y	Z	A	B	C	D	E	F	G	H	I
K	K	L	M	N	O	P	Q	R	S	T	U	V	W	X	Y	Z	A	B	C	D	E	F	G	H	I	J
L	L	M	N	O	P	Q	R	S	T	U	V	W	X	Y	Z	A	B	C	D	E	F	G	H	I	J	K
M	M	N	O	P	Q	R	S	T	U	V	W	X	Y	Z	A	B	C	D	E	F	G	H	I	J	K	L
N	N	O	P	Q	R	S	T	U	V	W	X	Y	Z	A	B	C	D	E	F	G	H	I	J	K	L	M
O	O	P	Q	R	S	T	U	V	W	X	Y	Z	A	B	C	D	E	F	G	H	I	J	K	L	M	N
P	P	Q	R	S	T	U	V	W	X	Y	Z	A	B	C	D	E	F	G	H	I	J	K	L	M	N	O
Q	Q	R	S	T	U	V	W	X	Y	Z	A	B	C	D	E	F	G	H	I	J	K	L	M	N	O	P
R	R	S	T	U	V	W	X	Y	Z	A	B	C	D	E	F	G	H	I	J	K	L	M	N	O	P	Q
S	S	T	U	V	W	X	Y	Z	A	B	C	D	E	F	G	H	I	J	K	L	M	N	O	P	Q	R
T	T	U	V	W	X	Y	Z	A	B	C	D	E	F	G	H	I	J	K	L	M	N	O	P	Q	R	S
U	U	V	W	X	Y	Z	A	B	C	D	E	F	G	H	I	J	K	L	M	N	O	P	Q	R	S	T
V	V	W	X	Y	Z	A	B	C	D	E	F	G	H	I	J	K	L	M	N	O	P	Q	R	S	T	U
W	W	X	Y	Z	A	B	C	D	E	F	G	H	I	J	K	L	M	N	O	P	Q	R	S	T	U	V
X	X	Y	Z	A	B	C	D	E	F	G	H	I	J	K	L	M	N	O	P	Q	R	S	T	U	V	W
Y	Y	Z	A	B	C	D	E	F	G	H	I	J	K	L	M	N	O	P	Q	R	S	T	U	V	W	X
Z	Z	A	B	C	D	E	F	G	H	I	J	K	L	M	N	O	P	Q	R	S	T	U	V	W	X	Y

A key is necessary for encryption and decryption. The key is written down until it matches the length of the text to encrypt and respectively decrypt (they have the same size). Encryption is performed by looking at each letter from the plain-text, taking its corresponding letter in the key, and replacing it with the letter found at the intersection of the row corresponding to the key letter and the column corresponding to the plain-text letter. Decryption is done by going to the row that corresponds to the key letter, identifying the encrypted text letter in the row, and using the column label as the letter for the plain-text.

The function that performs the encryption is called `vigenere_encrypt()`. It takes a plain-text and a key, encrypts the plain-text according to the method described previously, and returns the encrypted text:

```cpp
std::string vigenere_encrypt(std::string_view text, std::string_view key)
{
    std::string result;
    result.reserve(text.length());
    static auto table = build_vigenere_table();

    for (size_t i = 0; i < text.length(); ++i)
    {
        auto row = key[i%key.length()] - 'A';
        auto col = text[i] - 'A';

        result += table[row * 26 + col];
    }

    return result;
}
```

Its counterpart is called `vigenere_decrypt()`. This is a function that takes an encrypted text and the key used for encrypting it and decrypts the text using the method described previously, returning the resultant plain-text:

```cpp
std::string vigenere_decrypt(std::string_view text, std::string_view key)
{
    std::string result;
    result.reserve(text.length());
    static auto table = build_vigenere_table();

    for (size_t i = 0; i < text.length(); ++i)
    {
        auto row = key[i%key.length()] - 'A';

        for (size_t col = 0; col < 26; col++)
        {
```

```
          if (table[row * 26 + col] == text[i])
          {
              result += 'A' + col;
              break;
          }
      }
  }

  return result;
}
```

Both these functions use a third one, called `build_vigenere_table()`, which creates the Vigenère table by performing a Caesar encryption of the entire alphabet 26 times, each time with a new shift value. The table is represented as a single string:

```cpp
std::string build_vigenere_table()
{
    std::string table;
    table.reserve(26*26);
    for (int i = 0; i < 26; ++i)
        table += caesar_encrypt("ABCDEFGHIJKLMNOPQRSTUVWXYZ", i);

    return table;
}
```

These functions for encryption and decryption can be used as follows:

```cpp
int main()
{
    auto text = "THECPPCHALLENGER";
    auto enc = vigenere_encrypt(text, "SAMPLE");
    auto dec = vigenere_decrypt(enc, "SAMPLE");
    assert(text == dec);
}
```

90. Base64 encoding and decoding

Base64 is an encoding scheme used for representing binary data in ASCII format using an alphabet of 64 characters. Although all implementations use the same first 62 characters (A–Z, a–z, and 0–9), the last two values may differ. The symbols + and / are used in the MIME specification. A base64 digit represents 6 bits of data, and four base64 digits encode exactly three bytes (8-bit) of binary data. When the number of digits is not divisible by three, extra bytes with a value of zero are added before converting to base64. Padding the encoded text with == or = can be used to indicate that the final group of three bytes from the plain data actually contained only one or two bytes.

Here is an example of encoding the text cpp. The result, in this case, is Y3Bw:

Source ASCII	cpp
Source octets	0x63 0x70 0x70
Source binary	01100011 01110000 01110000
Base64 binary index	011000 110111 000001 110000
Base64 decimal index	24 55 1 48
Base64 encoding	Y3Bw

 The algorithm is described in detail on Wikipedia at https://en.wikipedia.org/wiki/Base64. You can use an online encoder, such as the one available at https://www.base64encode.org/, to verify that the results you get for base64 encoding and decoding are actually correct.

The class encoded, shown as follows, has two public methods: to_base64() encodes a vector of bytes to base64 and returns the result as a string, and from_base64() decodes a base64 encoded string to a vector of bytes and returns it. Two distinct tables are used for encoding and decoding. The table for encoding is actually a plain string called table_enc that contains the base64 alphabet. The table used for decoding is called table_dec and is an array of 256 integers, representing the index in the encryption table (table_enc) of each base64 6-bit digit:

```
class encoder
{
   std::string const table_enc =
"ABCDEFGHIJKLMNOPQRSTUVWXYZabcdefghijklmnopqrstuvwxyz0123456789+/";
   char const padding_symbol = '=';

   char const table_dec[256] =
   {
      -1,-1,-1,-1,-1,-1,-1,-1,-1,-1,64,-1,-1,-1,-1,-1,
```

```
        -1,-1,-1,-1,-1,-1,-1,-1,-1,-1,-1,-1,-1,-1,-1,-1,
        -1,-1,-1,-1,-1,-1,-1,-1,-1,-1,-1,62,-1,-1,-1,63,
        52,53,54,55,56,57,58,59,60,61,-1,-1,-1,65,-1,-1,
        -1, 0, 1, 2, 3, 4, 5, 6, 7, 8, 9,10,11,12,13,14,
        15,16,17,18,19,20,21,22,23,24,25,-1,-1,-1,-1,-1,
        -1,26,27,28,29,30,31,32,33,34,35,36,37,38,39,40,
        41,42,43,44,45,46,47,48,49,50,51,-1,-1,-1,-1,-1,
        -1,-1,-1,-1,-1,-1,-1,-1,-1,-1,-1,-1,-1,-1,-1,-1,
        -1,-1,-1,-1,-1,-1,-1,-1,-1,-1,-1,-1,-1,-1,-1,-1,
        -1,-1,-1,-1,-1,-1,-1,-1,-1,-1,-1,-1,-1,-1,-1,-1,
        -1,-1,-1,-1,-1,-1,-1,-1,-1,-1,-1,-1,-1,-1,-1,-1,
        -1,-1,-1,-1,-1,-1,-1,-1,-1,-1,-1,-1,-1,-1,-1,-1,
        -1,-1,-1,-1,-1,-1,-1,-1,-1,-1,-1,-1,-1,-1,-1,-1,
        -1,-1,-1,-1,-1,-1,-1,-1,-1,-1,-1,-1,-1,-1,-1,-1,
        -1,-1,-1,-1,-1,-1,-1,-1,-1,-1,-1,-1,-1,-1,-1,-1
    };
    char const invalid_char = -1;
    char const padding_char = 65;
public:
    std::string to_base64(std::vector<unsigned char> const & data);
    std::vector<unsigned char> from_base64(std::string data);
};
```

The method `to_base64()` is implemented as follows. This function appends = or == at the
end of the encoded string to indicate the actual length of the plain data:

```
std::string encoder::to_base64(std::vector<unsigned char> const & data)
{
    std::string result;
    result.resize((data.size() / 3 + ((data.size() % 3 > 0) ? 1 : 0)) * 4);
    auto result_ptr = &result[0];
    size_t i = 0;
    size_t j = 0;
    while (j++ < data.size() / 3)
    {
        unsigned int value = (data[i] << 16) | (data[i+1] << 8) | data[i+2];
        i += 3;

        *result_ptr++ = table_enc[(value & 0x00fc0000) >> 18];
        *result_ptr++ = table_enc[(value & 0x0003f000) >> 12];
        *result_ptr++ = table_enc[(value & 0x00000fc0) >> 6];
        *result_ptr++ = table_enc[(value & 0x0000003f)];
    };

    auto rest = data.size() - i;
    if (rest == 1)
    {
```

```
        *result_ptr++ = table_enc[(data[i] & 0x000000fc) >> 2];
        *result_ptr++ = table_enc[(data[i] & 0x00000003) << 4];
        *result_ptr++ = padding_symbol;
        *result_ptr++ = padding_symbol;
    }
    else if (rest == 2)
    {
        unsigned int value = (data[i] << 8) | data[i + 1];

        *result_ptr++ = table_enc[(value & 0x0000fc00) >> 10];
        *result_ptr++ = table_enc[(value & 0x000003f0) >> 4];
        *result_ptr++ = table_enc[(value & 0x0000000f) << 2];
        *result_ptr++ = padding_symbol;
    }

    return result;
}
```

The method `from_base64()` is also shown here. This function is able to decode both strings with and without padding:

```
std::vector<unsigned char> encored::from_base64(std::string data)
{
    size_t padding = data.size() % 4;
    if (padding == 0)
    {
        if (data[data.size() - 1] == padding_symbol) padding++;
        if (data[data.size() - 2] == padding_symbol) padding++;
    }
    else
    {
        data.append(2, padding_symbol);
    }

    std::vector<unsigned char> result;
    result.resize((data.length() / 4) * 3 - padding);
    auto result_ptr = &result[0];

    size_t i = 0;
    size_t j = 0;
    while (j++ < data.size() / 4)
    {
        unsigned char c1 = table_dec[static_cast<int>(data[i++])];
        unsigned char c2 = table_dec[static_cast<int>(data[i++])];
        unsigned char c3 = table_dec[static_cast<int>(data[i++])];
        unsigned char c4 = table_dec[static_cast<int>(data[i++])];
```

```
      if (c1 == invalid_char || c2 == invalid_char ||
          c3 == invalid_char || c4 == invalid_char)
         throw std::runtime_error("invalid base64 encoding");

      if (c4 == padding_char && c3 == padding_char)
      {
         unsigned int value = (c1 << 6) | c2;
         *result_ptr++ = (value >> 4) & 0x000000ff;
      }
      else if (c4 == padding_char)
      {
         unsigned int value = (c1 << 12) | (c2 << 6) | c3;
         *result_ptr++ = (value >> 10) & 0x000000ff;
         *result_ptr++ = (value >> 2) & 0x000000ff;
      }
      else
      {
         unsigned int value = (c1 << 18) | (c2 << 12) | (c3 << 6) | c4;

         *result_ptr++ = (value >> 16) & 0x000000ff;
         *result_ptr++ = (value >> 8) & 0x000000ff;
         *result_ptr++ = value & 0x000000ff;
      }
   }

   return result;
}
```

Since the `encoder` class encodes binary data to base64 and decodes to binary data from base64, a helper class is provided for converting a string to a sequence of bytes and the other way around. The class called `converter` in the following has two static methods; one called `from_string()` that takes a `string_view` and returns a `vector` of bytes with the content of the string, and one called `from_range()` that constructs a string from a `vector` of bytes:

```
struct converter
{
   static std::vector<unsigned char> from_string(std::string_view data)
   {
      std::vector<unsigned char> result;

      std::copy(
         std::begin(data), std::end(data),
         std::back_inserter(result));

      return result;
   }
```

```
static std::string from_range(std::vector<unsigned char> const & data)
{
    std::string result;

    std::copy(
        std::begin(data), std::end(data),
        std::back_inserter(result));

    return result;
}
};
```

The `encoder` and `converter` classes are used in the following sample to encode and decode to and from base64 data of various lengths. It validates that the result of decoding the encoded text is the same as the original:

```
int main()
{
    std::vector<std::vector<unsigned char>> data
    {
                { 's' },
              { 's','a' },
            { 's','a','m' },
          { 's','a','m','p' },
        { 's','a','m','p','l' },
      { 's','a','m','p','l','e' },
    };

    encoder enc;

    for (auto const & v : data)
    {
        auto encv = enc.to_base64(v);

        auto decv = enc.from_base64(encv);

        assert(v == decv);
    }

    auto text = "cppchallenge";
    auto textenc = enc.to_base64(converter::from_string(text));
    auto textdec = converter::from_range(enc.from_base64(textenc));
    assert(text == textdec);
}
```

Although the implementation of base64 encoding and decoding provided here is complete, it is not the most performant one. According to my tests, it performs similarly to the implementation available in Boost.Beast. However, I do not necessarily recommend that you use it in production code. Instead, you should use a more thoroughly tested and widely used implementation, such as the ones available in Boost.Beast, Crypto++, or other libraries.

91. Validating user credentials

A good choice for a free, cross-platform C++ library for cryptographic schemes is Crypto++. This library is widely used in both non-commercial and commercial projects, as well as academia, student projects, and others, for its industry-proven implementation of cryptographic functionalities. The library provides support for AES and AES candidates, as well as other block ciphers, message authentication codes, hash functions, public key cryptography, and many other features, including non-cryptographic functionalities such as pseudo-random number generators, prime number generation and verification, DEFLATE compression/decompression, encoding schemes, checksum functions, and more. The library is available at `https://www.cryptopp.com/` and will be used to solve the cryptography problems in this chapter.

 When you download the library, you will find several projects corresponding to different configurations of the library. The one you should use is `cryptolib`, which produces a static library. The dynamic library version, `cryptodll`, has been validated by NIST and CSE for FIPS 140-2 Level 1 Conformance. FIPS 140-2 is a series of US government computer security standards that specify requirements for cryptography modules. Because of this compliance, `cryptodll` does not contain anything else that does not meet the requirements, including DES and MD5.

To solve the problem, we will model a system that maintains a database of users. A user has a numerical identifier, a username, the hash value of his password, as well as optional first name and last name inputs. The following class, called `user`, is used for this purpose:

```
struct user
{
    int         id;
    std::string username;
    std::string password;
    std::string firstname;
```

```
    std::string lastname;
};
```

Computing the hash value for a password is done in the function `get_hash()`. This function takes a `string_view` that represents the password (or any text, for that matter) and returns its SHA512 hash value. Crypto++ includes a number of hash functions, including SHA-1, SHA-2 (SHA-224, SHA-256, SHA-384, and SHA-512), SHA-3, Tiger, WHIRLPOOL, RIPEMD-128, RIPEMD-256, RIPEMD-160, and RIPEMD-320, all in the `CryptoPP` namespace, as well as MD5 (in the `CryptoPP::Weak` namespace) if you use the static library version. All these hashes are derived from the class `HashTransformation` and are interchangeable. To compute the hash we must:

- Create a `HashTransformation`-derived object, such as `SHA512`.
- Define an array of bytes large enough to retrieve the hash digest.
- Call `CalculateDigest()`, passing the output buffer, the text to transform, and its length.
- The digest resulting from hashing the original text has a binary form. This can be encoded in a more human-readable form as a string containing hexadecimal digits. This can be done using the `HexEncoder` class. You can attach a sink, such as `StringSink` or `FileSink`, to accumulate the output.

The Crypto++ library uses the concept of a pipeline to flow data from a source to a sink. Within this flow, data can encounter filters that transform it before it reaches the sink. Objects within the pipeline take ownership of other objects passed to them via a pointer in the constructor and automatically destroy them when they are destroyed themselves. The following quote is taken from the library's documentation: *"If a constructor for A takes a pointer to an object B (except primitive types such as int and char), then A owns B and will delete B at A's destruction. If a constructor for A takes a reference to an object B, then the caller retains ownership of B and should not destroy it until A no longer needs it."*

Following is the implementation of the `get_hash()` function:

```
std::string get_hash(std::string_view password)
{
    CryptoPP::SHA512 sha;
    CryptoPP::byte digest[CryptoPP::SHA512::DIGESTSIZE];

    sha.CalculateDigest(
        digest,
        reinterpret_cast<CryptoPP::byte const*>(password.data()),
```

```
        password.length());

    CryptoPP::HexEncoder encoder;
    std::string result;

    encoder.Attach(new CryptoPP::StringSink(result));
    encoder.Put(digest, sizeof(digest));
    encoder.MessageEnd();

    return result;
}
```

The following program uses the class `user` and the function `get_hash()` to model the login system. `users`, as the name implies, is a list of users. Although this list is hardcoded, it could be read from a database. You can take it as an extra exercise to store the users in a SQLite database and retrieve it from there. After the user enters his username and password, the program computes the SHA512 hash of the password, checks the list of users for an exact match of the username and the password hash, and displays a message accordingly:

```
int main()
{
    std::vector<user> users
    {
        {
            101, "scarface",
"07A8D53ADAB635ADDF39BAEACFB799FD7C5BFDEE365F3AA721B7E25B54A4E87D419ADDEA34
BC3073BAC472DCF4657E50C0F6781DDD8FE883653D10F7930E78FF",
            "Tony", "Montana"
        },
        {
            202, "neo",
"C2CC277BCC10888ECEE90F0F09EE9666199C2699922EFB41EA7E88067B2C075F3DD3FBF3CF
E9D0EC6173668DD83C111342F91E941A2CADC46A3A814848AA9B05",
            "Thomas", "Anderson"
        },
        {
            303, "godfather",
"0EA7A0306FE00CD22DF1B835796EC32ACC702208E0B052B15F9393BCCF5EE9ECD8BAAF2784
0D4D3E6BCC3BB3B009259F6F73CC77480C065DDE67CD9BEA14AA4D",
            "Vito", "Corleone"
        }
    };

    std::string username, password;
    std::cout << "Username: ";
    std::cin >> username;
```

```
   std::cout << "Password: ";
   std::cin >> password;

   auto hash = get_hash(password);

   auto pos = std::find_if(
      std::begin(users), std::end(users),
      [username, hash](user const & u) {
      return u.username == username &&
         u.password == hash; });

   if (pos != std::end(users))
      std::cout << "Login successful!" << std::endl;
   else
      std::cout << "Invalid username or password" << std::endl;
}
```

92. Computing file hashes

File hashes are often used to ensure the integrity of content, such as in the case of downloading a file from the web. Although implementations of the SHA1 and MD5 hashing functions can be found in a variety of libraries, we will again use the Crypto++ library. If you did not follow the previous problem and its solution, *Validating user credentials*, you should do so before continuing with this one, because the general information about the Crypto++ library that was given there will not be repeated here.

Computing a hash for a file is relatively simple using the Crypto++ library. The following code uses several components:

- `FileSource`, which allows reading data from a file using a `BufferedTransformation`. By default, it pumps data in blocks or chunks of 4,096 bytes, although manual pumping is also possible. The constructor used here takes a path to an input file, a Boolean that indicates whether all data should be pumped or not, and a `BufferTransformation` object.
- `HashFilter`, which uses the specified hash algorithm to calculate the hash of all input data up to the first `MessageEnd` signal, at which time it outputs the resultant hash value to its attached transformation.
- `HexEncoder`, which encodes bytes in base 16 using the alphabet 0123456789ABCDEF.

- `StringSink`, which represents a destination of string data in a pipeline. It takes a reference to a string object where data is to be stored:

> `BufferedTransformation` is the basic unit of data flow in Crypto++. It represents a generalization of `BlockTransformation`, `StreamTransformation`, and `HashTransformation`. A `BufferedTransformation` is an object that takes a stream of bytes as input (this may be done in stages), does some computation on them, and then places the result into an internal buffer for later retrieval. Any partial result already in the output buffer is not modified by a further input. Objects deriving from `BufferedTransformation` can participate in pipelining, which allows data to flow from a source to a sink.

```
template <class Hash>
std::string compute_hash(fs::path const & filepath)
{
   std::string digest;
   Hash hash;

   CryptoPP::FileSource source(
      filepath.c_str(),
      true,
      new CryptoPP::HashFilter(hash,
         new CryptoPP::HexEncoder(
            new CryptoPP::StringSink(digest))));

   return digest;
}
```

The function template `compute_hash()` from the preceding code can be used as follows to determine various hashing values:

```
int main()
{
   std::string path;
   std::cout << "Path: ";
   std::cin >> path;

   try
   {
      std::cout << "SHA1: "
                << compute_hash<CryptoPP::SHA1>(path) << std::endl;
      std::cout << "SHA256: "
                << compute_hash<CryptoPP::SHA256>(path) << std::endl;
      std::cout << "MD5: "
```

```
                     << compute_hash<CryptoPP::Weak::MD5>(path) << std::endl;
    }
    catch (std::exception const & ex)
    {
        std::cerr << ex.what() << std::endl;
    }
}
```

It is important to note that the MD5 hash is obsolete and insecure and is only provided for backward compatibility. In order to use it, you must define the `CRYPTOPP_ENABLE_NAMESPACE_WEAK` macro before including the `md5.h` header, as follows:

```
#define CRYPTOPP_ENABLE_NAMESPACE_WEAK 1
#include "md5.h"
```

93. Encrypting and decrypting files

In order to solve this problem with the Crypto++ library, we need to use several components:

- `FileSource`, which allows reading data from a file using a `BufferedTransformation`. By default, it pumps data in blocks or chunks of 4,096 bytes, although manual pumping is also possible.
- `FileSink`, which allows you to write data to a file using a `BufferedTransformation`. It is the companion sink object to a `FileSource` source object.
- `DefaultEncryptorWithMAC` and `DefaultDecryptorWithMAC`, which encrypt and decrypt strings and files with an authentication tag to detect tampering. They use AES as the default block cipher and SHA256 as the default hash for the MAC. Each run through these two classes produces a different result due to the use of a time-based salt.

Two overloads are provided both for encryption and decryption:

- One overload takes a source file path, a destination file path, and a password. It encrypts or decrypts the source file, and the result is written in the destination file.
- The other overload takes a file path and a password. It encrypts or decrypts the file, writing the result in a temporary file, deletes the original file, and then moves the temporary file to the original file path. Its implementation is based on the first overload.

The functions that perform file encryption are shown here:

```
void encrypt_file(fs::path const & sourcefile,
                  fs::path const & destfile,
                  std::string_view password)
{
   CryptoPP::FileSource source(
      sourcefile.c_str(),
      true,
      new CryptoPP::DefaultEncryptorWithMAC(
      (CryptoPP::byte*)password.data(), password.size(),
         new CryptoPP::FileSink(
            destfile.c_str())
      )
   );
}

void encrypt_file(fs::path const & filepath,
                  std::string_view password)
{
   auto temppath = fs::temp_directory_path() / filepath.filename();

   encrypt_file(filepath, temppath, password);

   fs::remove(filepath);
   fs::rename(temppath, filepath);
}
```

The decrypting equivalent functions are basically identical, but instead of using
DefaultEncryptorWithMAC for the buffered transformation they use
DefaultDecryptorWithMAC. The two afore mentioned overloads are shown as follows:

```
void decrypt_file(fs::path const & sourcefile,
                  fs::path const & destfile,
                  std::string_view password)
{
   CryptoPP::FileSource source(
      sourcefile.c_str(),
      true,
      new CryptoPP::DefaultDecryptorWithMAC(
      (CryptoPP::byte*)password.data(), password.size(),
         new CryptoPP::FileSink(
            destfile.c_str())
      )
   );
}
```

```
void decrypt_file(fs::path const & filepath,
                  std::string_view password)
{
    auto temppath = fs::temp_directory_path() / filepath.filename();

    decrypt_file(filepath, temppath, password);

    fs::remove(filepath);
    fs::rename(temppath, filepath);
}
```

These functions can be used as follows:

```
int main()
{
    encrypt_file("sample.txt", "sample.txt.enc", "cppchallenger");
    decrypt_file("sample.txt.enc", "sample.txt.dec", "cppchallenger");

    encrypt_file("sample.txt", "cppchallenger");
    decrypt_file("sample.txt", "cppchallenger");
}
```

94. File signing

The process of signing and verifying is similar to encryption and decryption, although it differs in a fundamental way; encryption is done using the public key and decryption using the private key, while signing is done using the private key and verification is done using the public key. Signing helps a recipient that owns a public key to verify that a file is unmodified by using the signature and its public key. Having the public key, however, is not enough to change the file and sign it again. The Crypto++ library is used for solving this problem too.

Although you can use any pair of public-private RSA keys to perform the signing and verification, in the implementation provided here the keys are randomly generated when the program starts. Obviously, in practice, you would generate the keys independent of the signing and verification, and not every time you do that. The function generate_keys(), which is shown at the end of the following listing, creates a pair of RSA public-private 3,072-bit keys. Several helper functions, all shown here, are used for this purpose:

```
void encode(fs::path const & filepath,
            CryptoPP::BufferedTransformation const & bt)
{
    CryptoPP::FileSink file(filepath.c_str());
    bt.CopyTo(file);
```

```
      file.MessageEnd();
}

void encode_private_key(fs::path const & filepath,
                        CryptoPP::RSA::PrivateKey const & key)
{
   CryptoPP::ByteQueue queue;
   key.DEREncodePrivateKey(queue);
   encode(filepath, queue);
}

void encode_public_key(fs::path const & filepath,
                       CryptoPP::RSA::PublicKey const & key)
{
   CryptoPP::ByteQueue queue;
   key.DEREncodePublicKey(queue);
   encode(filepath, queue);
}

void decode(fs::path const & filepath,
            CryptoPP::BufferedTransformation& bt)
{
   CryptoPP::FileSource file(filepath.c_str(), true);
   file.TransferTo(bt);
   bt.MessageEnd();
}

void decode_private_key(fs::path const & filepath,
                        CryptoPP::RSA::PrivateKey& key)
{
   CryptoPP::ByteQueue queue;
   decode(filepath, queue);
   key.BERDecodePrivateKey(queue, false, queue.MaxRetrievable());
}

void decode_public_key(fs::path const & filepath,
                       CryptoPP::RSA::PublicKey& key)
{
   CryptoPP::ByteQueue queue;
   decode(filepath, queue);
   key.BERDecodePublicKey(queue, false, queue.MaxRetrievable());
}

void generate_keys(fs::path const & privateKeyPath,
                   fs::path const & publicKeyPath,
                   CryptoPP::RandomNumberGenerator& rng)
{
   try
```

```
    {
        CryptoPP::RSA::PrivateKey rsaPrivate;
        rsaPrivate.GenerateRandomWithKeySize(rng, 3072);

        CryptoPP::RSA::PublicKey rsaPublic(rsaPrivate);

        encode_private_key(privateKeyPath, rsaPrivate);
        encode_public_key(publicKeyPath, rsaPublic);
    }
    catch (CryptoPP::Exception const & e)
    {
        std::cerr << e.what() << std::endl;
    }
}
```

In order to perform the signing, we use a pipeline that starts with a `FileSource`, ends with a `FileSink`, and contains a filter called `SignerFilter`, which creates a signature over a message. It uses the `RSASSA_PKCS1v15_SHA_Signer` signer to transform the source data:

```
void rsa_sign_file(fs::path const & filepath,
                   fs::path const & privateKeyPath,
                   fs::path const & signaturePath,
                   CryptoPP::RandomNumberGenerator& rng)
{
    CryptoPP::RSA::PrivateKey privateKey;
    decode_private_key(privateKeyPath, privateKey);

    CryptoPP::RSASSA_PKCS1v15_SHA_Signer signer(privateKey);

    CryptoPP::FileSource fileSource(
        filepath.c_str(),
        true,
        new CryptoPP::SignerFilter(
            rng,
            signer,
            new CryptoPP::FileSink(
                signaturePath.c_str()))));
}
```

The opposite process of verification is implemented in a similar way. The filter used in this case is `SignatureVerificationFilter`, which is the counterpart of `SignerFilter`, and the verifier is `RSASSA_PKCS1v15_SHA_Verifier`, which is the counterpart of `RSASSA_PKCS1v15_SHA_Signer`:

```
bool rsa_verify_file(fs::path const & filepath,
                     fs::path const & publicKeyPath,
                     fs::path const & signaturePath)
```

```
{
    CryptoPP::RSA::PublicKey publicKey;
    decode_public_key(publicKeyPath.c_str(), publicKey);

    CryptoPP::RSASSA_PKCS1v15_SHA_Verifier verifier(publicKey);

    CryptoPP::FileSource signatureFile(signaturePath.c_str(),
                                       true);

    if (signatureFile.MaxRetrievable() != verifier.SignatureLength())
        return false;

    CryptoPP::SecByteBlock signature(verifier.SignatureLength());
    signatureFile.Get(signature, signature.size());

    auto* verifierFilter =
        new CryptoPP::SignatureVerificationFilter(verifier);
    verifierFilter->Put(signature, verifier.SignatureLength());

    CryptoPP::FileSource fileSource(
        filepath.c_str(),
        true,
        verifierFilter);

    return verifierFilter->GetLastResult();
}
```

The following program generates a pair of RSA public-private keys, then uses the private key to sign a file using the `rsa_sign_file()` function, and then uses the public key and the signature file to verify the file using the `rsa_verify_file()` counterpart function:

```
int main()
{
    CryptoPP::AutoSeededRandomPool rng;

    generate_keys("rsa-private.key", "rsa-public.key", rng);

    rsa_sign_file("sample.txt", "rsa-private.key", "sample.sign", rng);

    auto success =
        rsa_verify_file("sample.txt", "rsa-public.key", "sample.sign");

    assert(success);
}
```

12

Networking and Services

Problems

95. Finding the IP address of a host

Write a program that can retrieve and print the IPv4 address of a host. If multiple addresses are found, then all of them should be printed. The program should work on all platforms.

96. Client-server Fizz-Buzz

Write a client-server application that can be used for playing the *Fizz-Buzz* game. The client sends numbers to the server that answer back with fizz, buzz, fizz-buzz, or the number itself, according to the game rules. Communication between the client and the server must be done over TCP. The server should run indefinitely. The client should run as long as the user enters numbers between 1 and 99.

Fizz-Buzz is a game for children, intended to teach them arithmetic division. A player must say a number and another player should answer with:

- Fizz, if the number is divisible by 3
- Buzz, if the number is divisible by 5
- Fizz-buzz, if the number is divisible by both 3 and 5
- The number itself in all other cases

97. Bitcoin exchange rates

Write a program that displays Bitcoin exchange rates for the most important currencies (such as USD, EUR, or GBP). The exchange rates must be fetched from an online service, such as: `https://blockchain.info`.

98. Fetching emails using IMAP

Write a program that can get information from an email server using IMAP. The program should be able to:

- Get a list of folders from the mailbox
- Get unread emails from a particular folder

99. Translating text to any language

Write a program that can translate text from one language to another using an online service. It should be possible to specify the text that you wish to translate, the language of the text, and the language to translate to.

100. Detecting faces in a picture

Write a program that can identify people's faces from pictures. At a minimum, the program must detect the face area and the gender of the person. This information should be printed to the console. The pictures must be loaded from the disk.

Solutions

95. Finding the IP address of a host

Host information, including IP addresses, can be retrieved with system-specific network utilities, such as `gethostbyname()`. Although this is available on all platforms, the way it is used is different and the requirement is to write a program that works on all platforms. There are various open source cross-platform libraries for networking, such as *POCO* and *Asio/Boost.Asio*. *POCO* is a more complex library, with support for not only networking but also data access, cryptography, XML, JSON, Zip, and others. *Asio* is a stand-alone, header-only library with a consistent asynchronous I/O model for network programming. It is also available as part of the Boost library, and a standardization proposal based on it is under evaluation. In this book, I will be using the standalone version of *Asio*, because it is a header-only library and does not have additional dependencies and is, therefore, easier to use. *Asio* can be used for solving this task.

The stand-alone *Asio* library can be found at `https://think-async.com/`, although the latest version seems to be available only on GitHub at: `https://github.com/chriskohlhoff/asio/`. All you have to do in order to use it is clone or download and unzip the repository and include the `asio.hpp` header in your sources. If you do not want any Boost dependencies, then make sure you define the macro `ASIO_STANDALONE` before including the library header.

The `get_ip_address()` function shown in the following code snippet takes a hostname and returns a list of strings representing the IPv4 addresses for that hostname. To do this, it relies on several Asio components:

- `asio::io_context` provides core I/O functionality for async I/O objects.
- `asio::ip::tcp::resolver` provides the ability to resolve a query to a list of endpoints. Its member function, `resolve()`, is used to resolve host and service names into a list of endpoints. Although there are various overloads, the one used here takes a protocol (in this case IPv4, but it can also use IPv6), a host identifier (either the name of a numeric address as a string), and a service identifier (this can be a port number). If successful, this function returns a list of endpoints, otherwise, it throws an exception.
- `asio::ip::tcp::endpoint` represents an endpoint that can be associated with a TCP socket.

The `get_ip_address()` function is implemented as follows:

```cpp
#define ASIO_STANDALONE
#include "asio.hpp"

std::vector<std::string> get_ip_address(std::string_view hostname)
{
    std::vector<std::string> ips;

    try
    {
        asio::io_context context;
        asio::ip::tcp::resolver resolver(context);
        auto endpoints = resolver.resolve(asio::ip::tcp::v4(),
                                          hostname.data(), "");

        for (auto e = endpoints.begin(); e != endpoints.end(); ++e)
            ips.push_back(
                ((asio::ip::tcp::endpoint)*e).address().to_string());
    }
    catch (std::exception const & e)
    {
        std::cerr << "exception: " << e.what() << std::endl;
    }

    return ips;
}
```

The function can be used as follows:

```cpp
int main()
{
    auto ips = get_ip_address("packtpub.com");
    for (auto const & ip : ips)
        std::cout << ip << std::endl;
}
```

96. Client-server Fizz-Buzz

In order to solve this problem, we will use the *Asio* library again. However, this time we need to write two programs: a server and a client. The server accepts TCP connections on a particular port, opens a connected socket, and starts reading on the socket. When it reads something from the socket, it interprets it as a number for the Fizz-Buzz game, writes back the answer, and continues to wait for another input. The client connects to a host on a particular port, sends a number read from the console, and then waits to receive an answer from the server before printing it to the console.

On the server side, the implementation of the Fizz-Buzz game is rather straightforward and should not require additional explanations. The `fizzbuzz()` function shown in the following code snippet takes a number and returns the result as a string:

```
std::string fizzbuzz(int const number)
{
   if(number != 0)
   {
      auto m3 = number % 3;
      auto m5 = number % 5;
      if(m3 == 0 && m5 == 0) return "fizzbuzz";
      else if(m5 == 0) return "buzz";
      else if(m3 == 0) return "fizz";
   }

   return std::to_string(number);
}
```

There are two main components that we will implement on the server side. The first component is called `session`. Its purpose is to read from and write to a connected socket. It is constructed from an `asio::ip::tcp::socket` object and uses its `async_read_some()` and `async_write_some()` methods to read and write data. As the name implies, these are asynchronous operations and a handler is called when they are completed. After successfully reading from the socket, it writes back the result of the `fizzbuzz()` function for the received number. When the writing to the socket completes successfully, it starts reading again. The implementation of the `session` class is shown as follows:

```
#define ASIO_STANDALONE
#include "asio.hpp"

class session : public std::enable_shared_from_this<session>
{
public:
   session(asio::ip::tcp::socket socket) :
      tcp_socket(std::move(socket))
```

```
        { }

    void start()
    {
        read();
    }

private:
    void read()
    {
        auto self(shared_from_this());

        tcp_socket.async_read_some(
            asio::buffer(data, data.size()),
            [this, self](std::error_code const ec, std::size_t const length){
                if (!ec)
                {
                    auto number = std::string(data.data(), length);
                    auto result = fizzbuzz(std::atoi(number.c_str()));
                    std::cout << number << " -> " << result << std::endl;
                    write(result);
                }
            });
    }

    void write(std::string_view response)
    {
        auto self(shared_from_this());

        tcp_socket.async_write_some(
            asio::buffer(response.data(), response.length()),
            [this, self](std::error_code const ec, std::size_t const) {
                if (!ec)
                    read();
            });
    }

    std::array<char, 1024> data;
    asio::ip::tcp::socket tcp_socket;
};
```

The other component that we will be writing is used for accepting incoming connections. It is called `server` and uses `asio::ip::tcp::acceptor` for accepting new connections on the local host on a designated port. After successfully opening a new socket, it creates a `session` object from the socket and calls its `start()` method in order to begin reading data from the client. The `server` class is shown here:

```
class server
{
public:
    server(asio::io_context& context, short const port)
        : tcp_acceptor(context,
                        asio::ip::tcp::endpoint(asio::ip::tcp::v4(), port))
        , tcp_socket(context)
    {
        std::cout << "server running on port " << port << std::endl;

        accept();
    }

private:
    void accept()
    {
        tcp_acceptor.async_accept(tcp_socket, [this](std::error_code ec)
        {
            if (!ec)
                std::make_shared<session>(std::move(tcp_socket))->start();

            accept();
        });
    }

    asio::ip::tcp::acceptor tcp_acceptor;
    asio::ip::tcp::socket tcp_socket;
};
```

The following `run_server()` function creates an `asio::io_context` object and an instance of `server` that immediately starts accepting incoming connections, and calls the `run()` method of the context. This executes an event processing loop, blocking until all work has finished and there are no more handlers to be dispatched, or until the `asio::io_context` object has been stopped, with a call to the `stop()` method. The `run_server()` function runs indefinitely until an exception occurs:

```
void run_server(short const port)
{
    try
    {
```

```
        asio::io_context context;

        server srv(context, port);

        context.run();
    }
    catch (std::exception& e)
    {
        std::cerr << "exception: " << e.what() << std::endl;
    }
}

int main()
{
    run_server(11234);
}
```

On the client side, the implementation is a bit simpler. `asio::connect()` is used to establish a TCP connection with a host on a specified port. After the connection is established, the synchronous `write_some()` and `read_some()` methods of `asio::ip::tcp::socket` are used to send and receive data to and from the server. This is executed in a loop, based on the user's input to the console, and runs as long as the user enters a number between 1 and 99. The `run_client()` function shown in the following code snippet implements all of this:

```
void run_client(std::string_view host, short const port)
{
    try
    {
        asio::io_context context;
        asio::ip::tcp::socket tcp_socket(context);
        asio::ip::tcp::resolver resolver(context);
        asio::connect(tcp_socket,
                    resolver.resolve({ host.data(),
                                    std::to_string(port) }));

        while (true)
        {
            std::cout << "number [1-99]: ";

            int number;
            std::cin >> number;
            if (std::cin.fail() || number < 1 || number > 99)
                break;

            auto request = std::to_string(number);
```

```
            tcp_socket.write_some(asio::buffer(request, request.length()));

            std::array<char, 1024> reply;
            auto reply_length = tcp_socket.read_some(
                                    asio::buffer(reply, reply.size()));

            std::cout << "reply is: ";
            std::cout.write(reply.data(), reply_length);
            std::cout << std::endl;
        }
    }
    catch (std::exception& e)
    {
        std::cerr << "exception: " << e.what() << std::endl;
    }
}

int main()
{
    run_client("localhost", 11234);
}
```

The following image is a screenshot of the server (on the left) and client (on the right) outputs, side by side:

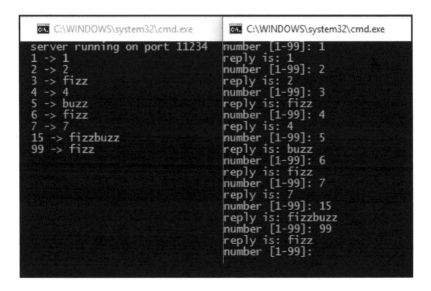

97. Bitcoin exchange rates

Various online services provide APIs for checking bitcoin market prices and exchange rates. A service that you can use for free is available at `https://blockchain.info/ticker`. A `GET` HTTP request returns a JSON object with the market price for various currencies. Documentation for the API can be found at: `https://blockchain.info/api/exchange_rates_api`. An excerpt from such a JSON object is shown here:

```
{
    "USD": {
        "15m": 8196.491155299998,
        "last": 8196.491155299998,
        "buy": 8196.491155299998,
        "sell": 8196.491155299998,
        "symbol": "$"
    },
    "GBP": {
        "15m": 5876.884158350099,
        "last": 5876.884158350099,
        "buy": 5876.884158350099,
        "sell": 5876.884158350099,
        "symbol": "£"
    }
}
```

There are various libraries that you can use for transferring data over a network. A widely used one is *curl*. This is a project that contains a command-line tool (*cURL*) and a library (*libcurl*), both written in C that supports a multitude of protocols, including HTTP/HTTPS, FTP/FTPS, Gopher, LDAP/LDAPS, POP3/POP3S, and SMTP/SMTPS. The project is available at: `https://curl.haxx.se/`. There are several C++ libraries on top of *libcurl*. Such an open source cross-platform library is *curlcpp*, which was written by Giuseppe Persico and is available at: `https://github.com/JosephP91/curlcpp`. We will use these two libraries for solving this problem and the ones that follow.

Instructions for building the *libcurl* and *curlcpp* libraries can be found in the documentation for the two projects. If you are using the source code for the book, everything is configured for you through CMake scripts. If you want to build the libraries yourself for other projects, then you need to do different things, depending on the platform you're building for. You can find building instructions for a debug configuration for Windows and macOS as follows:

On Windows, using Visual Studio 2017, you need to do the following:

1. Download *cURL* (from: `https://curl.haxx.se/download.html`), and unzip and locate the Visual Studio solution (it should be at `projects\Windows\VC15\curl-all.sln`). Open the solution and build the `LIB Debug - DLL Windows SSPI` configurations for the target platform that you need (Win32 or x64). The result is a static library file called `libcurl.lib`.

2. Download *curlcpp* (from: `https://github.com/JosephP91/curlcpp`), create a folder called `build`, and run CMake from it, setting the `CURL_LIBRARY` and `CURL_INCLUDE_DIR` variables. The former must point to `libcurl.lib`, and the latter to the folder with the CURL headers. Open the generated project and build it. The result is a static library file called `curlcpp.lib`.

3. In the Visual Studio project where you need to use curlcpp, add `CURL_STATICLIB` to the preprocessor definition, the path to the `curl\include` and `curlcpp\include` folders to the list of **Additional Include Directories**, and the output folders of the two libraries to the **Additional Library Directories**. Lastly, you need to link your project to the following static libraries: `libcurl.lib`, `curlcpp.lib`, `Crypt32.lib`, `ws2_32.lib`, `winmm.lib`, and `wldap32.lib`.

On macOS using Xcode, on the other hand, you need to do the following:

1. Download *openssl* (from: `https://www.openssl.org/`), and unzip and run the following commands to build and install it:

```
./Configure darwin64-x86_64-cc shared enable-
ec_nistp_64_gcc_128 no-ssl2 no-ssl3 no-comp --
openssldir=/usr/local/ssl/macos-x86_64
make depend
sudo make install
```

2. Download *cURL* (from: `https://curl.haxx.se/download.html`), and unzip and create a folder called `build` from which you can run CMake, specifying the `OPENSSL_ROOT_DIR` and `OPENSSL_INCLUDE_DIR` variables to pinpoint *openssl*. If you want to disable generating test and documentation projects, set the variables `BUILD_TESTING`, `BUILD_CURL_EXE`, and `USE_MANUAL` to `OFF`. The result for a debug build is a file called `libcurl-d.dylib`:

```
cmake -G Xcode .. -DOPENSSL_ROOT_DIR=/usr/local/bin -
DOPENSSL_INCLUDE_DIR=/usr/local/include/
```

3. Download curlcpp (from: `https://github.com/JosephP91/curlcpp`), create a folder called `build`, and run CMake from it, setting the `CURL_LIBRARY` and `CURL_INCLUDE_DIR` variables. The former must point to `libcurl-d.dylib`, and the latter to the folder with the CURL headers. Open the generated project and build it. The result is a file called `libcurlcpp.a`:

```
cmake -G Xcode .. -DCURL_LIBRARY=<path>/curl-
7.59.0/build/lib/Debug/libcurl-d.dylib -DCURL_INCLUDE_DIR=
<path>/curl-7.59.0/include
```

4. In the Xcode project where you want to use cURL and curlcpp, add `CURL_STATICLIB` to the preprocessor macros, the paths to the directories `curl/include` and `curlcpp/include` to **Header Search Paths**, the output directories of the two libraries to **Library Search Paths**, and the two static libraries, `libcurl-d.dylib` and `libcurlcpp.a`, to the list in **Link Binary With Libraries**.

Libcurl has two programming models (called interfaces): *easy* and *multi*. The *easy* interface provides a synchronous, efficient, and simple to use programming model for transferring data. The *multi* interface is an asynchronous model that provides multiple data transfers using a single thread or multiple threads. When using the *easy* interface, you first initialize a session, then set various options, including the URL and perhaps callbacks that will be called when data is available. After finishing the setup, you perform the transfer, which is a blocking operation that returns only when it's done. After the transfer has completed, you may get information about the transfer, and, in the end, you must clean up the session. Initialization and cleanup are handled according to the RAII idiom in the *curlcpp* library.

The following `get_json_document()` function takes an URL and performs a HTTP GET request. The response from the server is written to an `std::stringstream` that is returned to the caller:

```
#include "curl_easy.h"
#include "curl_form.h"
#include "curl_ios.h"
#include "curl_exception.h"

std::stringstream get_json_document(std::string_view url)
{
    std::stringstream str;

    try
    {
        curl::curl_ios<std::stringstream> writer(str);
        curl::curl_easy easy(writer);
```

```
            easy.add<CURLOPT_URL>(url.data());
            easy.add<CURLOPT_FOLLOWLOCATION>(1L);

            easy.perform();
        }
        catch (curl::curl_easy_exception const & error)
        {
            auto errors = error.get_traceback();
            error.print_traceback();
        }

        return str;
    }
```

When performing an HTTP GET to https://blockchain.info/ticker, we get back a JSON object, as shown earlier. The following types are used to represent the data returned by this API:

```
struct exchange_info
{
    double      delay_15m_price;
    double      latest_price;
    double      buying_price;
    double      selling_price;
    std::string symbol;
};

using blockchain_rates = std::map<std::string, exchange_info>;
```

We can use the nlohmann/json library for handling JSON data. Details about this library can be found in the Chapter 9, *Data Serialization*. The following from_json() function deserializes an exchange_info object from JSON:

```
#include "json.hpp"

using json = nlohmann::json;

void from_json(const json& jdata, exchange_info& info)
{
    info.delay_15m_price = jdata.at("15m").get<double>();
    info.latest_price    = jdata.at("last").get<double>();
    info.buying_price    = jdata.at("buy").get<double>();
    info.selling_price   = jdata.at("sell").get<double>();
    info.symbol          = jdata.at("symbol").get<std::string>();
}
```

Putting all of these together, we can write a program that fetches exchange rate information from the server, deserializes the JSON response, and prints the exchange rates to the console:

```
int main()
{
    auto doc = get_json_document("https://blockchain.info/ticker");

    json jdata;
    doc >> jdata;

    blockchain_rates rates = jdata;

    for (auto const & kvp : rates)
    {
        std::cout << "1BPI = " << kvp.second.latest_price
                  << " " << kvp.first << std::endl;
    }
}
```

98. Fetching emails using IMAP

The **Internet Message Access Protocol (IMAP)** is an internet protocol for retrieving email messages from an email server using TCP/IP. Most email server providers, including major ones like Gmail, Outlook.com, and Yahoo! Mail offer support for it. There are some C++ libraries for working with IMAP, such as *VMIME*, that is open source and cross-platform and supports IMAP, POP, and SMTP. However, in this book, I will use *cURL* (or more specifically, *libcurl*) to make HTTP requests to an email server using IMAPS.

The required operations can be achieved with several IMAP commands. In the following list, `imap.domain.com` is an example domain:

- `GET imaps://imap.domain.com` retrieves all of the folders in the mailbox. If you want to get the subfolders from a specific folder, such as `inbox`, then you should do a `GET imaps://imap.domain.com/<foldername>`.
- `SEARCH UNSEEN imaps://imap.domain.com/<foldername>` retrieves the identifiers of all the unread emails from the folder.
- `GET imaps://imap.domain.com/<foldername>/;UID=<id>` retrieves the email with a specified ID from a particular folder name.

TIP

If you are using Gmail, Outlook.com, or Yahoo! Mail as your email server provider, the IMAP settings are very similar. They all use the port 933 with TLS encryption; instead of, the username is your email address, and the password is your account password. What differs is the server hostname. For Gmail, it is `imap.gmail.com`, for Outlook.com, it is `imap-mail.outlook.com`, and for Yahoo! Mail, it is `imap.mail.yahoo.com`. Beware that if you're using 2-FA, then you need to generate a third-party application password and use that one instead of your account password.

These functionalities are implemented in the following code snippet as member functions of the class `imap_connection`. This class is constructed with the server URL, the port number, a username, and a password. The helper method `setup_easy()` initializes a `curl::curl_easy` object with authentication settings, such as the port, the username and password, and TLS encryption, as well as other common settings, such as the user agent (which is optional):

```cpp
class imap_connection
{
public:
    imap_connection(std::string_view url,
                    unsigned short const port,
                    std::string_view user,
                    std::string_view pass):
        url(url), port(port), user(user), pass(pass)
    {
    }

    std::string get_folders();
    std::vector<unsigned int> fetch_unread_uids(std::string_view folder);
    std::string fetch_email(std::string_view folder, unsigned int uid);

private:
    void setup_easy(curl::curl_easy& easy)
    {
        easy.add<CURLOPT_PORT>(port);
        easy.add<CURLOPT_USERNAME>(user.c_str());
        easy.add<CURLOPT_PASSWORD>(pass.c_str());
        easy.add<CURLOPT_USE_SSL>(CURLUSESSL_ALL);
        easy.add<CURLOPT_SSL_VERIFYPEER>(0L);
        easy.add<CURLOPT_SSL_VERIFYHOST>(0L);
        easy.add<CURLOPT_USERAGENT>("libcurl-agent/1.0");
    }

private:
    std::string    url;
```

```
        unsigned short port;
        std::string     user;
        std::string     pass;
};
```

The `get_folders()` method returns the list of folders in the mailbox. However, the function simply returns the string received from the server without actually parsing the content. You can take it as a further exercise to do that and return a list of folders. The function creates a `curl::curl_easy` object, initializes it with the appropriate parameters, such as the URL and authentication information, performs the request, and then returns the result from the server from the `std::stringstream` in which it was copied:

```cpp
std::string imap_connection::get_folders()
{
    std::stringstream str;
    try
    {
        curl::curl_ios<std::stringstream> writer(str);

        curl::curl_easy easy(writer);
        easy.add<CURLOPT_URL>(url.data());
        setup_easy(easy);

        easy.perform();
    }
    catch (curl::curl_easy_exception const & error)
    {
        auto errors = error.get_traceback();
        error.print_traceback();
    }

    return str.str();
}
```

Here is an example of what the output may look like:

```
* LIST (\HasNoChildren) "/" "INBOX"
* LIST (\HasNoChildren) "/" "Notes"
* LIST (\HasNoChildren) "/" "Trash"
* LIST (\HasChildren \Noselect) "/" "[Gmail]"
* LIST (\All \HasNoChildren) "/" "[Gmail]/All Mail"
* LIST (\Drafts \HasNoChildren) "/" "[Gmail]/Drafts"
* LIST (\HasNoChildren \Important) "/" "[Gmail]/Important"
* LIST (\HasNoChildren \Sent) "/" "[Gmail]/Sent Mail"
* LIST (\HasNoChildren \Junk) "/" "[Gmail]/Spam"
* LIST (\Flagged \HasNoChildren) "/" "[Gmail]/Starred"
```

The `fetch_unread_uids()` method is quite similar. This function returns a vector of unsigned integers representing the identifiers of unread emails from a specified folder. It performs the request in a similar manner as the previous function, except that it parses the result to create a list of email IDs. It also sets a `CURLOPT_CUSTOMREQUEST` option to `SEARCH UNSEEN`. The result of this is that the default `GET` method is replaced with the specified method (`SEARCH`, in this case):

```
std::vector<unsigned int>
imap_connection::fetch_unread_uids(std::string_view folder)
{
    std::stringstream str;

    try
    {
        curl::curl_ios<std::stringstream> writer(str);

        curl::curl_easy easy(writer);
        easy.add<CURLOPT_URL>((url.data() + std::string("/") +
                              folder.data() + std::string("/")).c_str());
        easy.add<CURLOPT_CUSTOMREQUEST>("SEARCH UNSEEN");
        setup_easy(easy);

        easy.perform();
    }
    catch (curl::curl_easy_exception const & error)
    {
        auto errors = error.get_traceback();
        error.print_traceback();
    }

    std::vector<unsigned int> uids;
    str.seekg(8, std::ios::beg);
    unsigned int uid;
    while (str >> uid)
    uids.push_back(uid);

    return uids;
}
```

The last method to implement is `fetch_email()`, which takes a folder name and an email identifier and returns the email as a string. This method is shown as follows:

```
std::string imap_connection::fetch_email(std::string_view folder,
                                         unsigned int uid)
{
    std::stringstream str;
```

```
    try
    {
        curl::curl_ios<std::stringstream> writer(str);

        curl::curl_easy easy(writer);
        easy.add<CURLOPT_URL>((url.data() + std::string("/") +
                              folder.data() + std::string("/;UID=") +
                              std::to_string(uid)).c_str());
        setup_easy(easy);

        easy.perform();
    }
    catch (curl::curl_easy_exception error)
    {
        auto errors = error.get_traceback();
        error.print_traceback();
    }

    return str.str();
}
```

This class can be used to fetch the requested content, as shown in the following code snippet. In this snippet, we read the mailbox folders, then retrieve the IDs of all the unread emails from the inbox folder, and then, if any exist, we fetch and display the most recent one:

```
int main()
{
    imap_connection imap("imaps://imap.gmail.com",
                         993,
                         "...(your username)...",
                         "...(your password)...");

    auto folders = imap.get_folders();
    std::cout << folders << std::endl;

    auto uids = imap.fetch_unread_uids("inbox");

    if (!uids.empty())
    {
        auto email = imap.fetch_email("inbox", uids.back());
        std::cout << email << std::endl;
    }
}
```

99. Translating text to any language

Text translation capabilities are available on many cloud computing services, including Microsoft Cognitive Services, Google Cloud Translation API, and Amazon Translate. In this book, I will be using Cognitive Services in Microsoft Azure. Azure Cognitive Services is a collection of machine learning and artificial intelligence algorithms that can be used to easily add intelligent functionalities to applications. One of the included services is *Text Translate API*, which provides capabilities such as language detection, translation from one language to another, and converting text to speech. We will also use *libcurl* for making HTTP requests.

Although there are various pricing plans for using the Text Translate API service, a free tier is also available. For text translation, it supports the translation of up to two million characters per month, which should be enough for most demo and prototyping purposes. In order to start using these APIs, you have to:

1. Have an Azure account. You should create one if you don't already have one.
2. Create a new *Translator Text API* resource.
3. After the resource is created, navigate to it and copy one of the two application keys generated for it. This key is necessary for making calls to this service.
4. The endpoint for calling the service is `https://api.microsofttranslator.com/V2/Http.svc`, not the one shown in the resource overview.

Documentation for the API for text translation is available at: `http://docs.microsofttranslator.com/text-translate.html`. To translate a text, you must:

1. Make a `GET` request to `[endpoint]/Translate`.
2. Provide the required query parameters (`text` and `to`) and possibly the optional ones such as `from`, for the language to translate from, which by default is English. The text to translate must not exceed 10,000 characters and must be URL encoded.
3. Provide the necessary headers. At a minimum, `Ocp-Apim-Subscription-Key` is required to pass the application key of the Azure resource.

As an example, the `GET` request for translating `"hello world!"` from English to French is the following:

```
GET /V2/Http.svc/Translate?to=fr&text=hello%20world%21
host: api.microsofttranslator.com
ocp-apim-subscription-key: <your key here>
```

What we get back in case of success is an XML string representing the translated text. The text is encoded with UTF-8. At this point, it is not possible to receive the result as a JSON. For the preceding example, the result from the server is:

```
<string xmlns="http://schemas.microsoft.com/2003/10/Serialization/">Salut
tout le monde !</string>
```

We can encapsulate the text translation functionality into a class that can handle application keys and endpoints in order to make the translation function simpler. The following `text_translator` class does exactly that. It is constructed from two strings, one representing the endpoint for the Text Translation API, and the other being the application key. As mentioned previously, the result from the server is returned in an XML format. The member function `deserialize_result()` extracts the actual text from its XML serialized form. However, to keep it simple, it just uses a regular expression to do so, and not an XML library, which should be enough for the purpose of this demo:

```cpp
class text_translator
{
public:
    text_translator(std::string_view endpoint,
                    std::string_view key)
        : endpoint(endpoint), app_key(key)
    {}

    std::wstring translate_text(std::wstring_view wtext,
                                std::string_view to,
                                std::string_view from = "en");

private:
    std::string deserialize_result(std::string_view text)
    {
        std::regex rx(R"(<string.*>(.*)<\/string>)");
        std::cmatch match;
        if (std::regex_search(text.data(), match, rx))
        {
            return match[1];
        }

        return "";
    }

    std::string endpoint;
    std::string app_key;
};
```

The `translate_text()` member function performs the actual translation. Its inputs are the text to translate, the language to translate to, and the language of the text, which by default is English. The input text for this method is a UTF-16 character string, but it must be converted to UTF-8. Also, the return from the server is text encoded as UTF-8 and must be converted to UTF-16. This is done with the helper functions `utf16_to_utf8()` and `utf8_to_utf16()`:

```cpp
std::wstring text_translator::translate_text(std::wstring_view wtext,
                                             std::string_view to,
                                             std::string_view from = "en")
{
    try
    {
        using namespace std::string_literals;

        std::stringstream str;
        std::string text = utf16_to_utf8(wtext);

        curl::curl_ios<std::stringstream> writer(str);
        curl::curl_easy easy(writer);

        curl::curl_header header;
        header.add("Ocp-Apim-Subscription-Key:" + app_key);

        easy.escape(text);
        auto url = endpoint + "/Translate";
        url += "?from="s + from.data();
        url += "&to="s + to.data();
        url += "&text="s + text;

        easy.add<CURLOPT_URL>(url.c_str());
        easy.add<CURLOPT_HTTPHEADER>(header.get());

        easy.perform();

        auto result = deserialize_result(str.str());
        return utf8_to_utf16(result);
    }
    catch (curl::curl_easy_exception const & error)
    {
        auto errors = error.get_traceback();
        error.print_traceback();
    }
    catch (std::exception const & ex)
    {
        std::err << ex.what() << std::endl;
```

```
    }

    return {};
}
```

The two helper functions for converting between UTF-8 and UTF-16 are as follows:

```
std::wstring utf8_to_utf16(std::string_view text)
{
    std::wstring_convert<std::codecvt_utf8_utf16<wchar_t>> converter;
    std::wstring wtext = converter.from_bytes(text.data());
    return wtext;
}

std::string utf16_to_utf8(std::wstring_view wtext)
{
    std::wstring_convert<std::codecvt_utf8_utf16<wchar_t>> converter;
    std::string text = converter.to_bytes(wtext.data());
    return text;
}
```

The text_translator class can be used to translate texts between various languages, as shown in the following example:

```
int main()
{
#ifdef _WIN32
    SetConsoleOutputCP(CP_UTF8);
#endif

    set_utf8_conversion(std::wcout);

    text_translator tt(
        "https://api.microsofttranslator.com/V2/Http.svc",
        "...(your app key)...");

    std::vector<std::tuple<std::wstring, std::string, std::string>> texts
    {
        { L"hello world!", "en", "ro"},
        { L"what time is it?", "en", "es" },
        { L"ceci est un exemple", "fr", "en" }
    };

    for (auto const [text, from, to] : texts)
    {
        auto result = tt.translate_text(text, to, from);

        std::cout << from << ": ";
```

```
        std::wcout << text << std::endl;
        std::cout << to << ": ";
        std::wcout << result << std::endl;
    }
}
```

Printing UTF-8 characters to a console is, however, not straightforward. On Windows, you need to call `SetConsoleOutputCP(CP_UTF8)` to enable an appropriate code page for that. But you also need to set a proper UTF-8 locale for the output stream, which is done with the `set_utf8_conversion()` function:

```
void set_utf8_conversion(std::wostream& stream)
{
    auto codecvt = std::make_unique<std::codecvt_utf8<wchar_t>>();
    std::locale utf8locale(std::locale(), codecvt.get());
    codecvt.release();
    stream.imbue(utf8locale);
}
```

The output for running the preceding example is as follows:

100. Detecting faces in a picture

This is yet another problem that can be solved using Microsoft Cognitive Services. One of the services available in this group, called *Face API*, provides algorithms for detecting faces, gender, age, emotion, and various face landmarks and attributes, as well as the ability to find face similarities, identify people, group pictures based on visual faces similarities, and others.

Similar to the Text Translate API, there is a free plan that allows up to 30,000 transactions per month, but only 20 every minute. A transaction is basically an API call. There are several paid plans that allow for more transactions per month and per minute, but for the purpose of this problem, you can use the free tier. There is also a 30-day trial that you can use. To get started with the Face API, you have to:

1. Have an Azure account. You should create one if you don't already have one.
2. Create a new Face API resource.
3. After the resource is created, navigate to it and copy one of the two application keys generated for it and the resource endpoint. These are both necessary in order to call the service.

Documentation for the Face API is available at: `https://azure.microsoft.com/en-us/services/cognitive-services/face/`. You should read the information about the `Detect` method carefully. In short, what we have to do is the following:

-   Make a `POST` request to `[endpoint]/Detect`.
-   Provide optional query parameters, such as flags for returning the face ID, the face landmarks, and a string to indicate what face attributes to analyze and return.
-   Provide optional and mandatory request headers. At a minimum, `Ocp-Apim-Subscription-Key` is required to pass the application key of the Azure resource.
-   Provide the image to analyze. You can either pass an URL to an image in a JSON object (with the content type `application/json`), or the actual image (with the content type `application/octet-stream`). The requirement was that the picture should be loaded from a disk file, therefore we must use the latter option.

In the case of success, the response is a JSON object containing all of the requested information. In the case of failure, the response is another JSON object with information about the error.

Here is a request to analyze and return the face landmarks, age, gender, and emotion, as well as the face identifier. Information about the identified face is preserved on the server for 24 hours and can be used with other Face API algorithms:

```
POST
/face/v1.0/detect?returnFaceId=true&returnFaceLandmarks=true&returnFaceAttr
ibutes=age,gender,emotion
host: westeurope.api.cognitive.microsoft.com
ocp-apim-subscription-key: <your key here>
content-type: application/octet-stream
content-length: <length>
accept: */*
```

The JSON result returned by the server looks like the following. Notice this is only a snippet because the entire response is rather long. The actual result includes 27 different face landmarks, with only the first two being shown in the following output:

```
[{
  "faceId": "0ddb348a-6038-4cbb-b3a1-86fffe6c1f26",
  "faceRectangle": {
    "top": 86,
    "left": 165,
    "width": 72,
    "height": 72
  },
  "faceLandmarks": {
    "pupilLeft": {
      "x": 187.5,
      "y": 102.9
    },
    "pupilRight": {
      "x": 214.6,
      "y": 104.7
    }
  },
  "faceAttributes": {
    "gender": "male",
    "age": 54.9,
    "emotion": {
      "anger": 0,
      "contempt": 0,
      "disgust": 0,
      "fear": 0,
      "happiness": 1,
      "neutral": 0,
      "sadness": 0,
      "surprise": 0
```

```
        }
      }
   }]
```

We will use the `nlohmann/json` library to deserialize the JSON object and *libcurl* to make HTTP requests. The following classes model the result from the server in case of success:

```cpp
struct face_rectangle
{
    int width = 0;
    int height = 0;
    int left = 0;
    int top = 0;
};

struct face_point
{
    double x = 0;
    double y = 0;
};

struct face_landmarks
{
    face_point pupilLeft;
    face_point pupilRight;
    face_point noseTip;
    face_point mouthLeft;
    face_point mouthRight;
    face_point eyebrowLeftOuter;
    face_point eyebrowLeftInner;
    face_point eyeLeftOuter;
    face_point eyeLeftTop;
    face_point eyeLeftBottom;
    face_point eyeLeftInner;
    face_point eyebrowRightInner;
    face_point eyebrowRightOuter;
    face_point eyeRightInner;
    face_point eyeRightTop;
    face_point eyeRightBottom;
    face_point eyeRightOuter;
    face_point noseRootLeft;
    face_point noseRootRight;
    face_point noseLeftAlarTop;
    face_point noseRightAlarTop;
    face_point noseLeftAlarOutTip;
    face_point noseRightAlarOutTip;
    face_point upperLipTop;
```

```
       face_point upperLipBottom;
       face_point underLipTop;
       face_point underLipBottom;
    };

    struct face_emotion
    {
       double anger = 0;
       double contempt = 0;
       double disgust = 0;
       double fear = 0;
       double happiness = 0;
       double neutral = 0;
       double sadness = 0;
       double surprise = 0;
    };

    struct face_attributes
    {
       std::string  gender;
       double       age;
       face_emotion emotion;
    };

    struct face_info
    {
       std::string    faceId;
       face_rectangle rectangle;
       face_landmarks landmarks;
       face_attributes attributes;
    };
```

Because a picture may contain multiple faces, the actual response from the server is an array of objects. The `face_detect_response` shown in the following code is the actual type of the response:

```
    using face_detect_response = std::vector<face_info>;
```

Deserialization is done as in other cases in this book, by using `from_json()` overloaded functions. If you have already solved the other problems involving JSON deserialization, you should be very familiar with these:

```
    using json = nlohmann::json;

    void from_json(const json& jdata, face_rectangle& rect)
    {
        rect.width = jdata.at("width").get<int>();
```

```
      rect.height = jdata.at("height").get<int>();
      rect.top = jdata.at("top").get<int>();
      rect.left = jdata.at("left").get<int>();
}

void from_json(const json& jdata, face_point& point)
{
      point.x = jdata.at("x").get<double>();
      point.y = jdata.at("y").get<double>();
}

void from_json(const json& jdata, face_landmarks& mark)
{
      mark.pupilLeft = jdata.at("pupilLeft");
      mark.pupilRight = jdata.at("pupilRight");
      mark.noseTip = jdata.at("noseTip");
      mark.mouthLeft = jdata.at("mouthLeft");
      mark.mouthRight = jdata.at("mouthRight");
      mark.eyebrowLeftOuter = jdata.at("eyebrowLeftOuter");
      mark.eyebrowLeftInner = jdata.at("eyebrowLeftInner");
      mark.eyeLeftOuter = jdata.at("eyeLeftOuter");
      mark.eyeLeftTop = jdata.at("eyeLeftTop");
      mark.eyeLeftBottom = jdata.at("eyeLeftBottom");
      mark.eyeLeftInner = jdata.at("eyeLeftInner");
      mark.eyebrowRightInner = jdata.at("eyebrowRightInner");
      mark.eyebrowRightOuter = jdata.at("eyebrowRightOuter");
      mark.eyeRightInner = jdata.at("eyeRightInner");
      mark.eyeRightTop = jdata.at("eyeRightTop");
      mark.eyeRightBottom = jdata.at("eyeRightBottom");
      mark.eyeRightOuter = jdata.at("eyeRightOuter");
      mark.noseRootLeft = jdata.at("noseRootLeft");
      mark.noseRootRight = jdata.at("noseRootRight");
      mark.noseLeftAlarTop = jdata.at("noseLeftAlarTop");
      mark.noseRightAlarTop = jdata.at("noseRightAlarTop");
      mark.noseLeftAlarOutTip = jdata.at("noseLeftAlarOutTip");
      mark.noseRightAlarOutTip = jdata.at("noseRightAlarOutTip");
      mark.upperLipTop = jdata.at("upperLipTop");
      mark.upperLipBottom = jdata.at("upperLipBottom");
      mark.underLipTop = jdata.at("underLipTop");
      mark.underLipBottom = jdata.at("underLipBottom");
}

void from_json(const json& jdata, face_emotion& emo)
{
      emo.anger = jdata.at("anger").get<double>();
      emo.contempt = jdata.at("contempt").get<double>();
      emo.disgust = jdata.at("disgust").get<double>();
      emo.fear = jdata.at("fear").get<double>();
```

```
    emo.happiness = jdata.at("happiness").get<double>();
    emo.neutral = jdata.at("neutral").get<double>();
    emo.sadness = jdata.at("sadness").get<double>();
    emo.surprise = jdata.at("surprise").get<double>();
}

void from_json(const json& jdata, face_attributes& attr)
{
    attr.age = jdata.at("age").get<double>();
    attr.emotion = jdata.at("emotion");
    attr.gender = jdata.at("gender").get<std::string>();
}

void from_json(const json& jdata, face_info& info)
{
    info.faceId = jdata.at("faceId").get<std::string>();
    info.attributes = jdata.at("faceAttributes");
    info.landmarks = jdata.at("faceLandmarks");
    info.rectangle = jdata.at("faceRectangle");
}
```

However, if the function fails for some reason, a different object is returned to describe the error. The `face_error_response` class is used for this purpose:

```
struct face_error
{
    std::string code;
    std::string message;
};

struct face_error_response
{
    face_error error;
};
```

We also need `from_json()` overloads to deserialize the error response. The implementation of these functions is as follows:

```
void from_json(const json& jdata, face_error& error)
{
    error.code = jdata.at("code").get<std::string>();
    error.message = jdata.at("message").get<std::string>();
}
```

```
void from_json(const json& jdata, face_error_response& response)
{
    response.error = jdata.at("error");
}
```

Having all of these defined so far, we can write the actual calls to Face API. Like in the case of text translation, we can write a class to encapsulate this functionality (where we can add more). This can help to easily manage the application key and endpoint (instead of passing them with every single function call). The `face_manager` class is used for this purpose:

```
class face_manager
{
public:
    face_manager(std::string_view endpoint,
                 std::string_view key)
        : endpoint(endpoint), app_key(key)
    {}

    face_detect_response detect_from_file(std::string_view path);

private:
    face_detect_response parse_detect_response(long const status,
                                               std::stringstream & str);

    std::string endpoint;
    std::string app_key;
};
```

The `detect_from_file()` method takes a string representing the path to an image on the disk. It loads the image, sends it to Face API, deserializes the answer, and returns a `face_detect_response` object, which is a collection of `face_info` objects. Because the actual image is passed with the call, the content type is `application/octet-stream`. We need to pass the content of the file into the `CURLOPT_POSTFIELDS` field with the `curl_easy` interface, and its length into the `CURLOPT_POSTFIELDSIZE` field:

```
face_detect_response face_manager::detect_from_file(std::string_view path)
{
    try
    {
        auto data = load_image(path);
        if (!data.empty())
        {
            std::stringstream str;
            curl::curl_ios<std::stringstream> writer(str);
            curl::curl_easy easy(writer);
```

```
        curl::curl_header header;
        header.add("Ocp-Apim-Subscription-Key:" + app_key);
        header.add("Content-Type:application/octet-stream");

        auto url = endpoint +
                "/detect"
                "?returnFaceId=true"
                "&returnFaceLandmarks=true"
                "&returnFaceAttributes=age,gender,emotion";

        easy.add<CURLOPT_URL>(url.c_str());
        easy.add<CURLOPT_HTTPHEADER>(header.get());

        easy.add<CURLOPT_POSTFIELDSIZE>(data.size());
        easy.add<CURLOPT_POSTFIELDS>(reinterpret_cast<char*>(
            data.data()));

        easy.perform();

        auto status = easy.get_info<CURLINFO_RESPONSE_CODE>();

        return parse_detect_response(status.get(), str);
        }
    }
    catch (curl::curl_easy_exception const & error)
    {
        auto errors = error.get_traceback();
        error.print_traceback();
    }
    catch (std::exception const & ex)
    {
        std::cerr << ex.what() << std::endl;
    }

    return {};
}
```

The `parse_detect_response()` method is responsible for deserializing the JSON response from the server. It does so based on the actual HTTP response code. If the function succeeded, the status is `200`. In the case of failure, it is a `4xx` code:

```
face_detect_response face_manager::parse_detect_response(
    long const status, std::stringstream & str)
{
    json jdata;
    str >> jdata;
```

```
try
{
    if (status == 200)
    {
        face_detect_response response = jdata;

        return response;
    }
    else if (status >= 400)
    {
        face_error_response response = jdata;

        std::cout << response.error.code << std::endl
                  << response.error.message << std::endl;
    }
}
catch (std::exception const & ex)
{
    std::cerr << ex.what() << std::endl;
}

return {};
}
```

To read the image file from the disk, the detect_from_file() function uses another function called load_image(). This function takes a string representing the path to the file and returns the content of the file in an std::vector<uint8_t>. The implementation of this function is as follows:

```
std::vector<uint8_t> load_image(std::string_view filepath)
{
    std::vector<uint8_t> data;

    std::ifstream ifile(filepath.data(), std::ios::binary | std::ios::ate);
    if (ifile.is_open())
    {
        auto size = ifile.tellg();
        ifile.seekg(0, std::ios::beg);

        data.resize(static_cast<size_t>(size));
        ifile.read(reinterpret_cast<char*>(data.data()), size);
    }

    return data;
}
```

At this point, we have all that is necessary to make calls to the `Detect` algorithm from Face API, deserialize the response, and print its content to the console. The following program prints information for the faces identified in a file called `albert_and_elsa.jpg` from the `res` folder of the project. Remember to use your actual endpoint and application key for your Face API resource:

```
int main()
{
    face_manager manager(
        "https://westeurope.api.cognitive.microsoft.com/face/v1.0",
        "...(your api key)...");

#ifdef _WIN32
    std::string path = R"(res\albert_and_elsa.jpg)";
#else
    std::string path = R"(./res/albert_and_elsa.jpg)";
#endif

    auto results = manager.detect_from_file(path);

    for (auto const & face : results)
    {
        std::cout << "faceId: " << face.faceId << std::endl
                  << "age: " << face.attributes.age << std::endl
                  << "gender: " << face.attributes.gender << std::endl
                  << "rect: " << "{" << face.rectangle.left
                  << "," << face.rectangle.top
                  << "," << face.rectangle.width
                  << "," << face.rectangle.height
                  << "}" << std::endl << std::endl;
    }
}
```

The image `albert_and_elsa.jpg` is also shown here:

The following is the program's output. Keep in mind that the actual temporary face identifiers will, of course, differ with each call. As you can see in the result, two faces were identified. The first is of Albert Einstein and his detected age is 54.9 years old. This picture was taken in 1921 when he was 42. The second face is of Elsa Einstein, the wife of Albert Einstein, who was 45 at that time. In her case, the detected age is 41.6 years old. From this, you can see that the detected age is only a rough indication, and not something that is very precise:

```
faceId:  77e0536f-073d-41c5-920d-c53264d17b98
age:     54.9
gender:  male
rect:    {165,86,72,72}

faceId:  afb22044-14fa-46bf-9b65-16d4fe1d9817
age:     41.6
gender:  female
rect:    {321,151,59,59}
```

Should the API call fail, an error message is returned instead (with the HTTP status 400). The `parse_detect_response()` method will deserialize the error response and print a message to the console. For instance, in case a wrong API key is used, the following message is returned from the server and displayed in the console:

```
Unspecified
Access denied due to invalid subscription key. Make sure you are subscribed
to an API you are trying to call and provide the right key.
```

Bibliography

Articles

- 1337C0D3R, 2011. *Longest Palindromic Substring Part I*, `https://articles.leetcode.com/longest-palindromic-substring-part-i/`
- Aditya Goel, 2016. *Permutations of a given string using STL*, `https://www.geeksforgeeks.org/permutations-of-a-given-string-using-stl/`
- Andrei Jakab, 2010. *Using libcurl with SSH support in Visual Studio 2010*, `https://curl.haxx.se/libcurl/c/Using-libcurl-with-SSH-support-in-Visual-Studio-2010.pdf`
- Ashwani Gautam, 2017. *What is the analysis of quick sort?*, `https://www.quora.com/What-is-the-analysis-of-quick-sort`
- Ashwin Nanjappa, 2014. *How to build Boost using Visual Studio*, `https://codeyarns.com/2014/06/06/how-to-build-boost-using-visual-studio/`
- busycrack, 2012. *Telnet IMAP Commands Note*, `https://busylog.net/telnet-imap-commands-note/`
- Dan Madden, 2000. *Encrypting Log Files*, `https://www.codeproject.com/Articles/644/Encrypting-Log-Files`
- Georgy Gimel'farb, 2016. *Algorithm Quicksort: Analysis of Complexity*, `https://www.cs.auckland.ac.nz/courses/compsci220s1c/lectures/2016S1C/CS220-Lecture10.pdf`
- Jay Doshi, Chanchal Khemani, Juhi Duseja. *Dijkstra's Algorithm*, `http://codersmaze.com/data-structure-explanations/graphs-data-structure/dijkstras-algorithm-for-shortest-path/`
- Jeffrey Walton, 2008. *Applied Crypto++: Block Ciphers*, `https://www.codeproject.com/Articles/21877/Applied-Crypto-Block-Ciphers`
- Jeffrey Walton, 2007. *Product Keys Based on the Advanced Encryption Standard (AES)*, `https://www.codeproject.com/Articles/16465/Product-Keys-Based-on-the-Advanced-Encryption-Stan`

- Jeffrey Walton, 2006. *Compiling and Integrating Crypto++ into the Microsoft Visual C++ Environment,* `https://www.codeguru.com/cpp/v-s/devstudio_macros/openfaq/article.php/c12853/Compiling-and-Integrating-Crypto-into-the-Microsoft-Visual-C-Environment.htm`

- Jonathan Boccara, 2017. *How to split a string in C++,* `https://www.fluentcpp.com/2017/04/21/how-to-split-a-string-in-c/`

- Kenny Kerr, 2013. *Resource Management in the Windows API,* `https://visualstudiomagazine.com/articles/2013/09/01/get-a-handle-on-the-windows-api.aspx`

- Kenny Kerr, 2011. *Windows with C++ - C++ and the Windows API,* `https://msdn.microsoft.com/en-us/magazine/hh288076.aspx?f=255MSPPError=-2147217396`

- Marius Bancila, 2015. *Integrate Windows Azure Face APIs in a C++ application,* `https://www.codeproject.com/Articles/989752/Integrate-Windows-Azure-Face-APIs-in-a-Cplusplus-a`

- Marius Bancila, 2018. *Using Cognitive Services to find your Game of Thrones look-alike,* `https://www.codeproject.com/Articles/1234217/Using-Cognitive-Services-to-find-your-Game-of-Thro`

- Mary K. Vernon. *Priority Queues,* `http://pages.cs.wisc.edu/~vernon/cs367/notes/11.PRIORITY-Q.html`

- Mathias Bynens. *In search of the perfect URL validation regex,* `https://mathiasbynens.be/demo/url-regex`

- O.S. Tezer, 2014. *SQLite vs MySQL vs PostgreSQL: A Comparison Of Relational Database Management Systems,* `https://www.digitalocean.com/community/tutorials/sqlite-vs-mysql-vs-postgresql-a-comparison-of-relational-database-management-systems`

- Robert Nystrom, 2014. *Game Programming patterns: Double Buffer,* `http://gameprogrammingpatterns.com/double-buffer.html`

- Robert Sedgewick, Philippe Flajolet, 2013. *Introduction to the Analysis of Algorithms,* `http://www.informit.com/articles/article.aspx?p=2017754seqNum=5`

- Rosso Salmanzadeh, 2002. *Using libcurl in Visual Studio,* `https://curl.haxx.se/libcurl/c/visual_studio.pdf`

- Sergii Bratus, 2010. *Implementation of the Licensing System for a Software Product,* `https://www.codeproject.com/Articles/99499/Implementation-of-the-Licensing-System-for-a-Softw`

- Shubham Agrawal, 2016. *Dijkstra's Shortest Path Algorithm using priority_queue of STL,* `https://www.geeksforgeeks.org/dijkstras-shortest-path-algorithm-using-priority_queue-stl/`

- Travis Tidwell, 2013. *An Online RSA Public and Private Key Generator,* http://travistidwell.com/blog/2013/09/06/an-online-rsa-public-and-private-key-generator/

- Victor Volkman, 2006. *Crypto++ Holds the Key to Encrypting Your C++ Application Data,* https://www.codeguru.com/cpp/misc/misc/cryptoapi/article.php/c11953/Cryptosupregsup-Holds-the-Key-to-Encrypting-Your-C-Application-Data.htm

- Yang Song, 2014. *Split a string using C++,* http://ysonggit.github.io/coding/2014/12/16/split-a-string-using-c.html

- *Decorator Design Pattern,* https://sourcemaking.com/design_patterns/decorator

- *Composite Design Pattern,* https://sourcemaking.com/design_patterns/composite

- *Template Method Design Pattern,* https://sourcemaking.com/design_patterns/template_method

- *Strategy Design Pattern,* https://sourcemaking.com/design_patterns/strategy

- *Chain of Responsibility,* https://sourcemaking.com/design_patterns/chain_of_responsibility

- *Understanding the PDF File Format: Overview,* https://blog.idrsolutions.com/2013/01/understanding-the-pdf-file-format-overview/

- *RSA Signing is Not RSA Decryption,* https://www.cs.cornell.edu/courses/cs5430/2015sp/notes/rsa_sign_vs_dec.php

- *RSA Cryptography,* https://www.cryptopp.com/wiki/RSA_Cryptography

- *Using rand() (C/C++),* http://eternallyconfuzzled.com/arts/jsw_art_rand.aspx

- *Crypto++ Keys and Formats,* https://www.cryptopp.com/wiki/Keys_and_Formats

- *INTERNET MESSAGE ACCESS PROTOCOL - VERSION 4 rev1,* https://tools.ietf.org/html/rfc3501.html

- *Internal Versus External BLOBs in SQLite,* https://www.sqlite.org/intern-v-extern-blob.html

- *OpenSSL Compilation and Installation,* https://wiki.openssl.org/index.php/Compilation_and_Installation

Library documentation

- *C/C++ JSON parser/generator benchmark,* `https://github.com/miloyip/nativejson-benchmark`
- *Crypto++,* `https://www.cryptopp.com/wiki/Main_Page`
- *Hummus PDF,* `http://pdfhummus.com/How-To`
- *JSON for Modern C++,* `https://github.com/nlohmann/json`
- *PDF-Writer,* `https://github.com/galkahana/PDF-Writer`
- *PNGWriter,* `https://github.com/pngwriter/pngwriter`
- *pugixml 1.8 quick start guide,* `https://pugixml.org/docs/quickstart.html`
- *SQLite,* `https://www.sqlite.org/docs.html`
- *sqlite_modern_cpp,* `https://github.com/SqliteModernCpp/sqlite_modern_cpp`
- *Ziplib wiki,* `https://bitbucket.org/wbenny/ziplib/wiki/Home`

Other Books You May Enjoy

If you enjoyed this book, you may be interested in these other books by Packt:

C++17 STL Cookbook
Jacek Galowicz

ISBN: 978-1-78712-049-5

- Learn about the new core language features and the problems they were intended to solve
- Understand the inner workings and requirements of iterators by implementing them
- Explore algorithms, functional programming style, and lambda expressions
- Leverage the rich, portable, fast, and well-tested set of well-designed algorithms provided in the STL
- Work with strings the STL way instead of handcrafting C-style code
- Understand standard support classes for concurrency and synchronization, and how to put them to work
- Use the filesystem library addition available with the C++17 STL

C++ Data Structures and Algorithms
Wisnu Anggoro

ISBN: 978-1-78883-521-3

- Know how to use arrays and lists to get better results in complex scenarios
- Build enhanced applications by using hashtables, dictionaries, and sets
- Implement searching algorithms such as linear search, binary search, jump search, exponential search, and more
- Have a positive impact on the efficiency of applications with tree traversal
- Explore the design used in sorting algorithms like Heap sort, Quick sort, Merge sort and Radix sort
- Implement various common algorithms in string data types
- Find out how to design an algorithm for a specific task using the common algorithm paradigms

Leave a review - let other readers know what you think

Please share your thoughts on this book with others by leaving a review on the site that you bought it from. If you purchased the book from Amazon, please leave us an honest review on this book's Amazon page. This is vital so that other potential readers can see and use your unbiased opinion to make purchasing decisions, we can understand what our customers think about our products, and our authors can see your feedback on the title that they have worked with Packt to create. It will only take a few minutes of your time, but is valuable to other potential customers, our authors, and Packt. Thank you!

Index

90396237R00183

Made in the USA
Middletown, DE
22 September 2018